Bangalore,
Britain
and Beyond
Connecting past and present

Debu Hosali (1910-1983)
Arti Kumar née Hosali (1946)

There are only two lasting bequests we can give to our children.

One is roots, the other is wings.

(Anonymous)

We shall not cease from exploration, and the end of all our exploring will be to arrive where we started and know the place for the first time.

Four Quartets: Little Gidding by T. S. Eliot (1888 – 1965)

It's the action, not the fruit of the action that's important. You have to do the right thing. It may not be in your power, may not be in your time, that there will be any fruit. But that doesn't mean you stop doing the right thing. You may never know what results from your action. But if you do nothing, there will be no result.

Mahatma Gandhi (1869 – 1948)

Contents

SECTION 2: PUBLIC SERVICES, PRIVATE ATTITUDES **65**

INTRODUCTION

A while back I was helping my son Umesh to move back from Hong Kong into his new home in London. As we unpacked crates full of his possessions, amongst his books and papers we came across a plain brown folder. Opening it was like finding treasure. Or rather, it was like re-discovering the key to a treasure-trove of memories from my growing-up days in Bangalore. For Umesh it brought back vivid memories of his childhood visits to India, where we spent time with his grandparents (my parents, Dada and Bhabi).

Nostalgia is a powerful magnet that draws us back to the relationships and landscapes of

our youth, the music of yesteryear, books and films which resonate with our personal and social histories. The past links with the present as we look at it through a contemporary lens. We make sense of how we have come to be as we are in present times, personally and collectively. And yet, for many of us, our treasured memories lie scattered among the debris of the past and the daily grind of the present.

So what exactly did Umesh and I re-discover in the said folder, which has bobbed up again in our lives, after lying dormant with him for several years? Well, we found numerous interesting articles, some of which you will find reproduced in this book. They were written by my father, Mr Devendranath Hosali, who was widely known in the public and private circles of Bangalore as Debu or Dada. He passed away exactly 33 years ago as I start writing this on 2 February 2016. It is said that writers never die, they just turn into their books. Dada was not a book author but he regularly wrote a weekly column during the 1960s and '70s in the magazine Mysindia.

"So much has changed since these columns were written," I say to Umesh as I turn pages in the folder, more than 45 years later. "The name *Mysindia* was chosen to represent the State of Mysore in the wider context of India. But Mysore was renamed Karnataka in 1973. *Mysindia* was entirely Dada's brainchild, produced in his printing press on South Parade, which was a beautiful wide avenue. It has now become Mahatma Gandhi (MG) Road – a traffic-congested road with a flyover carrying a metro line running above its entire length and beyond.

I fall into a reverie: "Bangalore (like many other anglicized place names) reverted to its indigenous name, Bengaluru, in 2015. As for the building which housed the Hosali Press, I tried to find it on a recent visit to Bangalore but it seems to have disappeared off the face of this earth. When I was growing up it provided our extended family with daily bread, so Dada had to try and run it as a business. I remember what a struggle he had sometimes to make ends meet. He was far more a man of art, literature and culture than a businessman. These articles he wrote every week provided an outlet for his creative abilities."

Umesh says, "Yes Mum, but some things never change. His columns are relevant and entertaining for a wide public even today, far beyond what our family might see in them. It's high time we published them. Bhabi always wanted us to do this – she said as much when she gave me this folder."

So yes, this book is not only a tribute to my dynamic father, but also to my dearly loved mother (almost universally called Bhabi). She passed away on 28 April 2013 but will always be with us in spirit and memory. Bhabi was a true soulmate to my father. She clipped out my father's articles every week and stored them in the said folder. They add up to a substantial evocation of the times: interwoven personal and socio-political perspectives that are sometimes serious and thought-provoking, but always written with that lighter Dada touch.

Many of my memories are also shared with my sister, Priya (family name, Rani). When Rani and I graduated from Mount Carmel College in 1963 and 1966 respectively, our first real jobs were at the Hosali Press. We both started our careers by co-editing *Mysindia*. There was not a computer in sight at the time. We typed all text on a tinny typewriter and passed it on to be manually type-set.

Four type-setters were employed for this express purpose, and all of them could recognize the metal shapes of English letters. They formed the words from our type sheets, even though they were mostly illiterate. They would then print out copies which we had to proof-read several times to eliminate errors.

After all this time I can still visualize Dada deep in thought – he might put his idea for a column into his cigar or his pipe and smoke it for a while. He then dictated it as I sat across the desk with pen and paper, trying to capture each word (luckily I'd taken a course in short-hand and typing). *Mysindia* styled itself as a magazine of local and national news, views and reviews. Every week it also included a serious editorial, a brilliantly clever poem touching on political themes of the day and a report on some local social event. In addition to these regular contributions, my job was to choose a short story and sundry articles from those that were submitted by members of the public. We gave many an aspiring author or journalist a fighting chance to get into print.

And it gave me a chance to learn about journalism, printing and publishing. It was always a thrill to go to the rear of the Press and see the many printing machines at work, churning out sheet after sheet of copy. I remember Dada's pride and pleasure in taking ownership of a new German machine that made high quality colour prints. The technical skills I learned are obsolete because printing technologies have advanced beyond recognition, but the generic skills and work ethic served me well as a foundation for my future career success.

As the second component of this book, I have added my own memories and thoughts alongside Dada's articles – looking at the lost world of my childhood in Bangalore through the lens of today's experiences. Where my memory is hazy (and where my thoughts go off at a tangent) I have filled in gaps with imagination, while staying broadly true to facts. I have changed some names so as to respect the privacy of certain individuals. If I unintentionally offend anyone I ask to be forgiven. I also bring in some perspectives from the UK, where I have lived, studied, worked and raised my children since 1970.

It strikes me that some of Dada's columns are amazingly contemporary and universally true – nothing much has changed – and in other ways that past world is truly and sadly lost. What amounts to nostalgia for me might be history for you, the reader – but much of it will no doubt resonate with the timeless part of your life.

So…step back in time and step forward again. Enter into our perspectives and retrospectives, enjoy them through words and pictures, and we hope you will find them emotionally and mentally relevant within your own world, wherever you are.

The style, structure and layout of this book

Let this book fall open at any page, dip into it at random at your leisure, and you will find something to make you think, make you laugh or even inspire you to write your own response. However you will make the most of this material if you start at the beginning and read through the four sections into which the book is structured. Dada's columns were originally written chronologically in the 1960s and '70s, but you will see I have not presented them here in date order. I have grouped them under four main sections, as they fall roughly into themes associated with

- family and social life
- public services, private attitudes
- politics and personalities
- gender issues.

I have then paired each of Dada's columns with my own corresponding news, views and reviews. My style of writing is of course different from my father's, and my perspectives are shaped by growing up in Bangalore as a daughter in his household. Inevitably my articles also come from experiences of studying, living and working both in India and in the UK, and travelling abroad. I have tried to respond to each of Dada's topics with my memories, and/ or my views on a historic parallel from my contemporary context. In some cases I simply use his topic as a jumping-off point for my article, so the link may seem tangential.

I hope the different visual layout for Dada's articles (presented here in columns) and my own text will prevent confusion as to who is 'speaking' the piece, and that the different voices, styles and time contexts will add interesting variations. You will see that Dada uses the majestic plural – the royal we – when referring to himself in the singular. This is his unique stylistic choice – a sort of echo from the plural Hindustani *hum* we often used in our family rather than the usual singular *mai*. Reading the articles today gives a strong sense of times gone by and I hope, as a reader, you enjoy this stylistic quirk, hearing the words as they would have been spoken by him.

SECTION 1: FAMILY AND SOCIAL LIFE

On fighting an election

27 March 1966

Over the years we have fought several elections, and almost every one of them successfully. In those early years of our youth our frank pronouncements, and our breezy, nonchalant attitude towards everyone – from the Diwan, Ministers, high government officials to the top business and professional men – made us a hero among a group of friends, and whenever we sought an office it came to us unanimously. That gave us a swollen head and we argued that if we could be the President of the Rotary Club of Bangalore, why not the Governor of the District? And thus, having assessed the strength of the contending forces, we filled in our nomination for this high office. But we soon found that this time we were pitched against an adversary it was not easy to defeat.

It all happened in the sylvan setting of Hotel Krishnaraj Sagar at Mysore in the year 1949. Car-loads of delegates from places as far as Waltair, Vijayawada, Kakinada, Guntur, Madras and Vellore arrived for the Rotary Conference. Now, frankly, we had not expected these friends from far-off Rotary Clubs to come to a remote place like Mysore and, when they joined one of the gayest pre-election beer parties given by our adversary, we were struck by fright. The conclusion was obvious – not one of these fellows was going to vote for us. So we decided on the next best thing. We said, if our rival was going to get the votes, let us at least get his beer, and we joined the beer party with great gusto.

But strange things happen in elections. When the exhilaration of the beer had worn off, sanity dawned on the delegates and, in the ballot that took place, an equal number of votes were cast, creating an impasse. Obviously, in the Constitution of Rotary International then, there was no provision to contend with an emergency of this type. And therefore the elders in Rotary told us to decide the issue by the toss of a coin. We promptly accepted the offer, but our rival would not. On some persuasion however, he also decided to take his chance. And lo and behold! In a fraction of a second the matter was decided in our favour. Destiny itself had conspired to make us the Governor of Rotary.

The Presidency of the Mysore Chamber of Commerce, although there was a contest, came to us without much trouble. But the election which we enjoyed most was when we contested for the Lok Sabha in 1951. We had no hope of getting in and were merely monkey-shining. We hired a couple of vans, fitted them with loud-speakers, coined a few slogans with biting sarcasm against the ruling party, and asked our stooges to shout themselves hoarse. The reward for such tomfoolery was utterly surprising: we scored 18,000-odd votes. What was shocking was two villages in Devanhalli cast 100% votes in our favour. Someone had started a rumour in these villages that we belonged to the caste of the voters there – and they were all Harijans.

Our recent adventure in electioneering at the Bangalore Race Club was equally tantalising. The Race Club has been for generations ruled by powerful men who have controlled large blocks of votes. Therefore we went to them and told them that we were going to have a stab at Stewardship, and solicited their support. We got a set answer from everyone: "No-one was to get group support, each one was working for himself, and that we should see the members and canvass their votes."

We thought it was a strange attitude for these powerful men to adopt and we said to ourself, "Each man for himself and the devil take the hindmost!" However, with so many friends in the Club whom we have known for so many years, we decided to leave the matter once again to destiny.

On the morning of the election we telephoned a friend and, on account of one of those quirks in these gadgets, we heard the following interesting conversation: "What, Debu Hosali? No, no. Tell all our friends to cut his name off the list. He has already been there for one year and if he is back again he will entrench himself deep, eclipsing all our chances for the future. Tell all our friends to cut his name off the list."

At this stage we butted in by saying, "Hello, hello." Our friend at the other end said, "Hello what? I am telling you to cut Hosali's name off in this evening's election. Did you get it or not?" And we answered, "Yes, we did get it!" A very mortified voice said, "Is it Debu? Of course, of course, you have all my support."

Destiny once again conspired to make our election a success. Strange things do happen in elections.

My father, Mr Devendranath Hosali: his public persona

Of course I first met my father in a private capacity the day I was born, but I've chosen to represent his public persona as the first article in this book because it was so dominant and dynamic. The vast majority of Bangaloreans became acquainted with him through his various public engagements, indicated through his experience of fighting elections. Further revelations follow as you read on, so now, in choosing to re-publish and annotate his weekly columns from *Mysindia*, I am once again making private material public in sharing it with readers. Here and now I write in retrospective as Dada's daughter, through my own experience of the impact his public life had on me and the family.

I remember well that he was President of the Rotary Club and later elected to the position of District Governor. He had actually joined the Rotary Club in Bangalore in 1943 (before I was born) and then occupied every possible office in that Club, with complete dedication to its many charitable contributions. They took up a large chunk of his time and energy, but he saw these as enjoyable opportunities rather than onerous work. His enthusiasm seemed to be infectious. He used to tell Rotarians that attending meetings should be an unfailing habit, as automatic as buttoning a shirt after putting it on.

Dada started *Rotary News* in 1953 for the whole of South-East Asia, and regularly edited and printed the magazine in his Hosali Press. It was imbued with his Rotary ideals and philosophy – his zeal for service and call to action.

Rotary played a substantial part in my family's life as I grew from childhood to adult-hood. I must have been about seven when Dada first went abroad to attend a conference of Rotary editors in Boca Raton, Florida. He brought back loads of fascinating stories of his experiences, and pictures which kept me occupied for weeks afterwards, absorbing scenes from a faraway land I never thought I would visit myself. Of course children nowadays are exposed to umpteen times more visual and mental stimuli on a daily basis, but I am going back to a time when we had no television or internet. Perhaps we made the most of what we did have though. Modern families have to cope with such a barrage of information from multimedia sources that sometimes much potential learning opportunity goes unnoticed and unused.

My husband too has been a Rotarian in recent times, in the UK – but family involvement and commitment here in the true Rotary spirit of service above self is not the same as it was in my childhood experience in Bangalore. My mother, my sister Rani and I accompanied Dada to conferences in neighbouring cities and had a wonderful time. At every one of these events I was proud of the thunderous applause he received when he addressed the audience. One of the Rotarians paid him the following tribute: "I was very impressed with the quality of his talk, the perfect diction, effortless flow of words, the Rotary content in the presentation and the total impact." And yet I recall his nervous pacing while he memorized his first speeches word for word – he had to write them meticulously first, but didn't want to refer to his notes when he spoke. In time he became such a confident and accomplished speaker that he could make impromptu speeches at a moment's notice.

Women were not admitted to the Club in their own right, but wives of the Rotarians in Bangalore were pioneers at the time in setting up their own Rotary-Anns club projects. I have a vague memory of being lifted up to a microphone at the age of two, at a charity event in the Bangalore Club. My mother prompted me: "Say that nursery rhyme you know, the one about Jack and Jill."

When I was done, an English lady came over and tried to start a conversation with me. My mother reminded me of this years later, recalling how I had answered the lady by reciting another nursery rhyme at her. It was the only small smattering of the English language I knew at the time. At least it goes to show that my two-year-old brain could recognise the difference between Hindi and English!

We boys and girls of Rotary learned and performed English and American songs from one of the Rotary Ann mums, Mrs Eswar, an English lady who was married to an Indian Rotarian. She was kind enough to play the piano and persevere through our caterwauling. But one not-so-fine day she pulled me up short: "Arti, you sing with too much abandon – the way you open your mouth so wide makes you look like a goldfish gasping for air!" Uh-oh, I was so mortified that I went to the other extreme and tried to sing with a closed mouth. I suspect that made me look like a ventriloquist.

Undaunted however, as time marched on I participated in modelling and dance shows, despite having no particular talent for such performances. Such fund-raising and social opportunities brought me into contact with a wonderful multicultural community of like-minded, philanthropic people from different parts of the world. I was always encouraged to volunteer and contribute. The habit has stayed with me to this day.

I also recall some day trips to an outlying village where the Rotary-Anns Club had set up a Rural Development Centre. The project aimed to educate rural women and children. Contraception was an important issue, as the population was increasing at an alarming rate, but birth control was controversial for villagers who wanted sons to work on the land and look after them in old age.

So imagine if you will my five-year-old self: an excited city girl looking forward to visiting a village one Saturday morning. My mother says, "I want you to come along and help me today. We are going to Whitefield[1] and we will take soap, toothpaste and shampoo to give to the village folk. We should tell them about washing hands, brushing teeth, getting rid of lice in their hair…"

---

1   Whitefield (at that time an outlying village) has now been drawn into the heart of the metropolis and is a thriving part of urban Bengaluru.

Okay. So I am grinning like a Cheshire cat on the bus ride over to Whitefield. Aunty Ila Bose (all my parents' friends were 'aunties' and 'uncles') – well, Aunty Ila cannot have children of her own, so she always gives me a cuddle and says she'd love to adopt me for that happy smile. But what do I do the moment we get to Whitefield? Run off to play and race around with the village children. They show me the crops and how rice is planted in the paddy fields. I am in the middle of a vegetable patch, entranced by carrots being dug out of the ground, when I'm suddenly scooped up by a pair of strong arms – but before I can howl in protest at this indignity I see the rattlesnake I've been saved from.

The strong arms (I couldn't tell you now if they belonged to a man, woman or older child) carry me off to a hut and bring me a glass of warm milk. I just remember asking, "Are those your pets?" pointing to the goat and the buffalo tethered in the yard. I am struck by the way in which this family live simply in a small space, right next to their big animals. And one of the girls then takes me by the hand and squats down with a bucket to show me how she milks the buffalo. I am too scared to go near – scared of the horns at one end and the legs that might kick me at the other – but the girl is comfortable and the buffalo is docile.

When I get back to my mother she asks, "Where have you been? I hope you've been helping like I said?" "Oh yes", I answer, but I am uncertain and hesitant, knowing full well that I've gained more than I've given that day.

I was five years old when Dada contested the Lok Sabha election that he refers to in his column. Oh, what immense excitement when Rani and I used to hear the election vans approaching with their blaring loudspeakers – which they frequently did for several weeks during the campaigning period. We would run out onto the first floor veranda of our house to catch a glimpse of all the election *tamasha*. Not that we understood the politics in any depth, but Dada's special message on 'housing for all' was symbolically conveyed by two substantial model huts mounted on the roof of his two campaigning vans. When the election was over one of these huts came to rest in our veranda and became a much-loved playhouse for my sister and me. And when we outgrew the playhouse it became a much-needed kennel for our Alsatian, Marcus.

When I think back to Dada's short foray into politics I can see he was persuaded to stand for election, but was really not up to the energy-sapping wheeling and dealing that often ends up as a menacing game. But in all the voluntary positions Dada occupied with so much integrity, wit, charm, energy and enthusiasm, I am proud of his willingness and ability to contribute to society and create benefits for people of all backgrounds. What this meant for us in the family was his frequent absence in many a long evening. After a day's work he would drive home, shower and change into a fresh white shirt, and drive off again to attend some meeting or other. He was a Councillor of the Corporation of Bangalore for 8 years, Master of the Bangalore Trades Association, President, Chamber of Commerce and President of the Mysore Printers' Association – not to mention his avid love of racing and long association with the Bangalore Turf Club as a Steward.

He writes frankly about himself in his columns, not disguising his flaws and opinions. That makes him jump off the page and live as a three-dimensional character. In reality he had a great presence when he entered a room – a charismatic presence that one couldn't ignore.

But he also did not ignore anyone if he felt they were floundering socially: if he noticed someone looking lost, someone who was new to a group, he would go up to them, draw them into conversation and introduce them to others.

This is a story to be continued, partly through Dada's own candid descriptions and partly through my parallel stories. Read on, and you will no doubt find his 3-D personality coming to life more and more in the pages that follow.

When did I say that?

10 Sept. 1967

In 1939 destiny itself conspired to make us the head of the family. Not that we were, by virtue of our wisdom or knowledge of worldly affairs, suited for this role, but our father was dead and we were the eldest among our brothers and sisters; and hence the title came to be conferred upon us.

But power does strange things to man. A *bania*[2] makes money in the black market and with it acquires the many material things of life – a nice house, good furniture, a good-looking wife, jewellery for her, a fleet of cars, a battery of servants, so on and so forth. All this gives him a complex of superiority over the others in the herd to which he belongs. He even starts thinking that he is endowed with better moral values, ability and wisdom, that his decisions are infallible and should, therefore, not be questioned by others.

Now that is exactly what happened to us. With the power that got vested in us as the head of the family, we developed the complex that we were an authority on everything under the sun and, therefore, no-one should question our decisions. Thus, over the years our management and mis-management, actions and inactions, decisions and indecisions, have brought to the family some good fortune (accidentally) and some considerable misfortune. And now, if there is any talk about what has happened in the past 28-and-odd years, as a result of our stewardship, and someone says, "It was your decision that was responsible for this unfortunate result", we say vehemently: "What nonsense! It was the decision of the family." If someone says you said such and such a thing 25 years ago, we assert, "When did we? In fact we never did!"

****

In 1947 destiny itself conspired to make some of our agitators in the freedom movement the leaders of India. Not that they were, by virtue of their wisdom or knowledge of worldly affairs, fitted for this role, but the British had packed up and they happened to be the tallest amongst a group of pigmies.

During the past 20 years, their management and mismanagement, actions and inactions, decisions and indecisions, direction and misdirection, have brought the country to the verge of ruin. The shibboleths of Socialism have created the worst class conflict. The three Five Year Plans have brought India to bankruptcy, the creation of Linguistic States have balkanised it into several parochial units. And now they are hell-bent on completing the disintegration by doing away with English and forcing

2   A *bania* is a merchant trader belonging to the business community in India

Hindi on unwilling linguistic groups.

Questioned about his assertion that in five years English will be replaced by Hindi as the official language in the High Courts and the Supreme Court, Minister Morarji Desai said the other day, "When did I say that? In fact I never did! It is a Cabinet decision."

My father, Dada: the private man

I think I constructed my Dada as my teddy bear early in childhood, loving him as all little girls love their teddy bears and their fathers. As I grew up I had to respect him too and I sometimes resented it. As described in his previous column, his word was law as the undoubted head of our household. He was in many ways a distant father, authoritarian and respected by everyone in the family.

At the same time our family was amazingly liberal – an oasis of critical and creative thought and deed in the midst of a very traditional national culture. This was largely because of the legacy that shaped Dada's personality. My grandfather (Panditji) had broken away from his Brahmin roots back in the 1890s. As a young man he was identified as a brilliant scholar with an incredible memory, so his Marathi community sponsored him to go to England and study Law at Oxford. The sponsors expected him to do them proud by joining the Indian Civil Service on his return. Getting recruited into an ICS position was reserved for privileged high-flying Indians at that time of the British Raj.

The story goes that Panditji qualified successfully and was called to the Inner Temple Bar in London. His personal behaviour was however another matter. He fathered a daughter with a young lady, Kate – I'm not sure if this was in or out of wedlock. Kate Hosali was clear that she would not return to India with Panditji when the time came for him to go back, but she vowed to raise their daughter, Nina, in her father's name. She never (re)married and remained true to her word.

The close mother-daughter bond between Kate and Nina was incredibly important and productive. They travelled together extensively in the Middle East and North Africa, and

Panditji with other students at Oxford

Kate Hosali

were appalled by the sorry plight of the donkeys they saw being treated cruelly as beasts of burden. This led them to study veterinary science on their return to London. In 1923 they started the charity SPANA (Society for the Protection of Animals in North Africa). Today, after more than 90 years, the work of SPANA in veterinary care, education and training centres is making the world a more compassionate place for countless working animals.

Returning to Panditji's story… apparently he disappointed his community back in Maharashtra on his return. They became aware that he had lived with Kate, eaten meat and drunk alcohol – all strictly forbidden to Brahmins. No-one would give their daughter's hand in marriage to him. I never knew Panditji because he had passed away in 1939, before I was born, but I used to ask my grandmother, Maji, how she had met and married him. Maji always deflected the question, saying she would write a book about it some day. She never did, so this has remained a mystery, especially because Maji was Bengali and Panditji was Maharashtrian – geographically from east and west coast of India, culturally and linguistically worlds apart. Inter-regional, inter-caste marriages were highly unusual in those times. There was surely a scandal in there somewhere, because society did not accept a flouting of caste and cultural traditions.

Panditji used his Law qualifications back in India to practise very successfully as a barrister until his death. One of his clients was extremely grateful to him for getting him off a murder charge and saving him from a prison sentence. He couldn't afford the fee however, so he gifted the printing press in Bangalore to Panditji. This inheritance was a great blessing for the Hosali family when Panditji died an untimely death and left a relatively young widow and seven children to fend for themselves. My father Dada was the oldest son; as tradition dictated, he had to take on the responsibility for raising his five younger siblings. His youngest sister was only seventeen at the time of their father's death.

This was a tremendous personal and financial responsibility for Dada, who was forced to become the head of the household when he was 29. He was unmarried and was happily pursuing a career in radio and music at the Gramophone Company in Calcutta – a job he loved. For a brief while there he played the harmonium for Kundan Lal Saigal, one of India's greatest singers of all time. Indian cinema was in its infancy in the 1930s and Saigal also acted and sang in those early films. Dada retained a lifelong interest in cinema, music and art, but he had to give all that up at the time and return to Akola where the family then lived. He was of an artistic and literary disposition and did not have a single business bone in his body. Despite this, he did manage to take over the Hosali Press as a business and combine it with his creative talents in writing and publishing.

It seems pretty incredible that Dada (at that time living in Bangalore, south India) heard about my mother (at that time living in Lahore, in the Punjab, northwest India). He was attracted by my maternal grandfather's Arya Samaji philosophy of fostering equality and valuing diversity – and uniting India through inter-regional, inter-caste marriages. But there was a distance of approximately 1,300 miles or 2090 km. between Bangalore and Lahore. Undeterred, Dada travelled three days and four nights by train to visit my mother and ask for her hand in marriage. They only saw each other across the table at lunchtime, and mutually agreed to marry, without having spoken a single word to each other. What she was agreeing to was a lifetime living with an extended family of mixed and dubious parentage and heritage, very different from her Punjabi roots. She had to join forces with Dada to bring up his younger brothers and sisters, getting them through school, college, training for jobs and marriage. Of course in India there is no welfare system and everything had to be paid for, including education and health. Such was her leap of faith.

My sister and I were born into this extended family – we lived with our aunts, uncles, pet dogs, rabbits and most of all with our grandmother Maji who ruled the roost with a rod of iron. In some of his articles Dada refers to Maji's imperious commands. And so the family continued to flourish, oblivious of religious and caste restrictions. We had friends from all sorts of backgrounds at different levels of social status – all accepted without judgment – and we were all (as young men and women) free to choose our occupations and marriage partners.

We were not well off though. Although Dada never talked about it, I saw at first-hand how difficult it sometimes was for him to make ends meet: to pay all his staff at the Press and look after the whole family. The responsibilities he shouldered for his immediate family extended in time to his nieces and nephews. During the summer holidays the entire clan would come to stay at our house in Basvangudi. We had fun times with our 'summer cousins' – giving up our beds and sleeping head to toe on big mattresses in the drawing room with an enormous mosquito net stretched over and above us.

My cousin Titli recently sent me a reflective email from her home, now in the USA:

"The images that float back into memory are my summer holidays in Bangalore. For some reason our holidays did not exactly overlap. You still had to dress and go off to school in the mornings in your green pinafore. They were long blissful summer days. I remember you and Rani playing the piano in the downstairs room off the staircase. Dada was so proud of you both and your musical skills. The lovely long walks we took to Lalbagh with Lucky romping alongside. The sitting room upstairs that had a library of leather bound classics. Maji, giving us *uptan* baths. The dining room with the blue chair near the sink where Dada and Maji would sit.

"I used to often go and spend the afternoon with Bhabi in her room - she had such a serene, peaceful aura.

"Krishna's delicious food - especially the *kaju ki mithai* that I would sneak down and eat when everyone was having an afternoon nap. Oh! and the monkeys that came around to eat the figs from the trees near the front gate. I loved watching them from the upstairs windows. In those halcyon days of childhood it was hard to believe we would ever be done with school – the future seemed so far away. If I had to write to my younger self now, I would have to advise her to enjoy every moment of childhood; it is a golden time."

Dada was Dada to everyone in the family – truly the elder brother in name and responsibility – and my mother was Bhabi (sister-in-law) to all, expected without question to fall in line and serve the family's interests. In due course these relationship terms extended far beyond the boundaries of the family, so that we grew up taking it for granted that our father and mother were Dada and Bhabi to all their friends and most of their acquaintances in Bangalore. I was truly blessed to have them as my parents.

Deafness sure has its compensations

5 April 1970

Friends often express sympathy with us on our growing deafness. But what is so very wrong with being deaf? For one thing, a very large part of the conversation of people is not worth listening to. For another, when somebody really wants you to hear what he's saying he comes close and speaks to you in your ear. And when such a person happens to be a pretty young girl, her very proximity and the whiff of her perfume gives you enough tantalization to be deaf all your life.

Now see what happened to us some time back. A friend of ours, who is Ambassador Plenipotentiary in an important country, came to Bangalore as he was escorting the President of that country on an all-India tour. We invited him for a cocktail party at the Bangalore Club. At 7:30 that evening, a number of smart ladies and gentlemen joined us at the party, but our Ambassador friend was late in coming as he had another appointment. Eventually, when he turned up along with a few European friends at about 8:30, everyone was quite high. And we were not only high but very deaf also.

As our friend came in, he introduced his European friends to us – the ladies and gentlemen – but we were quite unable to get their names. Neither did we bother to ascertain who they were; our only desire was to offer them drinks. And so we shouted for the bearer and ordered large whiskies and sodas, brushing aside the protests of the gentlemen by a friendly slap on the back and of the ladies by an affectionate peck on the cheek.

Thus the party proceeded and all barriers appeared to have broken down, what with the drinks, our back-slapping the gentlemen and affectionate peckings of the ladies! By 11 pm, when it had become one of the gayest parties of our life, and all our friends were in rollicking good humour, our European friends got up to take leave and, in so doing, mentioned how much they had enjoyed themselves. They extended the most cordial invitations to us to visit their country. At that we asked, "But what is your name, and which country do you come from?" When the card was presented to us, we realized with a shock that all the liberties we had taken were with the President of xxx and his wife.

****

This morning a gentleman came into our office. Having introduced himself, he started explaining the purpose of his visit. After ten minutes of talk, to which we listened attentively but were unable to understand a word, the talk having fallen on deaf ears, we divined with our sixth sense that he had called for some urgent printing. We said it was unfortunate that the Press was busy with high priority jobs, and we could not be of much help to him.

At that he cut us short and commenced another ten minutes of pleading. Having listened to him attentively once more, and not having heard what he was saying, we put on the quizzical expression we have perfected for such occasions – raised eyebrows and wrinkled forehead – and looked sternly in his face.

At that the man started talking rapidly once again. Our printing department manager, who was standing next to us, took a sheet of paper and wrote down: "His first offer for the job was Rs. 4,500, which he raised to 6,000, and is now prepared to pay Rs. 7,500."

In great animation we said, "Get the contract form."

Deafness sure has its compensations!

Silver linings

So Dada's deafness seemed to have some compensations for him, but I had to ask myself if that cloud also had silver linings for me. He found it difficult to hold normal conversations with my sister Rani and me, but he needed our quiet companionship and often played rummy with us. He always sat in the same chair he favoured at our dining table, and when I visualise him there he's often reading a book – like the novels in Readers' Digest condensed volumes. I definitely got my great love of reading from him and from the vast variety of books in our house, sent to him because he was an editor and proprietor of a printing press.

I think that I accepted his deafness pretty much as a normal part of himself because he accepted it. Although being hard of hearing was a constraint, he never used it as an impediment or an excuse. It did not stop him from seeking office, getting elected and being effective and productive in all his roles. It was typical of his personality that he could look at both sides of a situation and dwell on the brighter side. I absorbed this positive attitude subliminally, and grew up fundamentally accepting that everyone has abilities and disabilities, and that these lie along a spectrum of individual strengths and development needs.

In my teaching profession, this approach underpinned my interactions with all students, regardless of their type and level of study, age and background. The innovative pedagogies I developed and authored had one basic aim: to enable all students to identify, critically appreciate and use their strengths, and to integrate their personal, academic and professional development. In this role, for me, Dada's role-modelling of a can-do attitude was one of the silver linings in the cloud of his deafness. Inheriting a positive attitude in life is actually worth more than silver or gold – it is priceless.

Now witness this conversation that took place when I was teaching at the University of Bedfordshire:

Overseas student: "Professor, where does your accent come from? I cannot quite place it – or you – where do you come from?"

Me (tongue in cheek): "I come from planet Earth! It must be a mid-Atlantic accent!" But then I feel I should answer his question more honestly. "I've never thought about it, it's just the way I speak. My accent must have changed naturally from its origins in India, because I've lived in the UK since 1970."

Student: "Oh, really? The thing is, we often cannot make head or tail of what some other lecturers are saying. We foreign students thought we could speak, read and write English quite well – but that was before we arrived here in the UK. I often don't understand when English people speak to me. We are struggling to make sense of the accents and study material. Except for your class; we really like the way you speak and explain things."

Of course I was chuffed with this type of student feedback. Then, over the years, life unfolded several surprises. I confess I've always identified myself as a learner rather than a teacher – I feel energized in the midst of a community of learners where I watch and experience new things. Every day. So, back then I overcame obstacles I never thought I could, and achieved things I never dreamt I would. Enabling my students to learn, develop and succeed earned me awards such as a National Teaching Fellowship in 2005, followed by a MBE in the Queen's New Year Honours list in 2008 "for services to higher education". Winning awards opened up a range of opportunities and made a massive difference in my career. I can attribute at least some of this success to Dada's deafness: I had to compensate by learning early on to communicate clearly and choose my words carefully. When Dada really couldn't hear something important I was trying to convey he would ask me to write it in one or two sentences. These communication skills filtered into my teaching.

During Dada's lifetime I never got to tell him how much I valued his example and influence in my career success. I am sad that my awards were achieved after he had passed away. I like to think he is still somewhere in a spiritual world where he knows and is proud of me.

Naturally there was also something of a downside because he was hard of hearing. To some extent I experienced him as a distant father, out of touch with my feelings and aspirations. Imagine attempting a heart-to-heart confidential chat whilst shouting to make oneself heard!

I recall an incident when I was working at the Press with him. I finished early and decided to walk to the Bangalore Club for a game of tennis. On the way there I remembered I hadn't given him an important message and an address to which he needed to post an urgent letter. So I headed straight to the Club Library and asked the kind lady who had her admin table in one corner if I could make a telephone call (we had no mobile phones in those days).

So there I was, reading out the message over the phone to Dada, trying to make myself heard. After several repetitions, when it came to the address, I got to the line where the letter had to go to the county of Middlesex in the UK.

Dada says: "What's that? Speak up!"

I speak louder: "It's Enfield, in Middlesex."

Dada: "Middle …what?"

I unthinkingly shout "Sex – S-E-X!" – and suddenly realise that every pair of eyes in the library is turned on me. Lots of shocked stares and some silly sniggering.

Deafness sure has its embarrassing moments too!

On giving evidence in a Law Court

2 July 1972

We have a mortal dread of giving evidence in Law Courts and all through our life we have avoided doing so. But the other day, in a certain civil suit involving the title of a house, the Judge compelled us to do so on pain of putting us under arrest. And so, one morning at 11, we found ourself in the labyrinthine maze of the Bangalore District Courts. After some considerable exploration, being driven from pillar to post, from the north wing to the south wing and from the east wing to the west wing, we managed to locate the correct Court and waited for the Judge's call.

It was a long wait of several hours, but eventually the Court Clerk called our name, followed by the peon repeating it loudly, and we were ushered into the Court.

But things went wrong right from the beginning. Instead of getting into the witness box, we walked straight into the dock meant for the accused, much to the chagrin of the lawyer who had summoned us and the amusement of all and sundry present. However, after being salvaged from the ignominious position we had got into, we were installed in the witness box only to encounter the next hurdle – the oath which was administered in Kannada. We had never heard it before and so we were quite flummoxed by it. Our natural reaction to it was the exclamation: "What!"

The Judge, a very severe looking person, thundered: "What do you mean by 'What!' Don't you understand that oath?"

We were a bit more flummoxed at this, and not knowing the answer, gazed vacantly at the Judge, when the lawyer opposite prompted us and said, "Just say 'yes'."

The lawyer then asked us if we knew Mr Peer Mohammed, the owner of the house under dispute. We said, "Yes, we knew him."

The Judge butted in ferociously, "What do you mean by saying you knew him? Is he dead? Don't you know him any longer?"

We said, "Your Honour, we knew Mr Peer Mohammed but in 1947, on the partition of the country, he went away to Pakistan. Hence we used the past tense."

"Then who is this man standing in front of you?"

We said, "Oh, that fellow! He is Noor Mohammed, the younger brother of Peer Mohammed."

The Judge well-nigh exploded: "This man seems to be a terrible liar. Why was he summoned here to give evidence?"

At this stage a little explanation is necessary. We had not set eyes upon the Peer and Noor Mohammeds since 1947, and our recollection as to who was who had completely faded.

The Judge glowered at us and came out with a number of expletives in Kannada, to which we put in apologetically, "Beg your pardon, Your Honour!"

Now the anger of the Judge knew no bounds. He said, "What do you mean by 'Beg your pardon' – don't you understand Kannada?"

Our meek rejoinder to this was that we did not understand Kannada, but the Judge's reaction to it was absolutely maddening. He raved, "This man here, this liar with the name Hosahalli, a Kannadiga, tells me he does not understand Kannada! I don't want his evidence. Send him away."

The lawyer submitted that he had just one more question which he would like to ask, but as he spoke rather inaudibly we once again came out with our "Beg your pardon" request.

The Judge howled: "'Beg your pardon' again, eh?"

We put in meekly that we were very deaf and could not hear the question properly. But the Judge went real mad at this. He stood up and, having hammered his gavel on the table, said: "Remove this man from my Court. He doesn't understand Kannada, he is deaf, he thinks Peer Mohammed is in Pakistan and Noor Mohammed in India, he thinks white is black and black is white. He is the biggest liar that ever stepped into my Court. Remove him!" And thus our first – and we hope our last – appearance in Court to give evidence ended in an inglorious exit.

We are not so identityless – after all

24 July 1966

11 years ago, at a marriage reception in Calcutta, we were seated next to an elderly lady, when our host came and introduced us to her. We bowed casually and settled down in our seat. Our host, observing that the importance of the names had not registered in our brain, whispered in our ear, "That is Air Marshal Mookerji's sister". With some animation we turned to her and said, "Oh, you are Air Marshal Mookerji's sister? Pleased to meet you."

The lady, in obvious annoyance said, "You think it is an honour to be the sister of Air Marshal Mookerji? I am Renuka Ray, if that makes any sense to you!"

We tendered profuse apologies for the *faux pas* we had committed.

****

Last Saturday at the Races we were standing next to two portly dames who were looking into the official Race Card. Finding our name among the Stewards, one asked the other, "Who is this Hosali?" The other said, "He is IGP[3] Hosali's brother – Sita's husband."

Notwithstanding the highly non-Aryan complexion we have, we flushed a deep crimson mixed with dark brown.

A few minutes later we were introduced to a Steward of the Western India Turf Club, and as our name was mentioned to him he said, "Oh, IGP Hosali's brother? I have known

Satish for many years."

****

Later in the evening at a cocktail party at the West End Hotel, we were greatly obsessed with the feeling that we had no identity of our own. Just then our host introduced us to some of the guests, and we cheerily said, "We are IGP Hosali's brother." And minutes later, when we were presented to some of the ladies, we blurted out "We are Sita's husband." And they looked askance as to who this Sita could be that we were so proud of being her husband.

****

Just as we were ruminating over the happenings of the day, an old friend of ours from Bombay hailed us with great warmth, "Hey Dada, how very wonderful meeting you after these many years! And how is everything? How is the world treating you?"

Just as these pleasantries were being exchanged, a group of young men turned towards us and one of them said, "So you are the famous Dada Hosali? We have been wanting so much to meet you. Have we not heard of your exploits over the years... when you...fixed up so and so?"

We left the party with a glow of satisfaction that, after all, we were not so identityless!

3   IGP (Inspector General of Police)

Some thoughts about identity

I couldn't help but chuckle when I read the column above. As far as I'm aware Dada had no identity issues – he had a strong and authentic sense of self: as the head of the household in his private persona, a capable editor and printing press proprietor in his professional life, and a philanthropic contributor to the betterment of society and to nation-building in a newly-independent India. In his columns you can often see the interweaving of these identities. And you have no doubt noted the royal 'we' he uses with reference to himself throughout his writings.

But perhaps identity is a fragile concept – one that is subject to three inter-dependent dimensions. Firstly, identity is about self-perception. For example, if I ask my students to describe themselves, they mention physical, mental and emotional characteristics – and these represent the attitudes they hold towards themselves at that moment in time.

Secondly, the formation of identity crucially depends on how others perceive and interact with us. Humans are social animals and so the individual Self does not exist in a vacuum – it is shaped and defined over and over again throughout our lifetime by the feedback we receive from others and from different environments. There is a proverb among the Zulu people: *A person becomes a person through other people.*

Philosophers and scholars have discussed and developed many theories of the Self but, in any culture, observation and intuition alone can show us that this socially constructed aspect of Self is dependent on the validation and sustaining influence of others. Amongst neuropsychologists there is a view that any serious mismatch between our self-perception and the perception of others can contribute to a breakdown in mental health.

And the reverse is correspondingly true: self-esteem and wellbeing are enhanced when we receive positive and constructive feedback from significant relationships in our lives. For example, psychologists have reported the results of research with visually impaired individuals. Their findings show that success in life, education and jobs of individuals with these disabilities are directly proportional to the expectations that people have of them. The more capable others believe they are, the more they will develop. Because self-esteem, self-belief and self-image are crucially formed through social interactions it is important for all of us to encounter – and provide – empowering experiences. Teachers, parents and grandparents have particularly significant opportunities and responsibilities for encouraging students and children to develop a positive and authentic sense of Self.

I believe that we can all be more empowering in a positive and altruistic way for ourselves and for others if we are in tune with the third aspect of identity: our inner spiritual and humanistic Self – which truly differentiates Self from Ego. Deepak Chopra expresses this beautifully:

> *You must learn to get in touch with the innermost essence of your being. This essence is beyond the ego. It is fearless; it is free; it is immune to criticism; it does not fear any challenge. It is beneath no-one, and full of magic, mystery and enchantment.*

When our thoughts, decisions and actions are driven by spiritual humanism, we can be(come) free from the tyranny and the suffering caused by Ego. An appreciation of the difference between Self and Ego is essential but difficult. This is a profound and universal concept which I can only touch upon superficially here, so I will leave you with your own views and beliefs.

Continuing in a personal and more superficial vein, the following poem entitled *I Come From…* was composed as a result of my belonging to a group of retired folk here in the UK. We meet every week to chat over a cup of tea or coffee and get involved in various activities that are a wellspring of friendship and creativity. We spent a few weeks writing 'poetry as therapy' with wonderful Fran, who enabled us to discover hidden talents in ourselves and others. In one of these sessions she asked us to write a poem in which every fourth or fifth line was to start with the words 'I come from…' So here's my version. I include it here because it says something about the formation of my identity.

I come from …

I come from the love of a wise and wonderful mother
She was the best friend a naughty girl could have
She gave me the principles of SANE:
Sleep, Attitude, Nutrition, Exercise.

I come from the love of a dynamic but distant father
He was the respected head of our extended family
We lived, played and fought in a house of 15 rooms.

I come from bright sunshine and warm monsoon rain
In the garden city of Bangalore where no pain meant no gain
Now a cyber city of India that churns out new media.

I come from a love of pet dogs and rabbits
Although Marcus the Alsatian scarred me at age two
Jumbo my Labrador was loving and true.

I come from a love of books, words and pictures
Trying to make my own gives me pain and pleasure
I seem to experience both in equal measure.

I come from St Albans – the city of my adult life
Studying, working in Hertfordshire for 46 years
Raising sons and grandkids, trying to be a good wife.

I come from being anchored in family relationships
And I appreciate above all the value of friendships
Even the solace of simple companionship.

I come from unexpected failure, illness and injury
Broken ribs and collarbone, bullies, computer glitches
Oh yes, I've had to cope with some horrible witches!

I come from unexpected success and rewards
A National Teaching Fellowship for outstanding contribution
And then an MBE "for services to higher education"
But success is a journey and not a destination.

I come from the love of learning and teaching
Enabling all my students to SOAR to Success[4]
To connect Self with Opportunity, Aspirations and Results
Now that is the legacy I hope I'll be leaving.

---

4   This refers to the *SOARing to Success* model I developed and authored.
Main book/e-book: Kumar, A. (2008) *Personal, Academic and Career Development in Higher Education – SOARing to Success* London and New York: Routledge Taylor and Francis Companion web:
http://www.routledge.com/professional/978041542360-1/

Some exasperating situations

26 Dec. 1965

We have a knack of getting into tight spots; not that our understanding of human nature is subnormal, but our misfortune is such that, more often than not, we find ourself in situations which are at once comical, ludicrous and exasperating. Now see what happened to us today.

This morning we went to our lawyer to seek advice on the many problems that were vexing us. After half an hour's consultation with him, we emerged from his chambers more befuddled and confused than ever, got into our car and drove away.

A moment later we found a fellow in the car behind kicking up a big racket with his horn and wanting to overtake us. With the inherent dislike we have of anybody trying to overtake us, be it in any walk of life, we resented this very much, and so we put our car in third gear, revved up the engine to its maximum capacity, and speeded up. But the fellow behind us was in hot pursuit and appeared equally determined to overtake us. After a few minutes of mad chase the fellow, having the advantage of a more powerful engine, managed to go ahead of us, and in passing made certain gestures and said certain things which, being very deaf, we were unable to hear.

We felt greatly humiliated at this and said to ourself, come what may this fellow must be taught a lesson. Therefore, shifting the

car into second gear, we started the race again, but the fellow – having slowed down – we overtook him easily, pulled up our car in front so that he could not pass us, jumped out in great wrath and thundered in our loudest voice, "What the deuce do you mean by swearing at us?" A police inspector who was close by appeared on the scene and asked, "Did he abuse you, sir?" We answered in the affirmative.

The fellow in the car was completely foxed, but he managed to say, "Mr Inspector, I did not abuse this gentleman. For the past five minutes I have been trying to overtake him only to tell him that he has been driving on a flat tyre, but the harder I tried the faster he went. See the result, his tyre is in shreds now. And for having done a good turn he now alleges that I have abused him. This is strange indeed!"

We were dumbfounded as we glanced at the rear wheel of our car, but we were profuse in our apologies – almost to the extent of self-mortification.

****

Later in the day we went to the Parade Stores and, sighting a young fellow who we thought was a salesman, we shouted, "A pound of butter and a tin of cheese." The fellow looked over his shoulder, then looked at us and stayed in the inert position in which he was. We waited a full minute to see if our order had registered in his brain or not, but the fellow was standing unconcernedly, ignoring us completely. We thought this was most humiliating and so we caught him by the shoulder and asked him why he was not taking down our order. And, as we started sermonizing on the need for everyone to do his duty conscientiously in free India, and giving him a few tips on effective salesmanship, the young fellow,

greatly upset, said "What is all this? I am a customer just like you, and you come here bellowing your orders at me and giving me tips on salesmanship. There is no need for me to be a salesman. I am the son of the Minister without portfolio."

We offered our profoundest apologies to him, and asked him to convey them also to his father – the Minister without portfolio.

But the climax came later in the day when our secretary informed us that Mr X was on the telephone and wanted to talk to us. Now here was another strange situation: with our increasing deafness, the telephone has been of no use to us for years, and we have developed an intense dislike for the gadget. Be that is it may, Mr X insists on pestering us with his requests for petty loans over the telephone. We were, therefore, mad with rage and we told our secretary to tell him that we were dead and hence could not come to the telephone, little realizing that Mr X at the other end could hear our loud thunder. The next moment, however, we took hold of the instrument and started giving a thorough dressing down to Mr X. After we had blown off some steam, the voice from the other end said, "This is not Mr X, Debu Hosali, this is your friend, the Minister without portfolio. I rang up to invite you for dinner tonight."

Once again we felt terribly mortified, and offered to our friend – the Minister without portfolio – the most profuse apologies. Are these not comical, ludicrous and exasperating situations?

Exasperating technologies

"My new smartphone is too smart for me" I confess to my friend who, like me, has just turned 70 years old.

"I know just what you mean," she says. "My daughter bought me an iPhone for a birthday present. She insists I need it and should keep it on 24/7. Well, that's really just so I can be at her beck and call for baby-sitting the grandchildren at a moment's notice! I'm often tempted to chuck them in the nearest bin. Mobile phones I mean… not the grandchildren."

People of my generation didn't grow up with computers, smartphones and social media. It's hardly surprising that we often find ourselves at odds with email, ebay, facebook, twitter, instagram and suchlike – an alien world of new tools and techniques.

One example comes from a morning when my aunt was visiting and staying with us for a few days in the summer of 2009. I was running late so I had rushed off to work, leaving my desk computer on at home. I was bothered by the thought that this was an environmentally unfriendly thing to do as it would be consuming power all day long. So when I got to work I telephoned my aunt to ask if she would kindly turn my computer off. She asked me which button to press in order to do this, so I said "You will see an icon which says 'start' in the bottom left-hand corner …"

She interrupted and fired off questions at me while I was trying to talk her through the process, a step at a time, so the conversation went something like this:

Aunt: "What do you mean by 'icon'?"

Me: "It's a little image button on the screen…"

Aunt: "You are asking me to shut it down and then telling me to go to a 'start' button!?"

Me: Well, if you hover over that button …"

Aunt: "What do you mean by 'hover over it' – I am standing over it!"

Me: "Aunty, I mean you need to do that with the mouse…"

Now, even as I said this I knew how ridiculous it was for me to expect my aunt to comply with my request – she had never used a computer before, and she didn't have a jargon-buster handy. I heard a little shriek on the other end of the line. My aunt was saying: "You know I'm really scared of mice – where is this mouse?"

The upshot of all this was that I said please forget it, it's ok, not to worry, and hung up. I came home that evening to find my computer still on, signaling and flashing its little lights at me, but that was nothing compared to the tizzy my aunt was in about having to spend a day with a mouse in the house.

Then there's the morning my alarm didn't go off and I missed an appointment because I overslept. Strangely, I seem to start rhyming my thoughts whenever I'm upset or emotional. This time my thoughts crystallized into conversations with various younger members of my family – largely imagined, but based on what they really might say!.

Generationally irrelevant!

(Me, to my sons and teenage grand-daughter)

"I missed my 'flu vaccination today
Have to go back next week – hate this delay!
Why must we be so time-bound and rule-bound!
Must make sure my watch is wound…"

"Thama, set your alarm, watch the clock
You must avoid the shock
Of missing a vital rendez-vous
What might it have meant for you?!"

"Mum, did you forget the doctor's appointment?
Maybe you're dicing with life and death
Or simply sacrificing your chance of good health…"

"But for now, Mum, you can run for the bus
Simply stop making this ridiculous fuss!
Learn to love your new smartphone
If you absolutely must have a moan
You don't have to do it alone
Put it on Facebook, tweet it on Twitter…"
Believe it or not, life can be sweeter
If and when you embrace social media
You can find everything on Wikipedia
Enjoy the white noise of virtual chatter
Surf the net, browse and play
Get your retail therapy on eBay
Keep the world at your fingertips
While also keeping the real world at bay!"

It suddenly struck me. Did my children and grandchildren find my lack of IT ability as frustrating as I found my Aunt's?

Satnavs are yet another example of technology that can trip us up. One afternoon I had to drive to the Bedford campus of my University to deliver a presentation. This was an unfamiliar journey for me. I would normally have planned it in advance on a map, together with a few written notes. However I had recently bought a satnav – a portable Tom-tom. My car is ancient and doesn't have a satellite navigation system built into the dashboard.

So with some trepidation I entered the postcode of the campus on my Tom-tom and set off.

My son Manoj on the other hand trusts his satnav completely. He says he would drive off a cliff if it told him to. Luckily I can see that it hasn't told him to yet – and I hope it never will. Mine has on occasion driven me round in circles (and driven me nuts) when a particular road was closed and I had to follow a diversion which took me several miles off-route. As for Baldev, my husband – well he often drives me nuts as well. He often disagrees loudly with the directions being issued by the satnav, convinced he knows a better route. I once suggested, "You know you can always change the voice on the satnav. That woman's voice is too polite and patient. I think you would find it easier to listen to a man's assertive directions." Ouch!

But I digress. On the afternoon of my Bedford campus presentation, the woman's voice proved trustworthy and I arrived at the campus in time. I gave the gadget a thankful pat and put it into my handbag. It seemed to accept my gratitude quietly. Then, just as I was almost ready to start introducing my first powerpoint slide, I moved my bag out of the way; and the satnav suddenly piped up "Turn around when possible." The people in the front rows of my audience heard this – so I had to start my presentation with people laughing at me and me laughing at myself. "Oh dear," I quipped, "I hope you have more faith in this talk than my satnav has in me."

And, oh heck, there was the time when my University issued all of us staff members with a personal alarm. The issue was accompanied by an all-staff email that read:

> *Some of you may already know that a senior lecturer suffered a serious assault and injuries in the car park last week. We are sending out personal alarms for each of you, so make sure you receive yours. Please don't be alarmed (pardon the pun) but we advise you to take care and be especially cautious in the car park area.*

In our open-plan office my colleagues start discussing this news. "I wonder who got attacked," my friend says. "This is quite horrific. I'm going to be scared going to my car – it's really dark these winter evenings by the time we leave."

Well I'm quite relaxed about all this. I drop my little alarm into my handbag with no further thought, and get on with the day's work. All is well until a few evenings later. I'm feeling ultra-satisfied with the pleasant and productive day I've had as I head out to my car. I have my car keys handy and, just as I press the button to open the door, I feel a heavy hand on my shoulder. All in a flash all pleasant thoughts are replaced by sheer terror. I'm as wobbly as a jellyfish. But then a familiar voice attaches itself to the heavy hand, and I see that it's none other than the security guard.

"Hey, you're not being very vigilant, are you?" he admonishes me. "Even your handbag is carelessly slung over your shoulder – so any thief could snatch it and be gone by the time you realise..."

"You gave me such a jump. I thought you were the criminal" I admonish him in return.

But I accept that he is right, and begin to think that my personal alarm needs to be more accessible in the event of a real incident. What good could it do if I have to rummage for it in the bottom of my handbag while I'm in the grip of an assassin? I fish it out and attach it to the strap of my bag. I resolve to carry my bag firmly in front like an attachment to my tummy.

Luckily the next few months bring no further bad news and we are all beginning to relax. Even the daylight is now making steady advances over dark evenings so all's well when we leave work.

Yes, all's well and God is in his heaven. I'm excited about going to a conference in Birmingham but the train comes to a dead halt in the middle of nowhere. For many minutes there is no explanation for the delay. Then a voice over the intercom apologises and announces there's a body on the line and we must wait until the police and forensics have done what they have to do. This makes people look up from their laptops, tablets and smartphones and make eye contact with each other. The man across the table from me says, "Why do people have to use the train as their killer weapon of choice?"

"Why can't people commit suicide by overdosing in their own beds at home?" we wonder. But then we chide ourselves for having so little sympathy with the lost soul on the line.

Eventually I'm rushing late into the conference hall. I fling off my shoulder bag and wriggle out of my coat as I enter. And, as I do so, a shrill blast pierces my ears. "Uh-oh – that's all we need", is my first reaction, "we will all have to evacuate because the fire alarm has gone off." But then I see that the speaker is striding over and everyone in the audience has their eyes fixed on me. The realisation dawns: I must have set off my personal alarm!

Sure enough, the strap of my bag has broken, and the pin on my alarm has pulled out and pinged off somewhere. In the next few minutes I'm surrounded by people trying to stop this infernal din. I have no idea myself how to do this. I put my fingers in my ears and make ridiculous, frantic suggestions: "throw the alarm out of the window; put it in a bucket of water…" But then I join the couple of people who are scrabbling on the floor, and finally I find the pin and stick it back. What a relief! Normality is quickly resumed. But the flushed heat of embarrassment creeps over me from time to time and distracts me from the proceedings for the better part of this conference.

Years later I'm submitting an article to an online journal and I'm advised to speak to the editor. I call him and start to introduce myself, but he interjects with "Arti! I know you! How could I ever forget that alarming entrance you made to our conference in Birmingham – right in the middle of my keynote presentation!"

I wonder if exasperating incidents with technologies will stalk me all my life – and beyond. If I had a gravestone (which fortunately I will not) it might read: "Rest in peace, free from the tyrannies of computer glitches, smartphones, social media, satnavs and personal alarms."

On sending and not sending RSVPs

25 Sept. 1966

On Monday, as we started our work, we were mighty happy to find that our secretary had cleaned up our table, which had been cluttered for days with pending correspondence, unused manuscripts, files, magazines, books and what not. What pleased us most was the three invitations which rested placidly under the paperweight. One was for a cocktail party on Monday evening from our friend, the Nawab of Kuch Parwah Nahin, the second from a friend's wife inviting us and Sita to dinner on Tuesday, and the third from our German friend, Dr Brummel, for dinner and drinks on Wednesday.

We examined the invitations a little closely, and found that two of them – the one from the Nawab and the other from our German friend – required a response, the cryptic RSVP having been imprinted on them, but our friend's wife had taken it for granted that we had only to be invited for us to fill the vacant seats at her table.

Now this RSVP business has baffled us all through life. There was a time in our teens when we thought that it signified the menu in abbreviation: *Russam, Sambar, Vadai, Payasam*. But it was not long before general knowledge tests dinned into our ears that it stood for *répondez s'il vous plait* – a French expression. In later life, however, this cryptic business of RSVP has created many an embarrassing situation for us. Whenever we have decided to respond and accept we have felt too tired and fagged out to attend the party. But when we have not responded, all the buoyancy and exuberance of youth bubbles up and there we are at the party, creating problems for our hostess, rearranging the table.

And so this time we decided to be correct and proper. We thought there was no need for an RSVP for the Nawab's party as it was only for cocktails; the friend's wife did not expect it in any case, and so we dictated our acceptance of the third invitation on Wednesday.

But as we went into the Nawab's house, we were surprised to find the gaiety of a cocktail party missing. Even the light in the portico was off. But the Nawab was in the drawing room with half a dozen cronies already in a state of high inebriation. On seeing us he yelled a welcome like an aboriginal chieftain, and embraced us as though we were a long-lost brother. But on seeing Sita he was a bit taken aback, sobered down and escorted her to the zenana. A thought crossed our mind faintly whether we had not made a mistake about the date, as the Nawab's parties were always gay affairs with all the belles and bounders of the city attending. But, before we could say any-thing about this, the Nawab was there with a double whisky … and thus, from one drink to another, it was 11 pm and we returned home thoroughly inebriated, flummoxed and confused about this party.

****

On Tuesday evening, as we entered Mrs X's drawing room, much to our chagrin we found the atmosphere of a dinner party absent. Mrs X was sitting in a homespun sari with her face unmade and, although both Mr and Mrs X were genuinely surprised at our visit, they accorded us a great welcome. We settled down to a drink and Sita and Mrs X to their feminine confabulations.

By and by it was 9.30, but there was no sign of other guests and no sign of dinner. At 10.30 we asked, "What about the other guests?" Mrs X, thinking we were already under the influence of drink, said: "What other guests, Dada? We are all here." And a little later when we said, "How about some dinner?" she said, "Of course, we are going to have pot luck," and repaired fast to fry a few eggs.

Once again we returned home quite a bit flummoxed and confused about this party.

****

On Wednesday morning we had a visit from Dr Brummel, who seemed to be in a state of considerable embarrassment. But after composing himself he asked, "Are you coming to my house this evening?" And we answered cheerily, "Of course – with Sita."

"But", Dr Brummel said, "there seems to be some mistake. Did you receive an invitation from me for a cocktail party?" We said yes and, picking up the invitation, we held it before him. Dr Brummel took one look at it and said, "Ah, this is the invitation I sent you last year, on September 21st. How did you receive it now?"

The whole mystery about the parties we had attended became clear to us. Our secretary, in cleaning our table, had fished out the three invitations we had received for the 19th, 20th and 21st September last year, and placed them before us.

Party time!

Dada's article gives us a glimpse of the parties that were typical of the sixties amongst his social circle – it was a rollicking time! His sister-in-law, Pushpa, who was married to his younger brother Satish, wrote about her experience of going to a wedding in Bombay with him and Maji. Her account is reproduced here, with her permission, but just be aware that this is purely her personal perspective.

A Candid Profile of Unguarded Moments

Pushpa Hosali, 1966

Many doubtless know Dada Hosali as a serious minded Editor of *Mysindia*, a past Governor of Rotary, a past President of the Chamber of Commerce and the Trades Association, an ex-Councillor of the Corporation of Bangalore and presently a Steward of the Bangalore Turf Club; an owner of freak horses bought for next to nothing, but which have won lakhs of rupees in stake money. But how many know that side of his character which is utterly unpredictable, especially when he is in a joyous holiday mood?

It was to the metropolitan city of Bombay that Dada, Satish, Ma and I had gone to attend the wedding of our niece. Bombay, at all times, is a hectic city; and Dada added greater thrill to it every moment of our stay there. At the wedding reception he kept on inviting everyone he met to come to the Ritz Hotel, where we were staying, for a cocktail party. When the list started getting bigger and bigger, utterly unmanageable in a hotel suite, I gave him a dirty, disapproving look, but he continued to invite more and more people. He patted my shoulder reassuringly, said there was plenty of Scotch whisky, and totally ignored my protests – which he pretended not to hear.

At 9.30 pm, the lift was only shunting between the lobby and the fourth floor, to suite 405. Within half an hour, elders, adults and children were sitting on each other's laps for want of space, while Satish and I were playing hopscotch trying to pass drinks. Children wanted dinner, Ma was tired and hungry after a strenuous day, and the rest wanted their glasses refilled at an alarming pace. The waiters were rushed off their feet getting dinner, snacks, cold drinks, ice cream, etc. At 2 am Dada declared that it was a lovely party and it was time to open another bottle of Chivas Regal!

Another night, a friend invited us for dinner at The Rendezvous at Taj International. The dinner was in honour of Dada, and the date was fixed in consultation with him. But that evening Dada disappeared and later telephoned that he would join us in half an hour. We waited for him till midnight, but in vain. He did not keep his rendezvous.

The next morning, the floor waiter comes and reports to me very gingerly that Dada hasn't come back yet. So the hunt starts for him – frantic telephone calls to everyone who happens to know him in Bombay. At 12 noon he arrives at the hotel, shaves, bathes and changes at lightning speed, and we proceed to the races as though nothing has happened. Surprisingly he looks none the worse for a whole night's binge.

He needs not one but four secretaries to keep track of his appointments – which he makes and breaks with the greatest of ease. In one evening he invited two different groups of people for cocktails at 7.30 pm, and also accepted invitations for two cocktail parties and dinners starting at 8 pm. Two cars arrived to pick us up while we were entertaining our guests. In a tangled situation like this, there was nothing else to do except to take our guests with us to the first dinner party.

There Dada announced with great nonchalance that he had brought all his friends – "only for one drink". The fraught hostess protested, "But Dada, the fine food I have prepared will be wasted."

To which he replied, "Not at all. Keep it in the fridge, I shall breakfast on it tomorrow morning." After one round of drinks he hustled us out and rushed like a hurricane to the second dinner.

At the second dinner party the host and hostess were really flabbergasted to see so many guests, for whom they were not prepared. Dada once again announced breezily: "Don't you worry, I have made all arrangements for the food." With that he despatched the car to the house of the friends where we were supposed to dine first. He invited them to come over with all the food they could spare... And thus ended the two dinner parties.

Thursday night we told him to keep his hotel room door open, as he was to leave for Bangalore by the early morning flight on Friday. That night he took special care to bolt and lock the door! At 4 am the porter reported that Dada is not opening the door. I walked across to his room and banged the door hard for several minutes. There was immediate response, but not from him. People from the adjoining rooms came out in their dressing gowns and looked menacingly at me. I explained to them that he has a deaf ear. The banging continued from 4 to 5 am without pause, while Dada slept blissfully through it all. At 9.30 am he looked at his watch upside down, declared to himself that it was still too early to get up, and went back to slumberland. At 10.30 am he was sitting in my room with his airline ticket in one hand and his head in the other.

The following Tuesday, Bombay was *bandh*, and not a crow was seen flying across the skies without a pass or a permit. But several of our friends were staying at the Ritz. So we decided to play roulette in the evening. Dada was in a real gay mood. Not even knowing the game properly, wherever he put his money it was getting doubled, much to the consternation of the croupier, particularly when it was a hundred rupee note. As the game proceeded, more and more Scotch got consumed.

But all good things must end and so did that evening. As a grand finale, we came down in the lift for dinner. But Dada did not join us for several minutes. And so we started looking for him. We found quite a crowd at the lift waiting for it. The lift came down to the ground floor and then suddenly shot up to the fifth floor – and this happened again and again. For a while nobody could make out what was happening until, through the glass door, someone sighted Dada operating the lift. It was one hell of a problem to stop the lift and get Dada out of it. That was the obvious result of too much Chivas Regal.

After the dinner was over he called a waiter, "Hey, Mr Boy, come on." He tore off a small corner of a hundred rupee note and said, "Here's ten rupees for you." Likewise he tipped all the waiters present in the room. When I stayed his hand and asked, "What do you think you are doing?" he says to me, "I am tipping them." Then he tears two more small bits off that note and says: "Here's 20 rupees tip for you, be happy."

And happy I was. In this pandemonium, I got to know him better than ever, although I had known him for 33 long years. Underneath this exterior of his is a kind gentleman who loves life and people.

On fasts and fasting

25 December 1966

We can speak with considerable authority on fasts and fasting, as we mastered its technique early in life when we were hardly six or seven years old. We realised that when all our howling and shrieking, our tantrums and shindies, failed to secure the things we wanted, the weapon that always succeeded was the threat to go without food. That certainly brought forth an immediate response from our grandmother who, at the merest mention of it, relented and not only coaxed us into eating but also gave us what we wanted.

But as age advanced and we were eight or nine years old, our uncle called our bluff. Having kicked up a shindy over something, we had threatened to go on a fast unless our demand was conceded. When our uncle heard of this, he not only gave us a sound thrashing but ruled, "Let the scoundrel go without food for a day. He has enough fat to last him for a month and it will do him a world of good to go without a meal or two."

This put us in a serious quandary. Not only our mother but even our grandmother, on whose solicitude we firmly relied, appeared to have joined the enemy's camp. We had declared our threat in the morning but it was noon, in fact afternoon, and no-one made the slightest approach to cajole us into eating. And for the first time we were faced with the problem of really going without food.

How could we, having declared that we were going to fast unto death, beg for food? That would have meant humiliation of the worst order. And so we decided upon a brilliant idea. We sneaked out of the house and raided an orchard in which the guava trees were laden with rich, ripe fruit. Unnoticed, we climbed a tree and helped ourselves to the most delicious guavas we have ever eaten in our life. The problem of lunch was thus solved, but that of dinner stared us in the face. And so we decided to fill ourselves to capacity; we left the orchard only late in the evening as dusk fell.

When we returned home there was considerable commotion in the house about our having disappeared. All the concern and solicitude of our grandmother had reappeared, and she started coaxing us to eat at least a morsel or two. But how could we? The guavas had occupied all the space in our stomach. Therefore, with a great show of force, we stuck to our resolve and went to bed.

Guava is a good food when eaten in moderation but when you fill your stomach to capacity with it, it is lethal. By about 8.30 at night the guavas had started working havoc in our stomach and the worst colic that anyone can suffer from attacked us. To cut a long story short, the doctor was summoned and the fact came out that it was an excess dose of guava that had given us the colic. Thus it came about that in later years we had to give up the weapon of fasts.

Curiously enough, however, after our marriage this weapon once again came in handy and worked surprisingly well with our wife. But after we had tried it a few times it boomeranged back on us: whenever we threatened to go on a fast, our wife threatened to go on a counterfast.

****

As we think of these incidents from our life, of fasts and fasting, we are surprised that this puerile stunt is getting into fashion in the highest quarters and even *Sants* and *Shankaracharyas*[5] are taking recourse to it. Today there are not only fasts but counterfasts and counter- counterfasts. And to what extent is the help of guavas being pressed into service? What sort of colic are they going to give to our country? Is Prime Minister Indira Gandhi coming out with the threat of a counterfast or a counter-counterfast?

---

5   *Shankaracharya* is a commonly used title for the heads of monasteries in India.

Pub grub – food for thought

Dada's article on fasting has dredged up one of my long-forgotten memories: I did once tell a fib about fasting, but in very different circumstances.

Back in 1982, when I started my first teaching job in Hertfordshire, I was not only lacking in teaching skills and experience but also in my knowledge of English food. As it happened, both areas of deficit were dealt with in one fell swoop.

Imagine this scenario: I have been invited to deliver a teacher-training course that involves planning weekly sessions with a co-teacher – let's call him Pete for short. Pete has prior experience of delivering this course so I'm happy I have him to work with. Dennis, our course coordinator, tells us: "Set up a time in between each session so you can plan the course properly for each week. You can use one of the college rooms or the café to meet."

Pete says, "I always use the pub down the road to do any in-between work. It's fairly quiet on weekdays so we can always find a table in a corner."

Okay. I've never been in a pub before so this is an opportunity to see inside. I have often wondered at the origins of pubs and pub culture. There seem to be many with the same sorts of names: The Red Lion, White Lion, Golden Lion, Black Lion – I wonder why, in a land where lions never existed as far as I know. I've also noticed that many pubs have the word Arms on their signs: The King's Arms, Queen's Arms, Farrier's Arms, etc. – but why would I want to eat in anybody's Arms? And there are yet other pubs with the strangest dodgy names (Boggy Bottom, The Long Arm and Short Arm, The Slug and Lettuce, Booty Lane, for example).

Pete is calling the shots on most of our arrangements. At our first planning meeting in Ye Olde Fighting Cocks pub I am told that this is considered to be the oldest pub in England. Its foundations date back to 793 AD and the building (as it stands) dates back to the 11th Century. It has served a number of different functions over the years, including cock fighting as a sport (I am not a fan of this), but I'm pleasantly surprised at the low exposed beams, wooden chairs and tables making it feel cosy and homely. Sure enough, we find a table near the cheerful, crackling open fire.

There is a lot to sort out around the entire course and not just the next session, so Father Time takes us hostage and tips us over into lunchtime. Pete picks up the menu on our table and says, "We better order some grub. What would you like?"

For a start, I don't like the sound of 'grub'. To me it means a fat, slimy, worm-like creature. And when I look at the menu – shock horror! Do people here eat toad in the hole? What sort of hole is the toad cooked in? Not wanting to be horrified further, I drop the menu and ask the waiter to just get me another coffee.

"Hold on a minute," says Pete, sensing my discomfort, "are you vegetarian? Maybe you can have a ploughman."

Uh-oh, do the English eat the poor farm workers who plough their fields? "I'm not hungry," I falter, but my traitor tummy growls audibly in protest. In desperation I add another fib: "I'm supposed to be fasting today – you know, devout Hindus all fast on Tuesdays."

Despite myself I reach for the menu again. I don't want to look like a total ignoramus, nor falsely like a devout anything, but I can't help blurting out: "I wasn't aware that people eat toads here. I did have a taste of frogs' legs in Bangkok once, quite by chance. Actually they tasted pretty much like chicken."

Now is that a glint of amusement I see in Pete's grey-green eyes? I quickly scan the menu for anything vaguely vegetarian and say to the waiter, "Please may I have a quickie?" I'm surprised at the reaction to this simple request: the waiter initially seems a little shocked; then he and Pete are in splits of laughter as they look to see where my finger has come to rest on the menu. "Ah, that's a quiche," Pete corrects me, still grinning, "it's pronounced keesh." But then he simply ignores the quickie/keesh/quiche and orders two lunches: the dreaded toad in the hole for himself and a ploughman's for me. "We have to educate our young friend here on pub grub," he tells the waiter who has been hovering patiently at our table, but who now goes off, still chuckling. Sure enough I learn in due course that a ploughman's lunch consists of nothing more sinister than bread, cheese, sweet pickle and salad.

Well, the upshot is that the following week I'm persuaded to try shepherd's pie, and the week after that, bangers and mash. "A pie and a pint will put hairs on your chest" announces Pete imperiously. Well (a) I don't want hairs sprouting on my chest, thank you; and (b) I don't see any down Pete's open-necked shirt (not that I'm looking).

A couple of months down the line I'm not letting Pete call all the shots. I insist we work at least a few times in my kitchen at home, and I challenge both his taste buds and brain cells with chicken biriyani, aubergine pullao, lamb rogan josh and my extensive knowledge of Indian food and drink. After all, I'm successfully teaching courses on Indian cookery right across Hertfordshire at the time. And I can contribute my own ideas in planning and delivering our course.

But I'm also merrily devouring pub grub and finding it all harmless – just so long as I can divorce the animal on the plate from the animal in the field. Or the toad in the pond – but, as it turns out, toad in the hole has nothing at all to do with toads. It is actually a tasty sausage cooked in Yorkshire pudding batter. All thoughts and fibs about fasting have long flown out of the pub windows, along with doubts about English food and culture. After all, how can people who make such delicious chocolate fudge cake and lemon posset harbour wicked designs on my religiosity or integrity? I've crumbled and drowned, just like the apple crumble drowning in custard I'm tucking into, even as I write this.

In retrospect, I have observed over the years how pubs have changed. I still go into various pubs with the walking group I joined in 2010 when I retired from full time work. With this group I walk across fields, over styles, under trees – all in the lovely, well-managed Hertfordshire countryside. The walks are planned to be approximately 4 to 5 miles, about once a month. Each circular walk starts and ends in a quaint village pub that has retained its old-worldly charm. Pubs however are now faced with increasing competition from the sheer number and diversity of restaurants, and the many fast-food chains and coffee shops that have sprung up in more recent times. So pub grub has had to compete and diversify. Traditional favourites are still on the menu, but may be offered with a modern twist.

And more recently (9 November 2016) from the BBC News website:

McDonald's is suing Florence for €18m after it was blocked from opening a restaurant on one of the Italian city's most historic plazas.

The fast-food giant had plans for an outlet on the Piazza del Duomo. The application was rejected by Florence's mayor in June.

The McDonald's chain is claiming it has been discriminated against, and wants to recoup the €17.8m (£15.9m; $19.7m) it estimates it will lose over the next 18 years, according to the Italian newspaper 'Firenze Today'.

Welcome to the mad new world. If McDonald's does win its claim, this legal tussle between modern fast food chains and traditional independent enterprises could sadly become the norm.

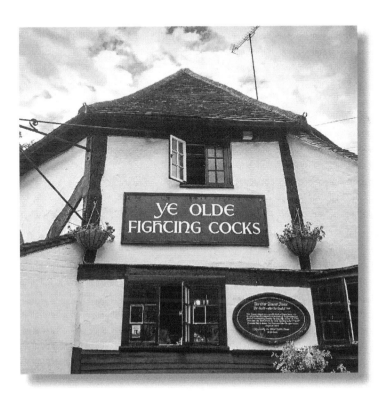

The do-it-yourself craze in me

21 April 1974

I have been a great believer in 'do-it-yourself.' There is not a piece of machinery or gadget that I have not tampered with in my life. I remember, when I was about seven years old, dismantling a grandfather clock, a proud heirloom of the family, and reducing it to its elemental state. When I pulled out its powerful spring, it un-sprung itself with such violence that it left a big gash on my right foot. The four-inch scar, which is still there, is a grim reminder of the thrills of the do-it-yourself credo.

****

And then there was the time when my mother asked me to take my younger brother to the barber's saloon for a haircut. I told her breezily that a four-year-old boy need not go to a saloon for a haircut, and volunteered to do it myself. Having procured my mother's tailoring scissors, I gave one snip and a big bald patch appeared on his head. Thus, snip after snip, the patches multiplied and, as I endeavoured to rectify the damage, I snipped off a bit of the skin itself from his scalp. The little fellow let out a big howl. My mother appeared on the scene and ordered me to take him immediately to the saloon.

The barber took one look at the boy's head and said: "Which bastard of a barber has cut his hair like this?"

The only way he could rectify the damage was to shave the head clean.

****

During the summer vacation, when I was a student, I used to spend hours in a tailor's shop, watching him stitch shirts, coats and pants for his customers, and it created a great interest in me for tailoring. I decided to try my hand at it, but who would entrust his precious cloth to me? The opportunity came when a servant boy bought some cloth for a coat. I told him not to waste his hard-earned money on tailoring charges, and that I would make him just as good a coat as any tailor. And thus started my new venture in making a coat. The results were astounding: the coat was too tight or too loose in places, and hung on the fellow like an old coat on a scarecrow. The fellow was however a country bumpkin, and was mightily pleased at the free tailoring he had got out of me.

****

A fortnight ago, my wife said that the ceiling lamp in the dining room was not lighting up and I should ask the electrician to come and repair it. I said that a small matter like a bulb not lighting did not need an electrician, and I would set it right myself. The ceiling, however, was 15 feet high and the problem was how to reach it. And so the dining table was shifted and another table went on top of it, and finally a chair perched precariously over it. With the servant holding this make-shift arrangement, I managed to make it to the ceiling. But, as I was fiddling with the holder, I got the shock of my life and came tumbling down to the floor. I had forgotten to put off the main switch. The chair and the smaller table broke. Somehow my bones remained intact, but the incident left a pain in the joints for a week or so.

****

Last week my wife said the servant's bicycle was out of order and should be sent for repairs. I examined the rickety 25-year-old war horse and found the hubs worn out, several spokes broken and the tyres in tatters. I went to the cycle shop and bought two brand new wheels, complete with the best Dunlop tyres and tubes. But when I fitted the wheels to the old frame, they presented a somewhat discordant appearance, which could be rectified only by putting in a new frame. Therefore I repaired fast to the cycle shop again and bought a brand new Raleigh frame. But the results were still not satisfactory, as the mudguards were badly battered. Thus, part by part, a new Raleigh emerged. My wife added up all the bills and said: "Your do-it-yourself craze has cost 60 rupees more than a new Raleigh would cost. Besides, what about all the time and labour you have wasted!"

The do-it-yourself craze in my family

What is it about the human male psyche? I'm pretty sure it's not just Dada, my husband and sons, but something built into the DNA of most men that motivates them to rise to a do-it-yourself (DIY) challenge. Admitting they cannot fix something seems like an unacceptable admission of failure.

DIY is a veritable little industry in its own right in the UK. We have here many large super-stores devoted entirely to encouraging us ordinary mortals (with no special skills) to do our own gardening, home décor and maintenance at the very least. Because it's expensive and difficult to get help for such jobs, most British men are handymen at least with basics such as changing light bulbs, making minor repairs and washing their cars. And women are not exempt – we have to do almost everything around the house and garden.

And so, trying to manage all these chores around our home in St Albans, when I say to my better half Baldev, "We need to get some help with pruning the honeysuckle and roses climbing over the pergola – they are running riot and getting entangled with each other," he says: "Oh we don't need to get help! I can do that."

At the weekend, while I'm busy vacuuming the carpets, washing down the hard floors, cramming laundry into the washing machine, shoving a chicken roast into the oven…I am suddenly alerted by a sharp shout from Bal out in the garden. I run out to find him struggling to lift himself out of the puddle he's fallen into, at the base of the step-ladder leaning against our pergola. "What on earth…" but I can see he is in immense pain, clutching at his right arm and shoulder. So I bundle him into my car and drive down to the Accident & Emergency department of our local hospital. Eventually they diagnose that he's dislocated his shoulder. "I just fell off the bottom rung of that damned step-ladder" he says ruefully. But at least he doesn't suggest he can fix his shoulder himself – that is not a DIY job. We wait for the expert consultant on duty to click it back into place. Ouch!

A few weeks later Bal notices that the ivy growing rampant on our west wall needs to be pulled back. "It can damage the brickwork," he tells me.

"Well, you and ladders are not the best of friends, Bal. No way am I letting you go up so high."

It so happens that Sanjeen, our eldest boy, comes over to visit the very next day together with Joseph, our three-year-old grandson. Now, whenever any of our grandchildren come round I drop all my own DIY chores and give them my undivided attention. Joseph knows this. He is already holding my hand and dragging me towards the corner where he knows

I keep a small stash of children's books. He picks out a handful of Mr Men books and we settle ourselves into the rocking chair which is just right for giving us both a tight hug. All is calm, all is bright – it is a beautiful sunny morning. It's very much in keeping with reading Mr Happy. I am just telling Joseph that if he wants to see a smiling cat or dog or mouse he needs to go to Happyland, where everybody is happy all day, every day.

But the peace of the morning is suddenly shattered by a shriek outside, followed by quite a commotion. Bal appears at the front door and shouts for me to come quickly – Sanjeen has fallen from the top rung of the ladder while pulling the clingy roots of the ivy out of our brick wall. It feels for a moment as if my heart has stopped beating. Joseph, bless his little cotton socks, is unwilling to interrupt the story. He resists getting off my lap, but I tell him, "It's Daddy, he might be hurt – come on Joseph, we must go and see."

Amazingly, Sanjeen is already standing upright and dusting himself off when we get outside. He says shakily, "I think I'm all right, mama, but I was actually right up there at the first floor window." It seems like a miracle that he is absolutely unhurt despite falling from such a height and landing flat on his back. He is just shaken by his unexpected descent into a bed of bracken and leaves, which appear to have cushioned his fall. I feel shaky too, just looking up at the height from which he's fallen. "It's clear that ladders are not your friends either," I say to him; "no more getting up there and pulling ivy. There's got to be a limit to these DIY escapades."

When we are safely back in the house having a hot drink each, little Joseph and I ensconce ourselves in the rocking chair and resume our story. "What happened in Happyland?" asks Joseph, "Did Mr Happy fall off a ladder?"

"I think he was Mr Happy because he didn't try to do everything himself," I say.

On giving evidence before commissions

5 June 1966

It isn't a small honour to be invited to give evidence before the various Commissions appointed by the Government. Invariably such honours go to eminent public men, experts in the field on which they have been asked to tender evidence. But sometimes, as a measure of doling out patronage, the Government confers it upon lesser fries like us.

Now we must admit that we are very poor at giving evidence. First of all we are slow on the uptake, which prevents us from coming out with a quick repartee. And this, coupled with our deafness, foxes us completely, so we commit many a *faux pas* in answering the questions put to us. See what happened to us when we were asked to appear before the Prohibition Enquiry Commission some 15 years ago.

We had decided to act the silent, strong man and not to volunteer any observation unless forced to do so. And therefore, as we went into the room, we kept our mouth shut. A few moments' silence completely flummoxed the Chairman and he said, "Are you Mr Debu Hosali?"

We nodded in assent.

"Do you welcome Prohibition or are you opposed to it?"

We said we loved our glass of whisky in the evening too much to welcome Prohibition. Besides, in the Hindu mythology, all the gods, the *suras*, drink; and the *asuras* don't. As we believed we did not belong to the latter category, we – like the *suras* – loved drink.

A member: "How do you know you are not an *asura*?"

We answered that question by asking another: "How do you know you are not one?"

The member: "You are a strange man."

We said: "So are you."

At this the Chairman looked in some surprise at the members and the members at the Chairman, and then he continued, "Do you think Prohibition has succeeded in Mysore?"

We said: "No, Sir. It has not."

The Chairman: "Why do you make such a sweeping statement?"

We said: "With due deference to you, Sir, it has not, as a good many in the Prohibition areas are perpetually drunk."

The Chairman: "If that is so, what are the police doing?"

We said, "They are doing damn all."

At this the DIG of Police, who was sitting in the room, jumped to his feet and said, "Sir, I strongly protest against that. It is a nasty insinuation and I want it expunged from the proceedings."

The Chairman thundered: "Order, order. You have no business to butt in. Sit down! I ask you all to sit down. And now, Mr Debu Hosali, have you any direct evidence to prove that people in Prohibition areas are drunk?"

We said: "Sir, what more direct evidence do you want? Only the other day we ourself were drunk like a coot in one of the Prohibition areas."

The Chairman thundered: "What! Were you drunk in a Prohibition area? No further evidence from you. You may go."

****

We betook ourself out of the room as soon as we could, and never again has the Government invited us to give evidence before any Commission.

On falling into a ditch

22 January 1967

In 1956 we acquired a Cadillac of rare vintage, and putting it in proper shape became the passion of our life. One evening we were getting its fuel pump repaired at Dozey's Garage. The matter being urgent, friend 'Swift' Dozey had asked his mechanic to work overtime. Although the man dismantled and assembled the pump a dozen times, the defect remained… and from 5 pm it was 6 and from 6, 7 pm. We were getting thoroughly bored observing the process producing no results.

We therefore called the watchman and asked him to fetch us from the adjoining Metro Bar some whisky and soda. And as the mechanic kept on dismantling and assembling the pump, we kept on helping ourself merrily to our drink.

At long last, at about 9 pm, the mechanic declared that the pump was ready and could now be fitted up. So, from a brilliantly lit room we came into the pitch dark yard of Dozey's Garage, following the mechanic closely on his heels and, as the mechanic passed between two cars, we found ourself descending into the abyss of an eight-foot concrete repair pit on which the two cars were parked.

To cut the story short, this unexpected fall into the pit was no small shock to us and caused no small injury to the various parts of our anatomy. What was a greater shock

was the sympathy and solicitude it elicited from all – friends, acquaintances, even strangers – when they got to know about it. What they did not know was the drink we had imbibed steadily that evening.

Now read about this other incident from our life that happened when we were on the water-wagon and, like an orthodox Brahmin, objected to having even a *nimboo pani* in any of the Clubs lest it be mistaken for alcohol.

A friend of ours invited us for dinner and said we could meet him at a certain Club where he was entertaining friends to cocktails and then dinner at his place. And thus we found ourself among a group of revellers who, by the time the Club closed, were as tight as tight could be. Eventually our friend took us to his place in his car, and a little past midnight he dropped us back at the Club. Most unfortunately, however, like all people who drive their own cars, we had taken out our car keys when we got into our friend's car, and put them in the cubbyhole in the dashboard. It was only after all the good-byes and salutations were over and when we got into our car that we realised our keys had been left in our friend's car.

It was pitch dark; the whole Clubhouse was locked; no telephone was available; and therefore the only alternative was to get a taxi. We therefore howled for the watchman and there appeared on the scene a rustic bum at whom we thundered our order for a taxi. But the bum, through his gestures, made it clear in no uncertain manner his resentment of our order. We offered him a bait of good money but still he refused. Now all this put us in a great rage. We took a couple of threatening steps forward at which the bum took to his heels. We gave him a hot chase.

Can you picture the scene? Mr Debu Hosali in hot pursuit of a bum in the dead of a pitch dark night, with the ground slippery with the heavy rains of the evening and another drizzle in progress. So far it is a matter to laugh at. But what followed is rather serious. The bum cleared a hedge and jumped over what looked like a puddle of rainwater. But, not knowing what was under that puddle, we landed into an eight-foot deep concrete tank full of mud and rainwater.

Well, we had the worst mud bath we ever had in our life, and after surmounting many difficulties we managed to get back home. The shock of what had happened to us that night was indeed great, but the way it was interpreted by our wife and mother dealt the worst blow. Our mother gave us a thorough dressing down for getting drunk and falling into a ditch, and our wife stopped talking to us for days.

Next morning, when we went to the Club to retrieve our car, no-one knew about the incident. And therefore, with our faith in the goodness of human nature restored, we ourself narrated to a few friends the serious accident we had met with the previous night. But look at the goodness of human nature – a few days later it was all over the town: "Mr Hosali got drunk and fell into a ditch."

The moral of this story is: If you ever get drunk and are likely to fall down, then choose the spot – the portals of a church or a temple. You can be sure of getting the sympathy of hundreds of devotees. But even if you are Morarjibhai, with a conscientious objection to drink, and are given to giddy spells, don't fall on the steps of a Club. All your cronies of the previous evening will join hands the next morning in assassinating your character. Even the steps of a prostitute's boudoir are preferable, as the woman in the hope of picking your pocket will at least render first aid.

The Bangalore Club

The real assassin of character

Uh-oh – in this flashback to my childhood, I experience the consternation in our family every time Dada gets into a scrape, but we just thank God he's had another lucky escape. He himself makes light of all his binge-drinking escapades. But we could draw a different moral to Dada's story: it's not about choosing where to fall when you are dead drunk – it's about choosing not to get drunk! Full stop. When you get to the point where you become legless and clueless, it's not friends and cronies who might assassinate your character – alcohol itself is the true assassin of character and of health. It is the fatal flaw, the Achilles heel. And there have been quite a few of these drunken incidents – I kid you not!

So when the telephone rings stridently before the crack of dawn it wakes me up and sets alarm bells ringing in my ten-year-old head. On this particular occasion I clamber out of bed and hang around at the top of the stairs to hear my mother's quavering "Hello?" as she picks up the receiver in the hallway below after several rings.

"Mrs Hosali, I've just seen Dada", says the voice at the other end. "I thought I better ring to let you know – he has sobered up and is on his way home now, but I'm sorry to tell you he drove his car onto the railway track during the night. He seems to have fallen asleep at the wheel… It's just a miracle – amazingly good kismet – that no train came along during that time. His car was parked right on the track for several hours."

It's also good kismet that the voice belongs to a policeman who is known to our family. Actually any police officer would be disinclined to enforce the prevailing drink-drive laws in Dada's case, as Dada's brother Satish was the Inspector General of Police at the time. But this particular policeman is genuinely sympathetic rather than critical. You would expect anyone to be astounded by the news he's conveyed, but Bhabi simply says, "Thank the dear Lord – and thank you, officer sahib." Now I hear the relief in her voice and run downstairs to keep her company because I know she still will not breathe easy until Dada actually gets home. So I snuggle back into bed with her and we talk and wait. By the time Dada's Triumph Herald turns in near our driveway, our cook Krishna is awake and ready to rush out and open the gate. This is one of his duties, no matter what time of the day or night Dada drives home, and sometimes that is in the dead of night when Krishna is woken up from a deep sleep. There's truly a lump in my throat when I think of the way we expected this from him, and took all our loyal servants for granted.

Dada is much the worse for wear when he unsteadily walks in. He doesn't want to talk about anything. He has a quick bucket bath, changes into his pyjamas and gets me to walk up and down on his hung-over, aching body. It's just as well that I'm a skinny creature so that I can do this foot massage, from which he always derives some comfort. And after a couple of hours in dreamland he's up and ready to go to the Press for a day's work as if nothing has happened.

Now picture this: Bhabi looks svelte and sweet in her silk sari, ready to go to a dinner party with Dada. Before every such social occasion I pick the little scented white jasmine buds from the obliging plant in our backyard, and string them up so that Bhabi can coil them into her hairstyle – she always wears her hair in a neat bun. Well then, by all accounts they enjoy a swinging party, but in different ways: Bhabi makes one fruit juice last forever while Dada downs one whisky after another at alarming speed. Trouble really starts on the way home. Dada starts driving round in circles, having completely lost his way in this unfamiliar part of town. There's nobody on the roads to ask for directions, as all sensible people are tucked up in bed. There seems to be a dim light in one of the houses so Dada stops and asks Bhabi to knock on that door. She gets out of the car reluctantly – but before she can do anything Dada has forgotten about her: he drives off, leaving her standing on the pavement in pitch dark!

At this, Bhabi doesn't know what to do – it's a scary situation. Rani and I hear about it the next day: she sits on the doorstep of a house for hours, waiting for a glimmer of dawn or some stirrings of life so that she can work out where she might be and how to get home. At the same time her imagination runs riot: what if a thief comes by? Even worse, a madman – or a rapist? She takes off her gold earrings and bangles and hides them in her sari, but she is prepared to bargain with them for her life if she is assaulted.

Eventually both Dada and Bhabi must have arrived back home safely, but I cannot remember the further details of this story. I may have blanked them from memory because I'm upset and appalled that my father could do such a thing to my lovely mother. But little did my young self understand that it was of course that assassin of character – that one-too-many whisky – that did such a dastardly thing.

The Club Sponge

24 September 1967

Having suffered a sharp rebuke from our old mother for having dropped a brick, in fact several bricks, at a cocktail party, we have been on the water-wagon for some time. In deference to her 77 years, we made an over-generous promise that we would not drink for three months. And the period of fasting was over yesterday. We, therefore, betook ourself quickly to the Men's Bar at the Bangalore Club.

Now this is one of the most hoary and ancient institutions of our country. Built almost a century ago, with its wooden carvings and panelling, it is almost a replica transplanted into Bangalore from one of the exclusive English clubs. Its musty and archaic odour is akin to the bouquet and aroma of heady wine and is, if anything, equally intoxicating.

As we walked into the Bar, we were greeted by the cheery voices of three of our friends – Doc the physician, Doc the scientist, and Sambu the chartered accountant – all old glassmates. What better atmosphere could one desire for an evening's pleasure? And thus, having joined our cronies, the party started off merrily. Drinks were ordered, glasses were clinked and, with the sparkling conversation of our friends, and our incapacity to hear it (because of our deafness), we were having a rollicking time when the Club Sponge made his appearance.

Now the mere presence of this man had a dampening effect, and the company fell suddenly silent. To the query from the Sponge, "How is everybody?" there was no answer. The Sponge therefore repeated: "I said, how is everybody?" and there was still no answer. Everyone sat glum. But the Sponge, who has no skin but buffalo hide, planted himself firmly behind us and our friend, Doc the physician, and extended his paws affectionately on our shoulders. Just as the embarrassment he had caused to everyone was reaching fever pitch, the barman brought a plate of cashew nuts and placed the plate on the counter. The Sponge guffawed heartily, extended his large paw and appropriated three-fourths of the plate for himself, with the observation: "Whisky needs a little blotting paper; otherwise it goes to your head."

At this, Doc the scientist remarked: "Blotting paper, eh? All the tissues in your body are made of sponge! Why d'you want blotting paper?"

The Sponge was obviously enraged at this. "You said made of sponge, eh?"

"So I did," rejoined Doc the scientist.

"Did you, eh?"

To put an end to this progressively unbecoming controversy, Doc the physician promptly asked the Sponge if he would care to have a drink. The Sponge brightened up and said, "Make it Scotch and soda."

And thus, from one round to another, the Sponge planted himself in our company – until it came to our turn to shout for the drink. We had decided to teach him a lesson and we, therefore, ordered one drink short. But before we could deprive him of his last free drink, the Sponge extended his big paw and appropriated the drink for himself, compelling us to order another for ourself. And, having downed the drink in one gulp, the Sponge said: "Thank you, gentlemen, for a nice time. My wife is waiting in the portico. I must be going now."

Nagging wives and henpecked husbands

26 May 1968

Why are some men so henpecked? Why should a hefty six-footer, all brawn and muscle, wielding great influence and power in his profession or business, quail at the merest glance of a little woman? She has only to say that he has had one too many and, whether he had them or not, he is out of the party even before the little woman has the time to pick up her handbag!

The other day we went to the Club, and in the ladies' lounge we spotted the said six-footer sitting with his petite and pretty wife. After the exchange of a few trivialities, we asked the man, "Why are you sitting here all by yourself?"

Before the man could answer, the woman said: "What d'you mean by 'sitting all by yourself' – am I not here?"

We answered that she was very much there but that she could go and play rummy with the ladies or have a look at the magazines. With that we dragged the fellow to the Men's Bar, much to the dismay of his wife.

The Men's Bar is an ancient and hoary institution. It is the sanctum sanctorum of all he-men, unsullied by the footsteps of any woman during the 100-odd years of its existence. In fact the Club rules are so strict that if the wife of any member were to barge into this special preserve of men, the husband's membership is liable to be suspended.

Finding himself in this rare atmosphere, this henpecked six-footer was greatly elated. With the absence of nagging, the free flow of drinks denied to him by his wife over the years, and with the hilarity, laughter and back-slapping, his inhibitions vanished into thin air – and even at the late hour of eleven he showed no signs of leaving.

In the meanwhile, his petite and pretty wife was fretting and fuming. When she could contain herself no longer she barged into the Men's Bar, much to the astonishment of all the buddies who were beating it up. But the astonishment was all the greater when the henpecked husband, instead of bolting through the other door, thundered: "Out, woman! You have defiled the sanctity of this hallowed institution. No woman has ever been allowed in here. Get yourself out before I lose my membership."

The woman fled, and from then on the man's henpeckedness has vanished, the relationship between husband and wife being quite normal now.

****

And now comes news from the Associated Press, London, that divorce was granted to a certain John Hatch, delivering him from the clutches of an excessively nagging wife. The complaint of Mr Hatch was that when he watched television he was made to sit on the floor lest the chair cushions got crumpled; when he undressed at night he was made to use the bathroom, as the bedroom curtains were always kept open to preserve the folds; he was not allowed to take off his jacket in the living-room because it would "cause dust"; he was asked to hand over his pay-packet unopened and was allowed only £5 per week, for which he had to render an account; he had to sit in the kitchen most of the time to avoid spoiling the furniture; and that, as a result of all this nagging, he had suffered a serious nervous breakdown.

Justice Sir Alan Orr agreed that this certainly amounted to cruelty, it went far beyond the ordinary wear and tear of married life, and therefore he granted a divorce.

****

It is a pity that this said John Hatch did not have a friend like us. One or two parties in his house with us and our cronies, with cigar ash all over the carpets, with a few broken ash-trays and half-a-dozen broken glasses and, last but not least, with plenty of drink in Mr John Hatch, all his henpeckedness would have disappeared, and he would have been spared the penalty of losing such a house-proud wife.

This love affair with Chivas Regal

Since Dada wrote in his usual candid and light-hearted manner about his trysts with alcohol, I feel free to comment on this topic myself. At the time though, in my childhood years, Maji (my grandmother) was the only one who dared to confront Dada on his drinking habits – not that it did much good. Chivas Regal is a soul-sucking, life-ruining drug – as powerful as any mistress who establishes a cruel hold on a man prone to addiction. Bhabi knew that Dada loved her, but she accepted with apparent equanimity that he loved Chivas Regal more. Perhaps she was wise to do so, as he would brook no opposition.

Dada had an intermittent and uneasy relationship with Chivas Regal. I never saw him bring that mistress home. He only ever drank socially, at parties and usually at the Bangalore

Club. At the Club, Mistress Chivas Regal resides in splendid bottles and reigns supreme in the sacrosanct Men's Bar. Woe betide any other woman who dares to enter! The Club is an old colonial institution which has inherited many of its attitudes from the British Raj. It upholds these traditional rules with religious zeal.

And so it transpires that Bhabi, Rani and I are left swatting mosquitos and waiting in the lounge outside the Men's Bar – whenever we happen to have gone with Dada to some social event or other. I'm usually more than half asleep on the lounge sofa when Bhabi would say to me, "I cannot go into the Men's Bar but you're little so you'd get away with it – you go in there and get him out." Normally a considerate and responsible husband and father, Mistress Chivas Regal would ensure that Dada's usual character was eclipsed by her hold on him. He would ignore our needs and feelings and we'd be waiting helplessly for him until the small hours of the morning.

As I grew older I got wise to the possibility that I may be stuck in this situation, so I used to take my school books with me and do my homework while waiting for him in the Club. I recall a time when his friend and glassmate, Mr Ghatge, caught me doing my exam revision in the lounge. He said to Dada, "Take her home – she has exams tomorrow" – to which he replied, "Oh, she's clever! She will pass her exams!"

In due course, when I was 16 and had learned to drive, he would hand me the car keys and expect me to get him safely home. There were not many other cars on the road at that time but I've got to say that driving on pot-hole-ridden, unlit roads was not my favourite pastime. Even so, I felt infinitely safer taking the wheel rather than Dada (under the influence of Chivas Regal) having control of the car.

And now, looking through an old photo album, I'm struck by so many photos of social occasions where that glass in the hand was a necessary appendage!

We get a drink on the house

17 May 1970

New York City, 11 April 1970

Our nephew came to see us at 7:30 in the evening at the Statler-Hilton Hotel where we were staying. He was only a boy when he left India, but during the eight years that he had been in the USA he had grown into a strapping young man. His visit was, therefore, an occasion for jubilation, and we decided to celebrate it by offering him a drink. The two of us walked into the fashionable Penn Bar and we shouted in our breezy manner: "Mr Barman, two whiskies and soda!"

Now let it be known that we are very deaf, and therefore cannot make out how loudly we are talking. This evening we must have shouted a little more loudly than we usually do, as the portly barman looked at us penetratingly and said: "Sir, I shall serve a drink for this young gentleman, but no more drinks for you tonight."

We were quite a bit surprised at his decision. He continued, "I think you should go to your room – sleep and sober up. You will thank me tomorrow morning for this suggestion."

We remonstrated that we had not taken a drink and that this was the first drink we were having. But it had no effect on him. He said, "They all say that, Sir, but I can see it in your eye." And he quickly mixed a whisky and soda for our nephew and said, "For you I have a very nice drink and it will be on the house."

We were considerably put out at this and, having asked our nephew to gulp down the drink, we left the Penn Bar and walked into another in the same hotel – a bar which was obviously not so posh but was meant for the plebeians. The drinks came, and from one round to another we kept on imbibing until it was 11 pm, when our nephew left.

We then tottered merrily into the Penn Bar and addressed the barman in an almost inaudible whisper, "Mr Barman, one whisky and soda please."

He eyed us suspiciously and remarked, "You seem to have sobered down! I think I better give you a drink."

We rejoined, "Yes, and let it be on the house."

Growing up with alcoholism

"I'm never ever going to touch alcoholic drinks," announces my cousin Titli, "and I'm not going to let my husband drink when I get married!" She has an extreme reaction to what we've seen and experienced as a result of Dada's love affair with Ms Chivas Regal. Titli has stayed true to her resolve: on a visit to Wolf Trap, Virginia, where she lives (more than forty years later) I see that she and Suresh, her husband, don't even order wine on special occasions. The subject is almost taboo.

Titli's reaction is similar to my own: I developed an aversion, almost a fear, of alcohol. When I was working with Air India, the crew usually met in the Captain's hotel room after a flight, straight after checking into our own rooms. Half bottles of Johnny Walker would miraculously appear and clink cheerily with tumblers. Alcohol flowed more freely than con-versation, but it was simply not a temptation for me. This nightcap drink was supposed to help us relax and sleep, but I never had problems falling into the dark and dreamless state of sheer exhaustion without it. However, living now in a culture where drinking is the norm amongst the majority population, I sometimes have a glass of wine on social occasions.

Umesh, our son who is an academic and professional high-flier, tells me: "I went drinking in local pubs with my University friends at Oxford because there was a lot of pressure to join in and be one of the lads". Of course! Alcohol-drenched socializing is typical of Oxford colleges. In his present job, Umesh is expected to order drinks for his clients and colleagues – and to join in so that he can feel a sense of belonging in his professional circle. When it's kept under control, a drink or two may help us lose some inhibitions and have a good time at a party, but all too often what starts like this gets steadily out of hand.

So, going further back down memory lane, picture this situation: Umesh is 17 at the time and working on a holiday job at Our Price Records in Hemel Hempstead – a neighbouring town. One fine day he says, "Mum, all the shop staff are going to a pub after work tomorrow, to celebrate someone's birthday. I'd like to go – but can you pick me up around 10.30?" I say OK, and we agree that he will wait for me in a particular car park at 10.30 sharp.

Now by that time of night I've changed into my pyjamas and slippers. It's fairly warm so I don't even bother to cover up with a jacket – I think it's only a matter of driving the eight miles or so to Hemel and picking him up. I get to the said car park in time but there's no sign of Umesh. I wait for 10 minutes, then 15… then decide I have to go and look for him. If you'd been to Hemel in the 1980s you will know there were several pubs along a stretch of the town-centre road – and so it happens that I've been into every single one of them in my pyjamas. Even if you are the sober one you end up feeling as confused and out of place as a drunk in a temple – or a frantic mother in pyjamas doing a pub crawl.

And on yet another occasion my abstinence doesn't let me off the hook. All of us – hubby and three sons – are at a slap-up wedding reception in London, enjoying the many dishes at dinner – and, in my family's case, over-enjoying the freely flowing drinks. Even I've had a glass of Sauvignon Blanc. We haven't discussed who is going to drive home – so when it comes to it I'm the only one sober enough. I get handed the car keys and have no choice. Oh dear, I'm not a happy bunny. I have no idea of the route to take back home. At one point I find myself driving round and round one-way streets, feeling like I'm trying to find a corner in a round room.

In Britain, drinking and driving is breathalyzed and penalized heavily: the laws against this 'crime' are strictly enforced. I'm sad to say one much-loved cousin of mine paid the price: he was deprived of his driving licence after three such offences – and indeed his alcoholism could have led to much more serious trouble. Another much-respected cousin, intellectually brilliant and a wonderful human being in every respect, became increasingly dependent on his daily intake of whisky. His addiction eventually robbed him of his liver, heart and brain function. It was heartbreaking to watch this decline.

The truth about alcohol is depressing and sobering. It emerges in statistics if not in one's personal experience: for example, in December 2015 it was estimated that alcohol misuse costs the UK economy £7.3 billion a year. More than 15,000 people die from alcohol-related illness in England alone. The National Health Service finds itself increasingly dealing with cases of alcohol poisoning in Accident & Emergency departments and hospital admissions. This at a time when the NHS is strapped for cash and resources to provide adequate care to an aging population with complex needs.

This morning a headline appears in one UK newspaper: "My Mummy's drunk. Please read to me". The news item reports that a child made this call to a helpline set up by the National Association for the Children of Alcoholics. Her parents were both drunk and unable to read her a bedtime story. Apparently 1 in 5 British children are affected by their parents' excessive drinking: research shows that they are more likely to struggle with school and homework, have more depression, anxiety, and risk of addiction themselves.

But why do alcoholics find it so hard to accept that their addictive habit is their Achilles heel? They find a number of justifications for turning to drink as a solution to their problems. Whisky actually means 'water of life'. Which it was in Britain in the long-ago past, along with beer, because water was too contaminated with nasty bacteria to drink. The mind boggles! I see a sign outside a bar near my house which says that "Alcohol is a solution: C_2H_60". According to chemistry, that holds true. According to cognitive, health and social psychology, alcohol is not a solution but a problem. And not just a problem in itself – it's the root of many another serious problem.

On absent-mindedness

27 August 1967

A story is told of two professors who went to the railway station to see off a colleague As they waited for the departure of the train on the platform they got so engrossed in a discussion that they hardly noticed the train had started moving. But as the train picked up speed, they made a dash for it and two of them managed to board the last compartment. The third was standing looking forlornly at the departing train when a railway official, obviously with the intention of offering solace to the professor, said "Sir, at least two of your colleagues could make it." The professor replied: "That's the trouble, my dear man. They had come to see me off!"

****

Now, this malady of absent-mindedness has during recent months taken some considerable possession of us, and has involved us in incidents which have brought serious trouble to us. We are not alluding to minor transgressions like lighting a cigar, throwing it away and putting the match in the mouth, but to more serious things. Please read on.

Some months ago we acquired a Dalmatian pup, and now it has become a routine with us to take it out for a walk after dinner. And, mainly to keep the beast on its good behavior, we carry a walking stick with us.

The other night, after returning from one of the said walks, we put the Dalmatian to bed, walked into our bedroom and did something which will go down as a classic story in the annals of absent-mindedness. We put the walking stick into the bed with due ceremony, covered it with the blanket, switched off the lights and stood ourself in the corner of the room. Just as we had started snoring, our wife walked into the room, put the light on and caught us in the most embarrassing situation of our life – standing in a dusty corner of the room and snoring away. With some effort she woke us up and demanded an explanation. But, despite all our endeavours to say that it was a case of absent-mindedness, she kept on repeating that we should see a psychiatrist.

Be that as it may, this incident did not create any serious repercussion as it did not involve anyone except ourself. But what happened last evening has created grave trouble for us. When we returned from the office our wife and daughters insisted that we take them out shopping. And so we drove them to Commercial Street. They walked into a shop and we followed them. As they were examining the various wares exhibited, the shopkeeper approached us and engaged us in a long conversation involving the policies of the Government and the problems they had created for trade and commerce.

Having talked to the shopkeeper for some ten minutes, we walked out of the shop, got into our car and drove back home to find that no-one was there. And so we shouted with some annoyance at the servants: "Where is everybody?" The servant was perplexed for a moment, but said a little later: "Sir, hardly half an hour back you took them out yourself."

The upshot of all this is that we have to see the psychiatrist with whom our wife has already fixed an appointment.

From hilarious to serious...

Haven't we all done it!? Done something absent-minded, which usually, luckily, didn't have any serious consequences? I've done things like... well, I've gone into a room to fetch a pair of scissors and come out 20 minutes later with a crying baby, all thought of scissors banished from my frazzled brain. Can't blame me for getting distracted!

There's an ad which appears on our TV from time to time: a busy young mother is getting lunch for her baby, who is sitting in his high-chair, drumming his little spoon hungrily on the tray table. Then we see the mother noticing that the pet dog is also hungry. Just then her telephone rings – she picks it up and, while chatting, simultaneously puts down lunch for her baby and lunch for the dog. It never fails to make me laugh when I see the baby's wondering expression as he examines the unfamiliar dog-food with which he has been served, and the puzzled look on the dog's face as he looks up from the baby bowl that's been put down for him. The ad is so funny that I always engage with its body language more than its message, so in fact I cannot recall what exactly it's advertising.

Absent-mindedness is usually related to multi-tasking in our busy, stressful lives. There is currently a big drive in the UK towards teaching mindfulness as an antidote to the constant pressures of modern lifestyles. Sessions on mindfulness and wellbeing are even offered in schools as one way of countering the increasing incidence of mental health problems. It is a sad fact that some primary school children as young as 6 and 7 are in counselling because they have issues with anxiety and depression. I fear it is a sign of our times that we cannot give all of them a childhood of carefree innocence, free from the stress that they will probably experience in their adult lives.

I do recall vaguely the incident when Dada forgot about us and left us in Commercial Street. The shops there have been superseded by the posh new malls that have mushroomed in Bengaluru, but Commercial Street was – and still is – one of my favourite places. Rani and I have birthdays three years apart but on consecutive days in May, so Bhabi was helping us choose our presents. We were happily engrossed in this delightful task, so when we did look round for Dada the shopkeeper said, "But Dada left about 10 minutes ago! I saw him get into the car and drive off."

However, Bhabi, Rani and I must have taken an auto-rickshaw home. Dada's absent-mindedness certainly didn't warrant any visit to a psychiatrist. Indeed his sense of humour is at its best in presenting its funny consequences. But what is happening on a large scale, with an aging population in the UK today, is sadly serious. What can I say? This poem I wrote recently may resonate with many people's experiences of someone they know:

Things left unsaid

The anguish of dementia as it takes its cruel way
Is far more than words can ever say
Between us, my dearest Bal, I deny that dreaded 'd' word
For it has the potential to destroy our personal world.

So things left unsaid swirl in smiles, gestures, eye contact
Creating a gulf between aspirations, reality and fact
A semblance of normality wraps round our spheres of solitude
As we move towards the unknown, still with hope and fortitude.

SECTION 2:

PUBLIC SERVICES, PRIVATE ATTITUDES

Keep your city clean

6 Sept. 1964

At a public meeting arranged by the Mayor of Bangalore to discuss the problem of keeping the city clean, a novelist and a social worker created a flutter when they crossed swords as to who was more responsible for fouling the streets, man or woman. The novelist alleged that women allow their children to defecate on the pavements, to which the social worker retorted that it was not uncommon to see men easing themselves on the roadside.

Leaving aside the question who got the better of whom, the debate has helped to focus attention on the attitudes to cleanliness in our cities. We are much given to taking pride in our ancient heritage, our glorious culture of a bygone era but, judged by any civilized standards, responsibility for public spaces and hygiene is almost non-existent. Why do so many people think it is acceptable to keep their houses spotless while they tip refuse right outside, into the street?

Take a trip to any of the crowded localities in the city area: the lanes and bylanes are littered with malodorous refuse, with myriads of flies flocking to it. It is a most revolting sight, quite apart from the disease it spreads.

****

But now let me tell you about the palmy days before 1950, when we had our own advertising representatives in New York. Later, when there was a steep decline in foreign advertising, we had to break our connection with them. But, when we were in New York last month, we called on them and they were very happy to meet us after a lapse of 20 years. Having entertained us to lunch, they asked one of their junior executives to show us the sights of the great city.

The junior executive, a pleasant young man, took us to many places of interest. Having visited India himself, he also talked about the things he has liked and disliked in our country. Among them, he said he was horrified to see children answering the call of nature on the roadside, and the cowdung that lay bespattered on the roads.

We explained to him that that was a feature of most economically backward countries where people could not afford private toilets, and even public toilets were not considered a priority. We then banished further talk about it.

At that stage our friend drove his car into Central Park and stopped it on the kerbside. It was the first flush of Spring and Magnolias, Camelias and Forsythias were in bloom. The park was an enchanting slight indeed.

Being early afternoon, a number of dog-owners with their pets on a leash were also out in the park. The dogs, little ones and larger ones, were busy paying attention to the lamp-posts, sprinkling them and then easing themselves on the pavement.

Our friend, remembering his earlier comment about the lack of cleanliness in India, felt a little embarrassed at this sight, but we put him at ease by saying, "Don't you worry. The only difference is in India it is little children and cowdung; here it is dogshit. If the Indian people venerate cowdung, we hope you Americans venerate dogshit as much."

All said and done, however, it is time we launched a campaign to wean people from dirty habits like those described above, and also minor ones such as spitting and throwing litter, sweepings and kitchen refuse into the streets. In the city of London, if a man is caught spitting, or even throwing a cigarette stub on the roadway, he is fined £5. Such a deterrent punishment is considered necessary in an enlightened society. In a country like India, with our ignorant masses, much more will have to be done, both in the matter of education and punishment.

Waging war against waste

Having lived in the UK for more than 46 years, I can testify to the truth of Dada's observation about London. While it's true that British cities are much cleaner than Indian cities, throwing litter is an ongoing problem here too, even though it is not tolerated socially and is a legal offence. The maximum fine for persistent littering is now £2,500 and local councils can impose on-the-spot fines generally ranging from £80 to £100 if so-called 'litter louts' are caught in the act. Police officers and litter wardens are trained to deal with offenders. And we, the public, are asked to report or challenge anyone we see throwing rubbish in the streets. Personally I shrink from challenging rowdy young people drinking outside pubs – it is an utterly scary prospect!

In Britain the local councils organize weekly collections of rubbish from every household. So every Thursday morning I get my bin-brain into gear: "Oops – the dustmen are coming. Time to sort the rubbish and put the right bins out! Now let's see… this week it's the turn of garden waste into the big green bin, and non-recyclables into the brown bin. Next week it will be paper and card in a black box, and other recyclable items – glass bottles and tin cans – in the big black bin."

In fact the complexity of sorting rubbish hit the BBC Breakfast News headlines this morning. Apparently people are not always getting it right, and the 50% recycling targets are being missed. There's a special box for food waste too. 7 million tons of food is thrown away in the UK. What a scandalous waste! Personally I don't tend to generate much food waste because we shop and plan meals carefully and we don't mind eating leftovers. We put all our fruit and vegetable peelings, tealeaves, etc. into a large composter in the back garden, and let the wonderful worms break it down into fertilizer for our plants. But there is also the option of grinding it down in the kitchen sink that is fitted with a waste disposal unit.

When the garbage truck comes round I am surprised to spot one of my graduate students collecting the bins.

"Hey, good to see you! But how come you're not using your degree?" I ask, and hastily add "Of course I know a dustman's job is important – if someone wasn't doing it we'd all be buried under a mound of rubbish."

"Yes – and I know everyone refers to us as dustmen, but the actual job title is 'refuse collector'. Actually we hardly come into contact with any refuse; and it's a very well paid job. I enjoy doing it."

He's right. I notice that the truck is fitted with mechanical arms that lift the bins and empty them effortlessly into the back of the truck.

From time to time the media focuses on the importance (and difficulty) of keeping Britain clean, and reports on the launch of special campaigns. At the start of 2016 Marcus Jones, the Communities minister, announced there was to be a new national litter strategy to "create a lasting clutter-free legacy for England". He said he wanted new fines of up to £150 to hit litter louts "in the pocket."

Mr Jones told *The Daily Telegraph*: "Dropping litter is the kind of antisocial behaviour that really gets people's backs up, and rightly so. It's thoughtless, selfish and ruins shared spaces for everyone. Not only that, litter clearance and disposal costs hundreds of millions of pounds for councils every year – money that could be going on other vital services."

The UK celebrated Queen Elizabeth's amazing reign in many ways during 2016, the year of her 90th birthday. As a tribute to her, slogans such as *Vacuum Your Village* appeared, and the campaign *Clean for the Queen* gathered momentum in the week before she turned 90. Adrian Evans, the chief executive of the campaign, warned that littering has become so commonplace in Britain that some people think it is their "human right" to drop rubbish. He said, "The key is enforcing the social unacceptability of littering, as much as the use of fines. Litter louts and fly-tippers need to be shamed into changing their ways, and fined until they do." A dedicated website was set up for the purpose of waging war against waste, and volunteers were recruited in all major towns and cities to pick up litter. They tweeted and competed by posting pictures online of the amount of litter they had picked up.

The UK is a nation of dog-lovers. We tax payers endorse the spending of our money by the local council to supply special bins in public parks, into which dog mess can be scooped up and deposited in small plastic bags. Most dog-owners are responsible people who comply. So much the better because, believe me, hell hath no fury greater than someone who has stepped inadvertently into vile and smelly dog poo. There are also signs to try and prevent such a tragedy: "If your dog does a poo, please put it into the litter bin." And then there's the man who made a point (and a photo opportunity) by showing what would happen if anyone followed that sign too literally: when his dog dared to poo in the park, he picked it up and went to dump it into the litter bin! Aaargh!

India may not have similar public services, schemes and sanctions to keep cities clean, but it makes perfect sense that changing personal and collective habits is the key to this problem. I find a parallel in India to the *Clean for the Queen* campaign in what Prime Minister Narendra Modi is doing to change people's attitudes. On 2nd October 2014, *Swachh Bharat* (Clean India) was launched throughout the length and breadth of the country as a national movement. "A clean India would be the best tribute India could pay to Mahatma Gandhi on his 150 birth anniversary in 2019," PM Modi said as he opened the Swachh Bharat Mission in New Delhi.

The Mission is indeed effecting a quiet revolution. In the past people were more willing to donate funds towards the building of a temple. But, a simple comment says it all: "You are more likely to feel relieved in a toilet than in a temple." Some 4000,000 toilets have been built and more are being built at a phenomenal rate of increase. 180,000 villages in 130 districts have access to toilets in private households.

On the subject of Modi's campaign, Roopali Sircar-Gaur, a college friend of mine who went on to become an inspirational head teacher, posted her personal experience on facebook:

"Shouting *Swacch Bharat, Swasth Bharat* (a clean India is a healthy India), *Mera Kitab Ghar* kids picked up brooms and filled garbage bags. They went berserk, cleaning the whole colony. People were forced to come out cheering in amazement.

If today our children do not hesitate to pick up brooms and mops it is because their teachers have taught them the dignity of all types of labour, they have been taught to keep their homes and surroundings clean. We salute them. It was a very satisfying day ... I feel blessed. Thirty kids, and of course the *rajma chawal* cooked by yours truly pretty early in the morning. Pressure cookers and rice cookers are so empowering. And yes, add to it a handy vegetable chopper! The tomato cucumber salad, with a lime dressing, chopped onions and some green chillies, was a hit."

This is democracy in India

22 October 1967

If you want the neighbourhood in which you are living cleaned up, the pot-holes in the roads filled, the pavements cleared of rubble and rubbish, the clogged underground sewers de-clogged, the storm-water drains (used over the years as dustbins) made storm-water drains – if you want water flowing in your taps 24 hours a day and, in fact, if you want all the inconveniences you have suffered over the past 25 years removed overnight, as though by a magician's wand, then you must get some VIP like the Vice President of India to build a house in your neighbourhood.

What a facelift the XV Cross of Jayanagar Extension, from the South End Road to the Madhavan Park, has received during the past few days! The whole area is metamorphosed. The road and pavements from the South End Circle to the Madhavan Park have been scrupulously cleaned. The tree trunks on both sides have been painted red and white, curb stones have been straightened and painted black and white, the compound walls have been whitewashed, and everything has been done to transform the area into what it should be under a well-administered Corporation. And all this has been achieved in a week or ten days!

What a miracle! And what is the reason? The Vice President of India has built a house opposite the Madhavan Park, and he is going to celebrate his son's marriage there shortly. Wherefore, the high and mighty person who, until a few years ago, was a trade union man spending his time in the slums, must be accorded the treatment India of the past gave to Rajas and Maharajas, and which we sneered at so contemptuously.

Here are a few more of the alterations effected to the neighbourhood. The bus stop in front of the Vice President's house has been shifted to the IX Main Road. Reason: it will be a source of disturbance to the Vice President. The road in front of the Kuchalamba Kalyan Mantap has been tarred overnight. Reason: the wedding is to take place there. The XVI Cross Road, hitherto in a deplorable state, has been tarred. Reason: the bride lives there, and the Vice President will have to perambulate on this road during the marriage.

The residents of Jayanagar have, for decades, cried themselves hoarse about these inconveniences, but they were crying in the wilderness. A small accident, however, like the marriage of the Vice President's son, has worked all these miracles. This is democracy in India.

(Based on a letter written to us by Mr C S Narayana Rao, 336 III Block, Jayanagar, Bangalore 11)

Self-reliance or reliance on the government?

Democracy in India is manifestly not congruent with the socialist ideals of equality. Indians are deeply entrenched in historic traditions of a hierarchical society. So if you are a VIP with power and authority, it appears to be expected and accepted by everyone, at all levels of society, that you will indulge your rights to power by some public shows of extravagance. The facelift in Jayanagar, which Dada describes in his article, is by no means an isolated incident. One could cite many such instances over the years and all over the country. One that I know of is the more recent example of Hichhan Bigha, a village in Bihar which had telephone connections installed, a new road built, a school renovated and 24 hour electricity supply – all work impressively carried out in less than a month. And how did this miracle happen, when in the state of Bihar hundreds of government servants had been deprived of their salaries for months?! Well, of course! The chief minister's daughter was to marry a man whose home was in Hicchan Bigha.

But let me continue on the topic of clean cities and civic responsibility … I came across an impressive Tedx Bangalore talk recently, which asks: *Why is India so filthy?* Encouraging a change of attitude is the main message of the talk. The speaker, Anamik Nagrik, says "I am a proud Indian but there is one problem I have with my country – we keep our houses clean but our streets dirty. We can send a rocket to Mars but we can't fix this problem… We say 'It's not my problem'. We are the undisputed champions of public filth."

He rightly identifies the specific cultural causes of our 'Ugly Indian' problem – a problem which has been recognized for decades (as in Dada's article) but which has stubbornly defied a sustainable solution. So what is it about the attitudes and the behavioural psychology endemic in Indian culture? We seem to take individual responsibility for keeping our personal, domestic spaces clean – but do we have no civic pride in our communal spaces? One thing is evident: we are not great at following rules, we don't like to be told what to do.

Mr Nagrik identifies two fundamental and universal aspects of psychology that both apply to this problem. Firstly, 'dirt attracts dirt': "If something is clean and beautiful we are instinctively inclined to respect it and keep it that way. But where we see garbage already littering a public space, overflowing a litter bin or simply dumped, we are likely to have no qualms in adding to it."

Secondly, we see the responsibility of cleaning public spaces as someone else's job. You have probably heard the story of four people named Everybody, Somebody, Anybody and Nobody. Everybody could see there was an important job to be done and was sure that Somebody would do it. Somebody got angry when he heard he was expected to do it, because he thought it was Anybody's job. Anybody could have done it, but he asked Nobody to do it. Nobody blamed Everybody for passing the job down the line. The end result was no result at all. So, behind this play on words there is a fundamental truth about human behaviour. Anamik Nagrik calls it the 'Tragedy of the Commons' because everyone complains about this common problem, but nobody owns the problem enough to do anything about it.

There is an encouraging trend afoot in Bengaluru that is breaking this vicious circle and attempting to deal with the The Ugly Indian syndrome. Volunteers fix the 'dirt attracts dirt' problem by simply getting out there and cleaning up their neighbourhoods, scrubbing down and painting walls, designing and installing functional and aesthetic litter bins, etc. They've decided to stop complaining and start acting: taking responsibility for public spaces, bringing communities together. Their example is a catalyst, spreading to other cities in India. *Mooh Bandh, Kaam Chalu* (keep your mouth shut, start working) is described in an extraordinary video with excellent examples of true, sustainable results.

Another recent inspirational example comes from Kendra Vidyalaya in Yelahanka – a school near Bangalore that has taken the Green Campus Scheme seriously and won an award for its successful, self-contained waste management. The students take pride in re-cycling all dry paper and rags to make useful and beautiful objects. They compost all organic material, incinerate sanitary towels – and spread the word to influence other schools and society at large. The way to go!

The dead are more important than the living

16 June 1974

At a recent Council meeting of the Bangalore City Corporation, our City Fathers expressed great concern for the welfare of the dead. Member after member waxed eloquent on the inadequacy of the facilities existing at the electric crematorium in Wilson Gardens to meet the needs of deceased citizens. After a marathon debate, the City Fathers resolved to set up two more electric crematoria, one at Srirampuram and the other at Kalpalli, at an estimated cost of Rs. 32 lakhs.

Doubtless, in the existing economic conditions in the country, this is a step in the right direction. Leaving aside the construction costs of the two crematoria buildings – say about Rs. 7 lakhs – the balance of Rs. 25 lakhs will represent the foreign exchange component for the purchase of the electric incinerators and other devices needed to burn the dead bodies. At a time when our industries cannot get licences to import spare parts and components to keep the wheels of their plants and machinery running, what is Rs. 25 lakhs in foreign exchange?! At a time when we are unable to import the nation's needs of crude oil, and petrol sells at Rs. 17 a gallon, what is Rs. 25 lakhs! At a time when power shortages, which have become endemic, compelling a cut of 25%, and even 50 % in some States, what are

a few thousand kilowatts of electric power! At a time when modern housewives have switched back to firewood and cowdung cakes from their all-electric kitchens, what are a few thousand kilowatts! No, of course Rs. 25 lakhs in foreign exchange and 100,000 kilowatts are a mere fleabite. After all, aren't we using them for the welfare of the dead?

Surprisingly, there was no mention in the Council debate if the death rate in Bangalore had shot up to the extent that would justify the commissioning of two more crematoria. From all reports, the death rate has remained static. However, if the new crematoria find that demand is lacking, the Corporation Council will no doubt take adequate steps to meet the shortfall. Haven't they, over the years, headed for this contingency? Slums abound, putrid water stagnates, millions of deadly mosquitoes breed, mountains of garbage accumulate at the dustbins, lepers and people infected with smallpox openly beg before the City and Cantonment markets, even before the five-star Ashoka Hotel, and propagate their deadly diseases. No, there will be no lack of demand for two more crematoria. The Corporation will take care, in its future plans, to fill the lacunae with enough dead bodies.

The dead are blameless while the living have many faults!

My maternal grandfather, Pithaji, was reading the newspaper as he always did every morning back in the 1960s when I knew him. His reaction to the obituaries section was to remark that people never spoke ill of the dead: "If they'd praised this man half as much while he was living that would have made his life so much happier."

On 6 December 2016 my Bishop Cotton alumni friends and I woke up to the news that one of our classmates had suffered a fatal heart attack at the age of 68. Emails amongst us began to fly back and forth. We knew her as a young girl who studied with us for a couple of years in school, way back. But now Jayalalitha Jayaram was famously known throughout India, and especially in Tamil Nadu where she served five terms as Chief Minister between 1991 and 2016. She had also starred in at least one hundred films before turning to politics. Both film stars and politicians inevitably acquire celebrity status in India, and Jayalalitha had certainly achieved that status with a glamorous on-screen life and a dramatic political life.

However the outpouring of shock and grief when her death was announced far surpassed the usual mourning at a celebrity's death. Social media and the newspapers carried images, videos and stories of immense crowds camping and wailing for days outside the Apollo Hospital where she was being treated. Her followers (members of the AIADMK party, Hindus and Muslims alike) were praying for her recovery and some were even self-harming in their desire to share her suffering. Amongst these vast numbers, women were prominent: Jayalalitha was an inspirational role-model and a champion of women's rights. She played a key role in the socio-economic development of Tamil Nadu, making it one of the most influential and progressive states in India.

Her powerful contribution was not without controversy during her lifetime. She was criticized for manipulating her followers into extreme devotion, encouraging them to call her *Amma* and prostrate themselves before her. Her lavish lifestyle aroused suspicion and accusations of corruption. A police raid on her home in the 1990s was said to have uncovered extravagant spending: 10,000 saris and 750 pairs of shoes. She was even imprisoned for short spells. When we were in school together we never imagined that anyone could need more than two pairs of shoes and a few outfits, apart from our uniform.

As I reflect with sorrow on the passing away of my former classmate, it strikes me that she had more ups and downs in her life than the Coney Island roller-coaster. Whatever the truth or misrepresentation of these extreme examples, I am moved to think of the impact these experiences would have had on her. The heights of adoration and depths of condemnation are both at the extremities of credibility. When she was indicted by the Supreme Court in 2001 on charges of corruption, it is reported that two of her devotees died of shock and eleven committed suicide. It seems to be a unique political phenomenon in India for followers of strong, charismatic leaders to demonstrate the most exceptional forms of loyalty! But I find it equally weird that Jayalalitha seemed to lap up this adoration. She provided details of how her "loving brothers and sisters" had killed themselves and become 'martyrs' for her: six by burning, three by hanging and two by taking poison.

Are the dead more important than the living? It does appear to be a general human tendency to exaggerate all the good things about a person after they have passed away. The eulogies and tributes that have come flooding in at Jayalalitha's death may be well deserved, but now she is actually being revered as a Goddess in Tamil Nadu.

Contaminated at the source

13 Sept 1964

25 years ago, the water supply of Bangalore was one of the best in India. Not many cities then were equipped with the Jewell filters, and people visiting the Waterworks at Tippagoondanahalli were shown round the place with great pride. Invariably a glass of crystal clear water was offered, with the comment that it was chemically, physically and bacteriologically 100% pure.

The same filters are in operation today and ought to filter and purify the water with the same efficiency as in the past. But seldom if ever do we find clear water coming from the taps. Often one finds, when the supply is resumed in the morning and evenings, that muddy water flows for 15 to 30 minutes before clear water starts coming out.

And now comes the news that the dead body of a man in a highly decomposed state has been found floating in one of the filters. Comment is unnecessary, as the fact itself speaks for the efficiency with which the works are now managed.

Anyone who has seen the operation of the filtering plant knows that each unit of the filter is filled and emptied at certain specific intervals, and the process is repeated several times a day. Assuming that there is proper inspection of the plant, the body of a man falling into the filter accidentally ought to have been detected within one or two hours, as every time the filter is emptied there is no water in it until the refilling starts.

The fact that the body was in a highly decomposed state proves that it had been in the filter for several days. That no-one sighted a big thing like the body of a man inside a filter no more than 20 feet in diameter and 20 feet deep proves the gross negligence of the supervisory staff.

There are certain functions which have belonged to the Government for a century past, and the supply of filtered water is one such. The alien Government of the pre-independence era, with its limited resources, managed to perform these functions with remarkable efficiency. It is a sad commentary that we have not only not maintained the old efficiency but brought about a general, all-round decline. This is true not only of Bangalore but even of bigger cities like Delhi, where the galloping epidemic of jaundice three years ago was traced to the underground sewers getting mixed up with the water supply lines.

If the citizen cannot have trust in the elementary functions of the Government, in the Government's ability to run simple things like the water supply, he certainly cannot have faith in the ability of the Government to do bigger things. It would be all to the good if our Governments at the State and Central levels were to put first things first and concentrate on performing their legitimate duties properly before they venture into wider fields.

Contamination causes casualties

My husband Baldev is from a farming family in the town of Abohar in southwest Punjab. In this area the soil is fertile but the ground water table has been rising year on year to the point where the land they own has suffered from severe waterlogging and salinization. It has been rendered largely unsuitable for cultivation, and this is not so much due to climate change or natural calamities but more because of the mismanagement of water sources.

The State of Punjab has come to be known as India's Breadbasket. While it occupies 1.57% of the country's geographical area, it produces over half the total amount of grain, through a system of wheat-rice cropping rotation. This system is supported by irrigation facilities from a vast network of canals that channel water from three major rivers and one seasonal river. This natural supply of river-water has made it possible for 83% of the land in the Punjab to be under agriculture compared to the national average of approximately 40%. And this has made a major contribution to India achieving self-sufficiency in food.

But there is a human price to be paid for the overuse of irrigation facilities in order to increase food production in this way, as indicated by the experience of my husband's family – and the suffering of many other families we know in the surrounding area. The mismanagement of resources led to a situation where fresh ground water was depleting at an alarming rate in the areas of wheat-rice cropping, alongside the severe waterlogging in southwest Punjab. This ecological disaster has had its parallels in human disasters. Some of our friends and fellow farmers lost their primary income source when their lands became unproductive and crops failed over a period of many seasons. Many fell into heavy debt and some committed suicide as they saw no way out.

The Government of India's Planning Commission set up an investigation into this situation in 2012. The resulting report in 2013 by high level experts found that this was a serious eco-systemic problem that would require a complex and sustainable solution to be implemented urgently. They warned that the whole area could turn into a desert if nothing was done, and made recommendations to rectify the imbalance caused by human activity. This is indeed a man-made catastrophe and it is one that should be averted by scientific means. India may be trying to implement the solution in its 12th Five Year Plan.

What is even worse for my in-laws and others living in the area is that the drinking water source is highly contaminated, not only by organic pollutants but also by harmful chemical and metal elements such as arsenic and uranium. Even though the family is very careful about boiling and filtering water for home consumption, they suffer from frequent tummy upsets and unexplained illness.

What a strange and inequitable world we live in! In the UK safe drinking water is taken for granted. It is an essential and basic expectation, and people use their democratic and human rights to complain if any deviation occurs. We have gone beyond expecting the basics, as proven by the recent news on Breakfast TV: residents in north London were complaining about fluctuating temperatures and tepid water flowing out of their taps, although it was still completely safe.

And then I come across another news item: the only five-star hotel in Belfast city centre has introduced a Water List alongside its Wine List on the menu. It is serving different types of bottled water that come with fancy price tags. The most expensive is water claiming to be harvested from icebergs in the Canadian Arctic. For the pleasure of drinking this you would pay £26.45 a bottle. They also serve water made from the sap of maple trees and harvested from rainforests.

The BBC (obviously a bit sceptical about this) decided to conduct an informal taste test, so they set up a table in the street for passers-by to blind-sample the iceberg water, the sap water and ordinary tap water. People were invited to guess which of these waters was the most and least expensive and to rate their preferences. The results showed that most people could not discern any difference in the taste of the special waters as opposed to tap water, and almost nobody said they would be prepared to pay the exorbitant price of £26.45 for the iceberg water.

The hotel, confronted with these results, said they considered it was valid to offer the different waters to suit different tastes and budgets. They felt it was a good idea to offer water that represented the place where it originated in the same way as wine carries the hallmark of its time and source-region.

Times demand that you sink a well before you build a house

18 Dec. 1966

Our grandfather was a great man. Patrician-looking, tall and handsome in his flowing *kurta* and *dhoti*, his was an arresting personality. Equally was he respected for his sane judgment on all things concerning men and matters. But, just as he had a strong regard for principles, he had his prejudices as well, and one came to us with great force when our ancestral home in Akola was being built. Said the old man, "Every sensible person must sink a well before he builds a house." And so, in that hottest place of India where the mercury touches 120°F in summer, the work of sinking a well started.

Now it is not easy to strike water in the arid region of Akola and, after months of toil, having gone down 100 to 120 feet, dynamiting rock after rock, he did strike water – cool, pure water from the bowels of the earth – and the day was celebrated with great gusto by the entire neighbourhood.

Small as we were then, it struck us as something incongruous that, when there was a first-class water supply system in Akola, with 24-hour running water in the pipes, the Herculean task of sinking a well 120 feet deep had preceded the building of the house. Therefore we asked our grandpa why he had undertaken the job of sinking a well instead of building the house first, and we remember vividly his answer even today. Said he, "The perfidy of the white man is such that one day he will shut off the water in the pipes and people would die of thirst like flies if we did not have the few wells we have in Akola."

****

That was exactly 50 years ago and there is little change in the situation except that the white ruler has been replaced by the brown or black one.

****

On Monday and Tuesday this week, on Sir M N Krishnarao Road where we live, there was not a drop of water in the taps. Obviously our rulers had taken it into their heads to turn off the water supply. So, having suffered the misery of two waterless days, we made bold to telephone the Water Supply Department. To the voice at the other end we said, "Notwithstanding the solemn assurances of our ministers to bring water from the river Cauvery, there is not a drop of water in the taps in our house for two days. We are dying of thirst and our body and soul are getting dirtier every minute."

The voice said, "Oh, that assurance! That is for bringing water from the Cauvery by 1972, not now – and in the meanwhile, if foreign aid does not come in, the scheme may have to be shelved until 1978."

"Good God!" we exclaimed. "What are we to do in the meanwhile – die of thirst?"

The voice answered with some annoyance, "My dear man, these businessmen have cornered the entire stock and created the present scarcity. From where do you expect to get water?"

We said, "What about the Americans? Can't they give us some immediate aid?"

"Oh, that!" the voice said. "We have already approached them but, despite two vast oceans – the Atlantic and the Pacific – they are so heartless that they are attaching all sorts of strings to their aid before they give us a drop. It is best not to count on their help. Let's be self-reliant."

We said, "What do you mean by self-reliance? Sink a well?"

"Exactly that," the voice said. "The perfidy of our present rulers is such that they would one day turn off all the water supply and people would die of thirst like flies." At this we were greatly shocked as the statement made by our grandfather 50 years ago came up vividly before us. We said, "You seem to be a very sensible man. Who are you?"

"Oh!" the voice said. "I am just another resident of Sir M N Krishnarao Road, waiting here in this office for the past six hours to catch the superintendent and to get him to turn the water supply on."

Water, water everywhere...

Having grown up in the house at Sir M N Krishnarao Road, I remember very well the scarce water supply that reached crisis level from time to time in Bangalore. We kids were taught to use water sparingly and to store it in every available bucket during the few morning hours before the taps stopped flowing.

It so happened that I had two pen friends around that time, when I was 10 years old – one in New Zealand and one in Canada. There was no email or social media then, so we exchanged long, newsy letters every few weeks by snail-mail. Oh what a joy it was to anticipate and receive those letters from a far-off world that I never thought I could personally experience.

One thing was clear from my correspondence with these pen friends: they did not suffer the same issues with water shortages. In fact one morning, to my sheer amazement and delight, the postman brought a small parcel together with the regular letter from New Zealand. My pen friend had sent me a birthday present – a beautiful emerald-green scarf with pictures of rivers on a map, and colourful native birds.

This led me to thinking that we too had this kind of beauty in Bangalore. A stone's throw away from our house we had what we called the 'tank'. The tank was (and still is today) a substantial lake near the west gate of Lalbagh, a vast, well-maintained botanical garden that was full of wonder for my 10-year-old self. I was aware of other tanks, rivers and streams in and around Bangalore, supporting a variety of birds, flora and fauna. And the monsoons bucket down gallons of rain over several days each year.

So I continued to wonder why we had this problem with our water supply. That night, in my prayers I asked God why he had created an unequal world in which some people have plenty of water and others' taps turn dry. As usual there was no reply from God. It was most frustrating.

The next day we had a Scripture lesson at school. In all such lessons, God came out of the Bible and no other source. The teacher said, "God is all-powerful and all-merciful."

I blurted out, "How can that be? If he had the power and the mercy to create a fair world, there would not be so much water in some countries and a shortage in others."

Teacher: "Don't ask silly questions, Arti. Even though God is merciful there is such a thing as hell. And when you question the Bible – well, that's blasphemy – and hell is where you're headed! Get out of the class and stand outside the door."

So I stood outside, punished but not cowed into submission. I wondered what 'blasphemy' meant and was not afraid of having my place in hell reserved. I had plenty of time to ponder the irrational and unjust behaviours of God and of my teacher. And anyway, being thrown out of class was a fairly regular occurrence for me at the age of ten. I used to spend most of my school time looking pensively out of windows – either from the inside out or the outside in.

Let's fast forward to the situation in our times. Instead of standing outside a classroom I am now standing outside India, with perspectives from the UK, but with much concern when my sister Rani tells me she has to buy water every summer in Hyderabad from a tanker that comes round. Friends from Bangalore tell me that the city will soon run dry.

With rising populations and greater need for water in both domestic and industrial use, it has been predicted that the wars of the 21st Century will be wars for water. India produces thousands of brilliant graduate engineers and scientists year on year and recently launched a spacecraft, but even today tap water is not safe to drink in many parts of the country. It is a sad fact that water – such a basic necessity and precious resource for mankind – is not prioritised and well managed. Taps remain dry for parts of the day and night in many large cities.

When I visit and travel around India I am appalled at the sorry state of many waterways that I see clogged up with plastic bags and debris irresponsibly thrown in. Quite apart from the sorry sight and stench that arises from some of these areas, there seems to be no awareness that plastic is not biodegradable, that it leads to environmental degradation and is hazardous for wildlife. People use waterways as one great communal dustbin for all kinds of waste.

On the other hand I was delighted to see on a visit to Bangalore in 2011 that the tank in Lalbagh was cleaner than I remember it from my childhood days, when it used to get clogged up extensively with a thick green waterweed. Those were the wonderful days when I walked and played in Lalbagh – my favourite gardens of all time – almost every day, and even did my homework sitting in one of the caves by the lotus pond. I knew every inch and cranny of Lalbagh, every beautiful old giant tree.

Women carrying water

I could name all the plants and flowers exhibited in the flower shows held in the Glass House. But I don't recall seeing flamingoes and cormorants in the big tank at any time in my younger days – and they were certainly much at home there on my visit in 2011.

Most heartening of all is the inspirational example of rain-water harvesting at the Barefoot College in rural Rajasthan, 100 km from Jaipur. Incredibly, this project was devised in 1986 by local illiterate people not thought to have the skills to succeed. But their success speaks for itself: they constructed an underground tank and connected it with a complex network of dome-shaped rooftop structures that collect up to 400,000 litres of rainwater. That would be enough to sustain their village of Tilonia through four years of drought.

What is more, the entire project is environmentally friendly. The leak-proof structures are made of local organic material. The entire 60,000 sq. ft. campus is lit by solar power. What an amazing inspirational example of rural development by self-reliant village folk!

The hazards of reading from right to left

9 June 1974

Mr W F Parsons narrates the following story in a recent issue of the Reader's Digest:

"To boost sales of a new washing powder in one Arab State, some eye-catching posters were displayed throughout that country. They showed on the left a dirty, blackened garment; in the centre its immersion in a mountain of suds; on the right its emergence clean and white.

Within days sales had dropped to almost nothing. Then the alarmed company realized why: Arabs read from right to left.

****

The recent detonation of a nuclear device by India has created a furore in many countries, particularly in Pakistan, and Mrs Gandhi has been at great pains to prove her peaceful *bona fides* and intentions in having blasted this nuclear gadget. In her endeavor to do so, an impressive exhibition of the various steps leading to India's success in this experiment was arranged in three sections at the United Nations. The section on the left displayed India's advance in nuclear science and technology, the manufacture of the device, its burial ten fathoms deep in the Rajasthan desert, etc.

In the central section was shown the earth-shaking blast, the mighty hillock and crater it created, and the dust cloud it raised.

The section on the right graphically described how clean, how free from radioactive fall-out, the explosion was, how it could be utilized for the purposes of peaceful development, of diversion of rivers into one's own country from the neighbouring ones, the conversion of deserts into lush corn fields, energy enough to turn the wheels of industry throughout the nation, mass sterilization and control of populations, cure for deadly maladies like cancer and leukemia and other diseases known and unknown which take such a heavy toll of human life.

The exhibition was widely acclaimed as one of the best of its kind, but when the photographs got published in the Pakistani Press they created an unprecedented scare among the people there. Immediate black-outs and air-raid practices were ordered in Karachi and Lahore, and Mr Bhutto swore vengeance on India by getting a similar device from China or the USA. The furore in Pakistan was entirely the result of the Pakistanis also reading from right to left.

The hazards of writing in abbreviations

I was hanging by the straps of British Rail as usual on the way in to London – there was never a seat on this early-morning commute. In the rush-hour crush of this particular morning I decided to let go of the straps and plant myself firmly in the middle of the other passengers, figuring I was so hemmed that I'd have nowhere to fall anyway, even if the train swung, swayed or jerked to a sudden halt. I managed to wiggle my phone out of my handbag and access my emails.

"There's a strange email from the boss," I said to my colleague Anna, who shared this journey with me most mornings, and was hemmed in next to me.

I showed her the message on my phone, which read: "Arti, are you interested in going to the MAD conference next month? I think it looks interesting and could be a good one to include in your staff development this term." The message didn't have an attachment to provide any further information on this conference.

"Now why on earth would she think I'm mad enough to benefit from a MAD conference?" I wondered out loud.

"Well, it's not inconceivable – you are rather mad," Anna remarks unhelpfully, "but that's good. I often think it helps to be perfectly loopy where we work."

"I know what MAD stands for," suddenly pipes up a strange voice behind me – one of the passengers has been looking over my shoulder and eavesdropping on our conversation. "It must be a conference on Mothers Against Drunk Driving. Now that would be interesting! Mothers can be quite rabid. But that would need to be MADD – with an extra D."

"Thanks," I say, "but I'm equally unconnected with that organization too."

"Then DEGT", says Mr Voice-behind-me, "and LOL. I will leave you to look up what that means!" He squeezes past us to hop out as the train reaches his stop.

"Cheeky Mr Expert-in-Textspeak!" I say to Anna. "Of course I know what LOL means – I put it at the end of many messages instead of writing out Lots of Love in full."

"Oh dear," she looks at me in disbelief; "don't you know that LOL means Laugh Out Loud?!"

Honestly, you can't take anything for granted! We do a Google search on the acronym DEGT out of curiosity, and find that it stands for Don't Even Go There.

Anyway, when I got to work I dropped in to see the boss, and discovered that the Aspire

Foundation was looking for mentors to join their growing numbers of volunteers to Make a Difference. The MAD event offered a chance to network with others and develop leadership qualities. Since that first encounter I've been in several mentor-mentee partnerships and enjoyed the various MAD experiences of meeting like-minded people.

Actually the greatest hazard of using an acronym has undoubtedly come from my variant take on the DOTS model, which defines careers education and guidance through four main components we all need in order to develop career maturity: Decision making, Opportunity awareness, Transition skills and Self Awareness. I like it. Except that, when we careers professionals attempt to apply the model in practice, we usually cover these components in a different sequence.

In a nutshell, we start with the S of DOTS, and place each individual Self at the start and heart of the life-career journey. We enable Self-assessment so that individuals will critically appreciate their authentic strengths, address their development needs, engage in suitable Opportunities, make realistic Decisions based on relevant information and implement successful Transitions. It's what we all need. The process is encapsulated by the resulting acronym SODiT.

Functioning in a cultural blind-spot, I was somewhat unaware of the unfortunate meaning of SODiT. It seemed perfect for the way I articulated and delivered career development programmes at my university. I even structured and presented a workshop at a national conference using this acronym – and everyone who attended was intrigued and amused. In fact my session attracted lots of academics, and they gave me positive feedback. And then I got a book proposal accepted with a prestigious academic publisher, using SODiT as the backbone of the contents.

It's not until I ran a session at my university with cross-faculty staff that I ran into trouble. A few of them objected to SODiT as if it was a vile disease. The session truly bombed and made me want to go home and console myself with death by chocolate. Because by then I was also well and truly into writing my book – using SODiT to structure the chapters and develop the associated skills. I looked up the real meaning of the expression and didn't like what I discovered. When I was done crying into my draft pages I contacted my editor and asked for her opinion. Well, she reassured me that I shouldn't worry or change anything because I was using SODiT as an acronym rather than a word. She simply wanted me to get the copy to her by the deadline.

But I decided that I didn't want to be linked with the word now that I knew what it meant – for heaven's sake, I'd be immortalized in print associated with SODiT! So I re-wrote the entire draft to fit with the acronym SOAR: Self, Opportunity, Aspirations, Results. *SOARing to Success* was born, and became the sub-title. Subsequently *SOAR for Employability* has been used extensively as a pedagogy and process to develop career management skills integrated with personal development planning and employability attributes.

And so I am saved from the hazard of writing in the SODiT abbreviation. Long live SOAR – as long as it does not soar into an ash cloud or fall to earth and get swept away by a tsunami!

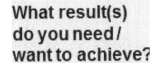

What result(s)
do you need /
want to achieve?

Own and align
personal goals with
graduate attributes
and professional
requirements – *SOAR*
for Employability

My Self
My Opportunities
My Aspirations
My Results

Man, monkey, golf and the 'twist'

20 August 1967

It was a lovely afternoon at the Golf Links. The sun peeped out of fleecy clouds, throwing its mild rays, and there was a rare coolth in the air. Several foursomes, ladies and gentlemen, were driving away on the golf course, following the ball, enjoying the afternoon's sport.

A mother monkey sat perched on a tree with a little baby monkey clutching its breasts. Asked the little monkey: "Why are those animals hitting that duck's egg and then following it across?"

Photo by Tycho Atsma (unsplash)

"Ssh," said the mother monkey, "don't call them animals. They are our distant cousins. But inscrutable are the ways of God. At a certain stage in the evolution of the species, God started being partial to this cousin of ours and helped him in every way to rise above the others. The result is that he now thinks he is the master of this earth, and all the others like us have to serve his interests."

"But why is he hitting that duck's egg and then following it, and why is he using those sticks instead of his hands?" queried the little monkey.

"Oh my son, that is not a duck's egg. It is a ball – a golf ball he calls it – hard as stone and quite inedible. Don't you ever bite it, it will break your teeth. The reason for his hitting the ball and following it is that, with the life of ease he leads, and the means of locomotion he has built for himself like the scooters, cars, railways and aeroplanes, he hardly gets a chance to exert himself and finds it very difficult to digest the food he has robbed from the rest of the creation. He must, therefore, walk around, take a little exercise, so that the food gets digested. It is only to create a wee bit of interest that he hits the ball and walks after it.

"But it will not be long before he loses the God-given skill of his limbs, like the hen having lost its ability to fly. Disuse will surely put them into disrepair; already he is unable to run and jump like us, and has to use a stick to hit the ball.

"But not only that: he has now become the laziest being in all creation. He works less and less, and exploits the other animals to do his work for him. He has even gone to the length of devising a science called cybernetics, and with its help made all sorts of automatic gadgets and machines – even an electronic brain which, he thinks, will take over the functions of his God-given brain. I despair for this cousin of ours. It is not long before he will turn into a robot. After all, can anybody avoid the Day of Retribution?"

****

With sundown, the Club was *en fete* with brilliant lights. In the spacious verandah sat ladies and gentlemen, dressed in their best finery, sipping drinks. Asked the little

Photo by Nandhu Kumar
(unsplash)

monkey of its mother: "What are they drinking, mama?"

"Oh, this cousin of ours, despite the nice time he is having, is always unhappy. After all the games he has played in the afternoon, he is still bored and is now trying to kill his ennui by drinking an artificial stimulant he calls whisky. But watch: after a few of those drinks have taken effect, he will be more like his primitive self and will start behaving normally."

And so it happened. The atmosphere became more and more gay; the band struck up; and the ladies and gentlemen started dancing the 'shake', 'jerk', 'twist' and the 'monkey'.

The baby monkey, observing this, said to his mother, "Even that our cousins cannot do properly. I think I better show them how to do it."

And before the mother monkey realised, the baby monkey had jumped off the tree and joined the fashionable set, creating such a pandemonium as had never been witnessed in the Club.

Photo by Andre Mouton
(unsplash)

More monkey business

I must have inherited Dada's helicopter perspective on life, standing back and making observations on the lifestyles we tend to adopt as humans. As it happens, I was in this sort of mood one morning when I was looking after my grand-daughter, Ishika – four years old at the time. We were watching one of those wildlife documentaries that David Attenborough is so brilliant at producing – and this one featured monkeys. I thought I might introduce Ishika to the theory of evolution at a level she could relate to. So I asked, "Ishki, do you think people are a bit like monkeys?"

She replied without hesitation, "Thama, you may be a bit like a monkey, but I am a princess!"

Well now – that sure backfired! It seems I just dis-proved the theory of evolution by regressing from Thama to ape status. But little Princess Ishika is sure to go far in life, don't you think?

I tell Ishika about one incident where a baby monkey actually did cause pandemonium by leaping into a group of us human beings, and I was at the centre of it. It happened when I had accompanied Dada to the Race Club on a Saturday afternoon in 1966. I had some unaccustomed money in my pocket from my first salary. Dada said I should enjoy the warm and pleasant afternoon at the Races and make the most of the delicious tea that was always served at these meetings. He also warned me: "Now don't you get into the *chakkar* of gambling. If you do you will always either be chasing your losses or celebrating your wins. In the end this is a mug's game."

Even so, I was studying the Race card and discussing the pros, cons and possibilities with some friends. Preoccupied as I was, I didn't notice the little baby monkey that had entered the members' enclosure. It seemed that everybody else did notice though – so people were scattering right, left and centre. I suddenly found myself with the monkey on my shoulder – it simply sat there, light and furry, while I completely froze. It was just a moment frozen in time when I didn't think of doing something or doing nothing – I was like a rabbit caught in the headlights of a car. So this monkey fiddled for a minute with a wisp of my hair that had come loose. It obviously didn't find me any more interesting than that (no lice in my hair), so it leapt off my shoulder and went its merry way – not sure where, but things returned to normal at the racecourse.

After that incident, when I went down to the paddock to look at the horses running in the next race, several young men accosted me. I realized they must have looked up from the general public area and witnessed the business with me and the monkey. "Congratulations on being so brave", they were saying – and some were asking me for tips as to which horse was going to win the next race, based on their reasoning that I must be lucky since the monkey god Hanuman had visited me up close and personal that day.

No such personal luck, though – every horse I backed came last or thereabouts. I actually began to think that I jinxed a horse whenever I backed it. I didn't dare tell Dada that I was going back home with an empty wallet. This experience cured me of going anywhere near horses and monkeys for a long while. Ishika listens to my story all ears and big eyes. She says, "But Thama, that baby monkey liked you. Could we get a baby monkey and keep it as a pet? Pal-eeez?"

I confess to my grandchildren, Ishika and Joshan, that I've never been brave around monkeys. Our neighbourhood in Basvangudi was home to rival gangs of aggressive rhesus monkeys, and they were the bane of my childhood years. Our toilets were in an outhouse at that time, basic brick walls covered with a corrugated iron roof. It is normal to feel relieved in a toilet, but not when a gang of monkeys suddenly decides to come by and jump on the iron roof, creating an almighty racket and a panic in the heart of the child inside. To make matters worse, some of these inquisitive little devils would poke their heads in and take a sneak peek through the gap where the brick wall didn't quite meet the roof. But it was not a pretty sight – for them or for me.

Our kitchen was also in an outhouse. I had the habit of climbing up a ladder to lie on the sloping tiled roof of the kitchen when I got home from school – simply to reflect on the day, dream and watch the changing shapes made by the clouds. My reveries were sometimes rudely broken by the sudden appearance of marauding monkeys. On many such occasions I almost fell from the roof, trying to clamber down the ladder in sheer terror of those bared monkey teeth.

Cooperative and non-cooperative eggs

2 May 1965

Next only to the fad of our Government in venturing into the field of commerce, industry, banking and insurance, comes Cooperation. If a group of contractors are unable to secure, say, road-building contracts, they have only to form themselves into a Road Workers' Cooperative Society, print a set of by-laws and register under the Cooperative Societies Act, and they forthwith become eligible for all sorts of concessions and special treatment. They have only to invest 100 rupees each, and on this meagre capital they succeed in getting not only contracts for lakhs of rupees but Government loans to boot. And all the while the same private business men are operating under the new guise of Cooperation.

Having seen the advertisements of the Grape Growers Cooperative Society announcing the sale of Anabshahi, Gulabi and other varieties of grapes, we repaired fast to Cubbon Park to buy some, and were greatly struck by the nice little painted booths and signboards of the Bangalore Cooperative Fish Marketing Union Ltd., etc. But when we wanted to buy some grapes we were told that the stock was exhausted and that we should come the next day.

In our disappointment therefore we went to the Egg Marketing Centre to buy some eggs instead. The signboard announced the time of sale as 9 am to 12 noon, and,

as there were still ten minutes to 12, we stood in the queue at the window for the payment of the purchase price. But, to our dismay, the man said that time was up. We pointed out that there were still ten minutes to 12, but his rejoinder was that, if he were to continue receiving money up to 12 noon, the man at the delivery counter would have to work overtime. We therefore interjected, "So what? Are you not interested in selling your goods?" The man's answer was, "Yes, but not after hours."

That appeared to us to be a very strange attitude on the part of anyone trying to push sales and make more money. We therefore asked him if he was not a Cooperator, and did his attitude not work to the detriment of his Society? He said, "No, we are non-cooperators – only hired men, getting a pittance at the end of the month. We couldn't care less what happens to the sales."

After two disappointments therefore we went to the Russell Market, and the Muslim vendor selling eggs welcomed us with outstretched arms as if we were a long-lost brother. "O Sab, it is such a long time since I saw you. Come, come, buy some of these special eggs I have for you. They are really wonderful. A special selected variety."

Being struck by the gushing welcome, we started examining the eggs and enquired what the price was. We were told it was only Rs. 3.50 per dozen. We thought that was rather atrocious, as the Egg Marketing

Centre in Cubbon Park was selling eggs at Rs. 3 per dozen. The vendor embarked on a tirade against the Egg Marketing Centre. "Oh Sahib, they are merely selling Government property, and no-one cares whether there are profits or losses. Here we look after the poultry, grow these special eggs, transport them from villages and make them available to the people. And for rendering this service the so-called Cooperative Societies are under-selling and ruining our business."

To cut a long argument short, we paid Rs. 3.50 for a dozen eggs and explained to ourself that the extravagance of 50p was well worth paying for courtesy. But when we reached home our wife questioned us as to why today of all days we had bought a dozen eggs, and for how much? We said we had paid only Rs. 3.50, to which she rejoined that we were an egghead, and that the village woman who comes to the door in the morning sells them for Rs. 2.75.

Russell Market - Thinking about eggs

Independent enterprises

Dada's article begs some big questions about what really motivates enterprising behaviours: are independent businesses more likely to provide better quality and courtesy to customers? Is it better for the economy when government policies allow free trade and competition to flourish, or when they intervene to provide concessions and promote cooperation?

Here in the UK (as most often elsewhere) it can be difficult for small enterprises to compete with their larger counterparts. My son Umesh posted a comment on Facebook which expresses a view related to these questions:

"Why would anyone, given a free choice, select a restaurant that is part of a chain over one that is independent? Yet the other day that is precisely what I did. Strolling around St Katherine's Docks at lunchtime I elected to go to a Café Rouge, reasoning to myself that they could not screw up the classics – a confit de canard or a (rib eye) steak frites. Wrong! They managed to destroy both dishes (through sheer complacency if nothing else). I quickly relocated to Kilikya's, a family-run Turkish restaurant which has a refreshingly chain-free atmosphere and the best Iskender kebab and Baklava this side of the Bosphorus. The experience was infinitely better in every respect."

This is not to say that all chains are rubbish and all independents are great; just that in many cases the latter will produce a more rewarding experience. And, even if a particular restaurant does not, we should support the entrepreneurial drive which keeps these places alive and kicking. It seems that sentiment is strong in the UK where over 60% of retail outlets are now (apparently) independent (a reflection of popular demand).

Indian cities of course have a veritable army of footpath entrepreneurs. Since there isn't the financial safety net of a social welfare system to support the jobless, this harsh environment encourages a diverse range of creative improvisations. So I find myself in Delhi wandering down a street with my broken *chappal*, looking for a *mochi* who will sew the strap back on. Just ten minutes later, and ten rupees down, I can put my *chappal* back on again. Next I'm looking for someone to mend my bead necklace, but the self-acclaimed jeweller sitting cross-legged on the dusty roadside doesn't have the right colour thread to complete the job. He isn't going to let that defeat him. He whips out his mobile phone and calls his mate a little further down the road. Sure enough, that jeweller comes up trumps, and a few minutes later I have a necklace looking good as new.

With no safety nets provided by the state, such 'footpath businessmen' have to use their initiative to make money. And make money they do, despite all the challenges of bureaucracy. They open small shops, tea stalls or *dhabas*, drive auto-rickshaws or taxis, polish shoes and shave men's beards. The street is the largest employer for millions of street-smart men and women. With modern technologies added to old techniques, and the propensity of Indians to repair, re-use and recycle things, examples of Indian enterprise are endless.

For example, the two photos reproduced below were taken by my son Manoj while he was travelling in India. A picture paints a thousand words, and his photography certainly does that.

Street dentist in Abohar

Bangle sellers

Dual standards of judgment:
O Tempora! O Mores!

17 April 1966

The species which goes by the name of homo sapiens is well known for its dual standards of judgment. These are observable in his conduct on the individual, communal, national and international levels, the yardstick of judgment being: what is good for me, my family, my community and nation is right, and everything else is wrong. Extrapolating this a step further: what is good collectively for homo sapiens is right and the billions of other creatures who inhabit this earth are wrong. They exist only to be annihilated, to make his life on this planet a little more comfortable.

See how well this is brought out by a recent report in the papers which reads:

> MURDEROUS FISH. April 12: A live fish choked a five-month-old child to death in Bombay today. The mother of the child had brought home a basket full of fish and left it near the baby. A fish jumped out and landed in the mouth of the child. She tried to pull it out but the fish penetrated deeper into the baby's throat. The child was rushed to hospital but it died of asphyxiation on the way.

The question arises: who is the murderer? The little fish that the hand of God lifted from the basket and deposited in the throat of the child, choking it to death, or the homo sapiens who is daily annihilating some billions and trillions of fish – and this is only one species, not to mention the depredation caused to the lives of other animals, birds, insects and the vegetable kingdom. Does not the goat and sheep exist only to appease the ravenous hunger of man, and is not the purpose of the cow and buffalo to provide milk and beef for this privileged animal?

The argument need not be extended further, as man – with the level of civilization he has reached – assumes glibly that this planet belongs to him, and that every other creature inhabiting it has been created by God only for his benefit. When the day of retribution comes there will be a long line of multitudes of animals, birds and other wildlife, demanding justice at the hands of God. One shudders to think what awaits man in the other world. Here is food for thought for Russells, Radhakrishnans and other philosophers.

****

With this sort of philosophy, is it any wonder that amongst the *homo sapiens* themselves, the Marxists or the anti-Marxists think that they have the sole right to exist on this earth, and the others must be liquidated. With this sort of philosophy, is it any wonder that our rulers, closer to home, think that whatever they do is right, and the large mass of people exist only to be fleeced and bled white? *O Tempora! O Mores!*

Multiple standards of judgment

We humans are complex and capable of incredible extremes. I'm sure you will not have to think too hard to identify examples of great kindness and great cruelty. Our standards of judgement can be rational or emotional, thoughtful or thoughtless, responsible or irresponsible – and ambivalent behaviours are evident in many of our interactions. But when it comes to children we are hopefully always on the side of responsible, nurturing, loving kindness due to some deeply-held human instinct. And if we are not, social approbation and legal penalties might deter us from negative or negligent actions.

So imagine this scenario: a young mother wakes up to a fine summer morning on 30 May 2016. She decides to take her three-year-old son to the Cincinnati Zoo, along with some of his friends. A visit to see exotic animals is always an exciting prospect for children. They set off in good spirits and all is well at the Zoo until they get to Gorilla World. In this enclosure they are thrilled to see Harambe, a huge and heavy silverback gorilla who weighs in at 400 kg. The three-year-old tells his mother he wants to get nearer to the gorilla. The mother says "No, no – you can't" but, before she can prevent him from doing so, he crawls through a barrier and falls 15 feet into the moat which surrounds the exhibit.

What does Harambe do? Well, he grabs the boy, pulls him out of the moat and seems to protect him. Witness accounts and photos taken at the time depict the behavior of a gentle giant rather than a dangerous monster. Gorilla mothers in the wild are known for their close and loving bonds with their young, and there is no reason to believe that Harambe would harm the little boy who has suddenly landed in his territory. But the onlookers start screaming, and that may be why Harambe pulls the boy further away from the frantic crowd. Of course this frightens the onlookers even more. In about ten minutes the decision is made to shoot the gorilla in order to rescue the boy.

So who was the actual murderer in this case? The little boy? His mother? The crowd of onlookers? The Zoo director who gave the command to fire the shot? The Zoo director later expressed remorse for having to shoot the silverback. He said "Harambe was a good guy" – and a valued member of an endangered species. As for the little boy, he was relatively unhurt but was taken to hospital, probably because of injuries sustained by his fall rather than any harm Harambe deliberately inflicted.

The killing of Harambe provoked immense outrage on social media sites. The backlash unmistakably blamed parental negligence for causing his death. A Facebook page, *Justice for Harambe*, was set up, calling for the parents to be charged with neglect. The page attracted 4,500 likes. But I would say that Yama[6], the god of death, came in the guise of Fear – and Fear was responsible for this totally avoidable shooting.

When it comes to animals, our double standards can hit the extremities of good or evil. On the one hand, groups of conservationists are going to enormous lengths to protect endangered species. If evidence were needed of our interest in wildlife, one only has to marvel at David Attenborough's amazing and popular documentaries, and stand in awe of the photographers who wait patiently for weeks to catch a glimpse of some elusive animals in their habitat and gain insight into their lives. All kinds of new technologies such as drones and electronic devices are now being used to capture them on camera and broadcast them to the world.

On the other hand, wildlife crime is on the increase. From time to time there are horrific scenes on TV that show great piles of tusks taken from elephants that have been poached and killed for ivory. Or rhinos brutally killed for their horns. Absolutely unforgiveable evil personified! But Yama does not just come in the guise of Evil. He also comes as Greed and Indifference, when people just want to profit from illegal trade in animal body parts. Or Yama comes as Ignorance when people buy such products, unaware that an animal has been killed to make them. Look at the case of seahorses: traditional Chinese medicine would have us believe that these appealing little marine creatures are aphrodisiacs, purely because they mate for life and stay loyal to one partner. If romance is dead in your own life, flog a dead seahorse! Such attitudes and beliefs put many creatures in danger of extinction.

Surely then, what Dada wrote about as a sign of his times is actually a trait of homo sapiens from time immemorial.

---

6   Yama is the god of death in Hindu mythology. It is said that Yama did not want to accept his status as the god of death when different roles were being allocated to the gods. He was advised not to worry, because nobody would blame him for a death. And so it is – we humans nearly always look for the cause elsewhere.

Corruption plus bravado

30 July 1972

Some years ago, when we were a Councillor of the Corporation of Bangalore, we were sitting in a barber's saloon in Basvangudi, waiting for our turn to have a haircut, when an important-looking fellow, obviously an official, walked in and started throwing his weight around.

"Have you sterilized those razors?" he queried. "Where is your Dettol? Why are the towels so dirty?"

The pompous proprietor followed the angry official with folded hands, from one corner of the saloon to the other, saying "Yes Sir; No Sir." The official said, "I belong to the Health Department of the Corporation. I'm Assistant Supervisor for Barbers' Saloons, and I'm going to cancel your licence for keeping your saloon so filthy."

The barber beseeched the official with ejaculations like "Yes Sir; No Sir." Eventually he pulled out a ten-rupee note and offered it to the aggrieved official. Just as the money was about to change hands, the eyes of the official fell on us, much to his chagrin. But, having regained his *sang froid*, he approached us with a beaming smile and said, "Sorry, Sir. Couldn't recognize you in your *jubba*. You're always so nicely dressed in a suit and tie." After a moment he continued, "I was not taking that ten-rupee note from him. I only wanted t frighten him out of his wits for keeping the saloon so dirty." And with that, with added *sang froid*, he walked out.

Later, when the official had left, we said to the barber, "At least our presence saved you ten rupees today." The barber said, "No, Sir. As you are short of hearing, you could not hear when he asked me in a whisper to keep the note for him. He is going to collect it later."

Corruption plus churlishness

In 1973 I decided to take my three little boys to visit my parents, and so I booked the journey from St Albans to Bangalore. The route was not covered by a direct flight at the time. The first leg of the journey, from London Heathrow to Bombay, was with British Airways. And then we were to connect with Indian Airlines from Bombay to Bangalore.

When you are travelling with young children, no-one on the plane wants to sit next to you – or even anywhere near you. Manoj was a babe in arms at seven months, Umesh was just short of two years old, and Sanjeen – at the grand old age of seven – was expected to be my right-hand man on this journey. Understandably, as we were trying to find our seats and I was carrying both Umesh and Manoj tucked into my right arm and left arm, other passengers looked in consternation at this three-headed, six-armed monster advancing slowly down the aisle. All no doubt were praying that we wouldn't be seated near them.

And then I discovered that BA – in their infinite wisdom and kindness(!) – had not allocated the baby crib I'd requested, and they had initially promised, for Manoj. I had worked as an airline stewardess myself so I knew that airline regulations entitled me to a crib and special assistance, especially as I was travelling with two infants under the age of two. Instead, BA saw fit to allocate cribs to some celebrity I could see up front, and no doubt to someone else deemed more important than myself and my children. They squashed the four of us together in three seats. I was left having to cope with the restless energies of a seven-year-old and a toddler, while holding a baby in my lap throughout the long flight.

A long flight? Worse was to come. Think back to what was happening in 1973. The Yom Kippur war was in full swing. In mid-flight the pilot announced that it would be too risky to fly the usual route through certain airspace over the Middle East, due to unexpected escalations on the war front; that we would have to make an emergency stop to re-fuel; that the diversion and additional stop-over would add several hours to our scheduled journey.

As you can imagine, that felt like the voice of doom to my ears. I had already refused a meal because I was worried the tray would be knocked over by my little ones, sending chicken curry, rice and salad flying all over the place. While feeding baby Manoj I couldn't stop Sanjeen and Umesh from romping in the aisle and getting in the way of the crew. One of the stewardesses looked pointedly at me and made a cutting remark: "Some people don't know how to control their children." To cut a long story short, the flight turned out to be a nightmare lasting 16 hours in total. Try getting a toddler to sit quietly strapped into a seat for 16 hours! Luckily we had a crew change after one of the stop-overs and the new crew were kind and helpful.

We arrived eventually into Bombay. I was fully aware that we had missed our domestic connection because of our delayed flight. BA took no responsibility for our onward journey. So the three-headed, six-armed monster, with seven-year-old trailing behind – bedraggled, beleaguered and much the worse for wear and stress – presented itself at the Indian Airlines counter. The adult head of the monster requested seats on the next available flight.

Passenger service agent: "Madam, there are no seats available for the next few days. The route to Bangalore is very busy and it's completely sold out."

Adult head: "But… but I wasn't expecting to be stranded in Bombay! Where do you expect me to go? My parents are in Bangalore and I haven't any money here to stay in a hotel or anything…"

"You will have to make your own arrangements and just wait – let me see, I can probably put you on a flight at the end of this week."

I didn't think I was going to get anywhere arguing with this churlish official, so I gathered up my children and what remained of my adult-hood, and marched out of the terminal. I remembered my Vitha Aunty who lived in Bandra – wow, I had her telephone number in my address book, what a stroke of luck! I called her from a telephone booth and relief flooded into me from head to toe when I heard her voice: "Take a taxi and come straight over. Of course you can stay with me."

True to her word, she welcomed all of us with open arms. Best aunt in all the world! When she had fed and watered us, we discussed next steps. She said, "I'm sure there are seats available – they always hold some back for last-minute VIP bookings. You haven't lived in India for quite a while so you were not aware that this agent saw your plight and expected you would come up with a substantial bribe to line his pocket. He expected you to slip him money discreetly under the counter. They are crooks – one and all."

OMG. This possibility hadn't struck me at all. Should I have offered a bribe, even if I had the money? Vitha Aunty didn't advise me to be complicit in the culture of corruption. She said I should go to the Indian Airlines city office the next day and speak to the manager. And she offered to baby-sit while I did so. "What, all three of them?" I asked in disbelief and wonderment at this kind offer; "I could take one of them with me." But Vitha Aunty was confident she could take care of the kids, and insisted I should go alone.

And so, with some trepidation, I left them in her care and took an auto-rick into town the next morning. The Manager Sahib turned out to be quite sympathetic, but even so I told a series of fibs and poured out a sob story. I described the truly stressful experience of being suddenly stranded in a strange city with three young children, no Indian currency, no accommodation. I said I'd had to leave my three in the care of a complete stranger – while my parents would be waiting for me to arrive in Bangalore.

"Okay, *bas*" he smiled and cut me short, "go and get your children and go to the airport this afternoon. I am issuing you with tickets for the next flight."

My faith in human nature restored, I was thankful not everyone was corrupt and churlish.

Travel under 'Control Raj'

3 Jan. 1965

As one travels in Western Europe today one finds that the trend is towards the abolition of passports, customs examinations and the like. In fact one can travel all over the Common Market area without being questioned by any official. The same is true of the United States of America. But these are countries whose citizens breathe the free air of democracy.

What is happening in India today? Ours is supposed to be a democracy and a free country but its freedom and democracy exist only in name. To realise the truth of this one has only to travel by motorcar to Madras.

A member of our staff going by road to Madras last week was stopped at half a dozen check posts. At the first check post he had to get down in heavy rain, go into the temporary hutment where the officials sat with registers, fill in the numerous columns, and explain where he was going and what he was carrying. A few miles away, at another check post, he was stopped. It now being dark, the police flashed torches inside the car, and questioned again if he was carrying any prohibited articles like liquor, rice, etc.

This process kept on repeating until, some 25 miles from Madras, there was a long line of car owners who had been stopped for the final examination. A few of them were compelled to unload their baggage, open their bags, and allow their goods to be searched.

This is free India, and this is the freedom its citizens enjoy. In a short journey of 200 miles between two states of the same country, officials have to interrogate an honest citizen half a dozen times as if he were a thief.

Why is it that the life of the citizen is being subjected to such restrictions in independent India – restrictions which did not pertain even when India was a colonial country? The answer is not far to seek. Do away with controls and the necessity of official intervention vanishes. But introduce controls and, in order to make them effective, checks and counter-checks on the conduct of the citizen become inevitable: it is taken for granted that every citizen is a swindler, smuggler, jaw-breaker and criminal until proved otherwise. That is the reason why there are so many checks on a 200 mile journey between Mysore, Andhra and Madras. If we do believe in democracy and freedom, and if we wish to make it a reality, it is only a large scale drive towards the abolition of controls that will make this possible. The sooner we make a beginning towards it the better.

Travels in a world of terrorism

"I'm truly cheesed off with easyJet," my friend Viera tells me. She has just returned from a trip to Vienna and seems to be more frustrated than a wheelchair user in a dance competition. "The queues were as long as my patience was short. Just to get to the check-in counters! And then they wouldn't allow me to take my handbag in addition to the carry-on case. Would you believe it, I had to try and squash it into the cabin bag! It wouldn't fit in, so I stripped almost to the bare bones. People were looking askance at me, but I was so annoyed I deliberately created a scene. I removed a fair number of clothes from the case and put them on one by one, including an extra jumper, jacket and... and ... honestly I looked like a pregnant bacon-pig!

"But also, to make matters worse, I nearly had my bottle of perfume confiscated – you know, they've introduced this thing about liquids. You can't take more than 50 ml of anything on board."

"You did know about that ban on liquids and gels, Viera. That has been around for at least the past ten years – ever since some idiot terrorist tried to blow up an airliner with liquid nitroglycerine or something. It happened to Umesh as well – he had a bottle of gin confiscated. Why didn't you put your perfume in your check-in bag?" I ask.

"Because I don't pay to check in baggage when I just go to European cities for a week! I manage to take all my toiletries in small sample containers – they all fit into my cabin bag. I forgot about the big bottle of perfume not being allowed. I had bought a £30 Roger & Gallet Rose Eau Fraiche as a gift for my friend. So when they warned me in the security queue, I just went to the loo and put the bottle down my knickers. It was too expensive – I just had to do this – and I actually got it through that way."

"At least it's been easy to hop, skip and jump across to European destinations on budget airlines," I remind her. "But now that Britain has voted to leave the EU, what's going to happen? Will we have to get a separate visa for every single EU country we visit?" Viera and I end up discussing our several 'don't knows'.

So where has this freedom of movement gone, since Dada wrote his article? I remember when Dada was late in dropping me at the Bangalore airport in 1968 and I actually ran straight from the car to the plane, which was already revving its engines. Traveling by air in those days was an easy pleasure. But all that was brought to an achingly tragic and traumatic end by the attack on the twin World Trade Towers in New York on 11 September 2001. Travel has never been the same since. It is fairly commonplace now to see armed police patrolling sensitive sites such as airports.

Just this morning (17 March 2017), there is breaking news on BBC Breakfast TV that yet another incident has caused major disruption. It is reported that a 39-year-old, French-born, radicalized Muslim man injured a female police officer in northern Paris before he stole a car at gun-point and drove across the city to Orly Airport. There he assaulted a patrol of three armed air force soldiers. He wrestled to the floor one of these soldiers, who was a woman, and the other two soldiers shot and killed him to protect her as well as other airport users in the area. Although, in the context of terrorism in our world today, this was a relatively minor incident and nobody else was injured at Orly, an investigation was immediately launched to determine whether this was part of a larger terrorist plot. About 3,000 people were evacuated from both airport terminals and all flights suspended for the better part of that day. Minor incident perhaps, major disruption!

And now (22 March 2017) we hear that electronic devices such as laptops and tablets are going to be banned in carry-on baggage. Some airlines are already implementing this ban, on flights from some Middle East countries. This is due to a new scare that terrorists are planning to hack into such devices and incorporate explosives into them. Viera is again upset: "How can I trust that my laptop will be safe in the hold? Someone could steal it and get my sensitive banking details – and I'd have to back up all my data just in case, each time I travel. Also, I don't think insurance covers unattended items. I could really do without this added headache. As if it isn't stressful enough to travel nowadays!"

Infinitely worse are the attacks on railways, buses and on our streets that come totally out of the blue. India has suffered enough from these. The horrific infiltration into the Taj Hotel in Bombay was widely reported here in the UK too. A subsequent TV documentary showed graphic details of the attack, focusing on the selfless, heroic efforts of staff: their actions in trying to save hotel guests were moving and inspiring. This stirred a deep personal chord in me because I used to go with a group of friends to the disco at the Taj while training with Air India, back in 1968. I also stayed there for a week in 2010, with a group of 'Asian Women of Achievement' – we were all finalists in a UK-wide contest, and were later offered the opportunity to go to Bombay on an action-packed business-related visit. I have never before or since experienced better hospitality and service than that provided by the Taj staff at every level. In the wake of this terrorist attack my heart went out to them.

More recently, a string of bombings, stabbings and shootings have been carried out in the name of fundamentalist Islamist groups, for example in Brussels, Zurich, Berlin and Paris. How can one foresee and prevent a suicide bomber or lone madman from using a vehicle as a weapon of mass destruction: driving it suddenly into innocent people, with the incredibly brutal and shocking aim of killing and injuring as many as possible?!

That is what happened in Nice, and on 22 March 2017 it happened in central London. A British-born man, who had converted to Islam and had a history of violence, hired a car and deliberately drove it into pedestrians on the pavement of Westminster Bridge. One young teacher, who worked in a nearby college was going to pick up her children from school – she was killed at the scene. Another lady fell into the River Thames and later died in hospital. Two others have also lost their lives as I write this, and more than 30 others are being treated in hospital for injuries.

The attacker also stabbed and killed an unarmed policeman who was guarding Parliament. He was however quickly arrested and shot before he could get very far into Westminster and do any more damage. Amazingly, the entire incident took just 82 seconds. What mayhem can be caused in such a short time capsule! And what inspiring examples too, of people rising up to help, emergency services rushing within minutes to the scene, communities coming together in sympathy, reinforcing positive British values and refusing to allow terrorism to win.

Even so, a survey conducted for a TV discussion programme found that 30% of Brits had changed their travel plans due to fear of terrorism. Some of my elderly friends believe it is simply safer not to travel abroad at all. We are certainly living in a more inconvenient world, with more hassle for us ordinary law-abiding citizens. And more of our taxes have to be spent on keeping us safe. Crash barriers and bollards have been put up on London Bridge after the carnage that was delivered there.

What would Dada make of these tragic incidents and largescale disruptions, the amount of time, effort and energy devoted by intelligence agencies to foil such attacks, and the many restrictions in our world as it has become today? What would he make of the trade-off in travel regulations between individual privacy and collective security, so visible in airports? What would he make of the panic – and the heroism – that follows every nasty terrorist incident, when innocent people live with the fear of losing their loved ones and their own lives?

Brats on the rampage

9 Oct. 1966

Brats all over the country, male and female, school and college, are on a rampage. In their insensate fury, they are hammering the teachers, burning the schools, the post offices, police stations, collectorates – leading to cane and *lathi* charges, firings, bloodshed and magisterial enquiries. The conflagration seems to be widespread – Bombay, Ujjain, Bhopal, Agra, Lucknow, Kanpur, Patna and God knows what other places are in the grip of this mad fury. The most surprising thing is that no-one knows the cause for which this rioting is going on.

****

We shall paint before you an imaginary picture: Brat A and Brat B are sitting together, apparently studying for their examinations, when Brat A suddenly flings his book out of the window and says in great wrath, "To hell with this wretched Leibniz. If he had been living today, I would have twisted his neck for having devised his Differential Calculus and written his fantastic theorem, bringing misery to generations of students. Try as hard as I may, I cannot understand head or tail of it; and I wonder if the teacher, who presumed to teach it, understood it either."

Brat B: "I say, the exam is next week. You will fail and your career will be ruined."

Brat A: "To hell with my career. The moment I look at those equations, Vimala's face comes up before me and I cannot concen-trate. Let's go out and practice aiming at the streetlights."

And so the two go out and start aiming at the streetlights. The beautiful globe, along with the bulb, cracks, making the noise of a minor bomb explosion. The men on the pavement look round to see what has happened, when a *khaddar*-clad congressman, a self-appointed custodian of public morals and property, takes hold of Brat A and questions him menacingly, "Why did you break that light?" The Brat answers: "Who broke it?"

The congressman: "You did."

Brat A: "I didn't. You did it. I saw you throwing that stone."

The congressman: "I threw that stone, eh? You crook! I'll teach you a lesson you'll never forget. Call the police."

As the limb of the law is approaching, Brat B takes a sharp aim at his head and the policeman reels with a deep gash on his forehead. People look for the culprit and see Brat B running a 100-yard dash through the lanes and by-lanes.

To cut the story short, a crowd collects and multiplies from hundreds into thousands and from thousands into several thousands. Word goes round that a student has been arrested by the police, and the entire student population in their solidarity chuck their books aside and join in the fray, aiming at street lights, shop windows, road transport. At this stage, the antisocial elements take over. The Car and Bus Overturners' Association joins in; the arsonists, looters and knife-happy start practising their skill; the police appear on the scene in force; and the rest is known to you.

This is what is happening since independence, and the question arises why the tragedy is being enacted year after year. This is not the first time in the history of our country that students are punished for their lapses, certainly not the first time that a lady teacher used an adhesive tape to seal the lips of a girl, probably for having put pins on her chair and for using bad language later. After all, it was too mild a punishment for the damage the pins must have done to her posterior. Then why this rebellion – even on the part of girl students?

****

It is only in a police state that force and violence keep the citizen on good behaviour. In free, democratic societies, it is the moral law that governs his conduct. By implication, this means that those at the helm of affairs, the leaders of our social, political and business life, conduct themselves according to the highest canons of ethics and morality. But alas, since independence, with death mowing down the great veterans in the Congress Party, it is left today with those who jumped upon the bandwagon for the loaves and fishes of independence. 19 years of freedom have completely vitiated the social fabric of the country.

The students know that, today, means do not matter – it is the end that counts. They observe the beggars of yesteryear becoming the leaders of today by all sorts of shady and devious means. They know that a political party which is trying to entrench itself for another five years will not take any action against them, for fear of losing a sizable chunk of votes which are theirs. Therefore do they go on a rampage at the slightest pretext in this pre-election year. And wherefore do we congratulate them for having raised the slogan "Quit Congress."

Brats defying the police - Cubbon Park Police Station

Only snakes were on the rampage

Diary entry: 5 September 1978, back home in St Albans after a holiday in Bangalore:

My youngest son Manoj is starting school today. He's blissfully unaware of all that this new beginning will mean for him. We are both just out of bed and I'm ironing his uniform shirt when he calls out from the hallway near the front door: "Mum, can I go out to play?"

No Moji, not this morning. And not for most mornings from now on. The summer we have spent staying with Dada and Bhabi in Bangalore is sadly and quickly going to disappear into the back of beyond. The weather was warm and pleasant enough to play outdoors almost all day, every day. I'm just a tad sad that my 'baby' is embarking on this new phase of life, which to some extent spells the end of that wonderful carefree age of 'playing barefoot in the garden'. There will be a hole in my own weekdays where my sons have been, in their childhoods of innocence and affection.

"Have you got your shoes on?" I call out to Manoj, because I cannot see him from where I am ironing in the kitchen.

"No."

"Have you got your socks on?"

"No! But I have got my feet on!"

Flashback to my first day at school, Bangalore, August 1951

"*Arré*, keep still", my mother says as she crouches down to help me wiggle and tug my feet into my new school socks and shoes. "I can see you are so excited!"

"I've waited all my life for this day" I tell her, with all of my five and a quarter-year-old life behind me, and all my future adventures stretching ahead of me.

"Yes, school can be fun." She smiles up at me, but the smile doesn't reach her eyes and there is no joy in her tone. I do not understand her feelings at the time, but sense that she will miss me. I put my arms around her head and then she lifts me off the chair and gives me a hug. "Come now, get your blazer on – the bus will be here soon."

The uniform in Bishop Cotton Girls' School consisted of a green tunic over a white blouse and big baggy green bloomers. I can't remember if we had to wear the green and gold tie in kindergarten, but it was definitely part of our uniform later. I resented the noose-like school tie just as I always resented imprisoning my feet in socks and hard school shoes. All through my pre-school years I'd played barefoot and romped with our pet dogs through the house and garden in Bangalore. But school was an exciting prospect that first morning. My friend Satish had already been in kindergarten for a whole year. I could have started too, at the age of four and a half, but Dada said he didn't believe in making children grow up too soon.

"Be good now," Bhabi says at the gate as she waves me into the rickety green and brown school bus. I spot Satish at the back of the bus and try to get to him, but the bus is crowded and I have to sit down before I fall down.

Bishop Cotton Girls' School accepted boys in kindergarten until they turned seven. After that they all went off to the Boys' School down the road. But having Satish in my class was great at the time. That first morning he warned me that we couldn't speak Hindi at school, not even in the playground. We would be smacked if we were overheard speaking in any language other than English. I did get smacked with a ruler on my shins anyway, because I was still playing outside after the bell rang. I sharply felt the injustice of this.

So I sought Satish out in class and the two of us scrambled out the minute the bell rang for our first mid-morning break. Joy ran free and fast on our little legs to the playground. Here we were soon joined by other children. A few of us began a game of hide and seek. Satish and I and a couple of others hid in the grass next to the hockey pitch. The grass had grown so thick and high that we couldn't be seen if we crouched down low. But suddenly Satish stood up tall and shouted "Arti, run – get up and run! There's a snake."

"We will be caught," I hesitated. And by the time I did get up and run the snake had bitten me on my shin. I barely saw it slithering away.

The other children took a look at my shin and Satish said we had to go quickly and tell the teacher. I didn't want to tell anyone and get into trouble on my very first day. But the snake and I seemed to be high drama for the others and they raced me back to our class. Our teacher then raced me to the office, and the Principal rang Dada immediately and asked him to come over – she said time was of the essence. Luckily Dada's printing press was not far from school and I didn't have to wait long. But one look at his grim expression when he appeared was enough to make me quail.

"I don't know what the fuss is about," I muttered, "I'm not ill – I feel fine."

"Just get into the car," Dada ordered.

I knew where we were going. Every medical matter – a big, bad emergency or a tiny hiccup – ended up in the Cash Pharmacy. I wondered where my snakebite would fall along this spectrum. Dada seemed sure that Dr M would deal with it – he was not only our family doctor but one of Dada's best buddies. And Cash Pharmacy was literally a three minute drive down the road from our school.

Dr M was with a patient when we got there so we had to wait. Dada paced the floor and I began to think how his faith in his doctor-buddy was entirely without foundation. To me Dr M was not unlike a snake himself – not a thin one but a toxic, fat, self-satisfied python that has swallowed a whole goat. He could certainly squeeze the life out of you. His hugs and forked tongue were those of a fake friend – and you certainly need to fear those more than open attacks from an enemy.

When he finally opened his door and ushered us in his voice boomed and echoed round the clinic: "Dada! What brings you here? How is life treating you?"

Meanwhile I'm trying to hide behind Dada's legs... I'm trying not to notice the surgical smells that waft around the room. Eventually he fires questions at me:

"At what time did you get bitten? What did the snake look like? Why were you playing in that grass? Is the snakebite painful? Tell me what the pain feels like…"

I tell him (as truthfully as I can) that it was a green grass snake; I feel just fine; the sting was not painful – not like the bee that had stung me last month or the bite on my arm from Marcus, our Alsatian. He takes one good look at my leg and my face, and announces breezily to Dada: "That snake couldn't have been very poisonous. She isn't foaming at the mouth or losing consciousness. Anyway, if it had been a venomous snake she would be dead by now."

To be on the safe side he makes an incision around the bite to withdraw any venom that might be there. He advises Dada to take me home and keep an eye on me, basically to see I don't fall asleep, as any venom that might be within me would take a hold if I did.

When I return to school the next morning my classmates whoop and cheer. Satish has already said on the bus that he's glad I'm not dead. The teacher, somewhat stony-faced, tells us all to calm down and settle down. The snakebite is never officially referred to by anyone in authority. When we go out to play I see that the grass has been cut down to its roots.

Of course I understand in retrospect that we brats were never allowed to go on the rampage, but snakes on the rampage in school would have been terrible publicity for Bishop Cottons.

At the end of Manoj's first day at school I can't wait to pick him up.

"How did it go, Moji?" I ask.

"Good" is all I can get out of him.

"Did you get bitten by any snakes?"

"No. There is a rabbit in our school," he tells me, shaking his head. He is just impatient to get home and get his bare feet into the garden again. But this is England, Moji. We wear socks and shoes here, and the garden is usually colder than the one in Bangalore. As for snakes – not likely!

Thinking now about that first encounter I had with the school snake, I'd say it was the most benign. My grandmother Maji always said that snakes – even the king cobras in her village – were never a problem if you just respected them and left them alone. They used to sometimes curl themselves around the large earthenware pots that held drinking water in her kitchen. She firmly believed that all snakes become blind in the presence of a pregnant woman. And Maji spent a good deal of her childbearing years being pregnant. (Dada was one of nine children.) She said the worst types of snakes are of the human variety and I have to fervently agree with her. One human snake in more recent times nearly did kill me. But that is another story – a long story that I will tell in future. But then again, that will have to remain a definite maybe.

Photo by Dil (unsplash)

Parents on the rampage

16 Oct. 1966

In our childhood the dictum "Spare the rod and spoil the child" was not a mere dictum but was very much put into practice. The hand of the teacher or the parent descended heavily on the miscreant at the slightest transgression of discipline. Terms like 'frustration', 'instability', 'adjustment', 'rejection' and 'acceptance' were unknown, as psychology was still a science unborn and no-one bothered about the young growing into distorted personalities through the use of corporal punishment. Strangely enough, the people of these times have grown into balanced personalities and are occupying some of the highest positions in our social, political and business life.

****

But see what is happening today, despite the know-how which psychology has placed in our hands! Notwithstanding dozens of commissions which have sat during the past two decades, cogitating on our educational system, casting and recasting its methods, news comes from a theatre of war somewhere in India, where battle is still raging between the students and the police, that in a certain school, boys – as a measure of punishment – were deprived of their pants and made to don skirts. We do not know if the opposite procedure was adopted in the case of girls.

Now the story runs that a mother, a hefty 16-stone virago, having learnt of the indignity to which her son was thus submitted, was much infuriated. She picked up her biggest broom and repaired fast through the streets of the village or town, whatever it was, muttering obscene oaths and invoking the curses of the 100 crore demons of Hindu mythology on the teacher who had the temerity to put her son to such shame. The people, seeing the wild sight, asked the woman what had happened and, being appraised, joined the woman in her wrath. By and by, a biggish procession carrying brooms, brickbats, sticks and other miscellaneous weapons descended upon the school.

****

We have no factual report on the treatment that was meted out to the poor teacher, but we have it on good authority that, after the woman had subjected him to a severe treatment of the broom, he was denuded of his manly apparel and made to wear a sari. He was then paraded through the streets, with all and sundry joining in the *tamasha*. Mysteriously, however, as the procession was wending its way through the main street, brickbats started flying, damaging street lights, shop windows, cars, buses and the heads and limbs of many people.

The inevitable then happened. The police arrived on the scene with their canes and *lathis*, rifles and bullets, and after they had fired into the air in self-defence, killing a few people, the village has now become quiet. It is nourishing its wounds and grievances and shedding many crocodile tears — obviously as a result of the teargas shells of the police.

****

It is rumoured that there is a move to appoint a high power commission; consisting mainly of the right and left communists, to re-indoctrinate people into the mechanics of causing such trouble, and a special sanction of 100,000 rupees for preliminary expenses is awaited from the Government.

Parents – and brats – on the e-rampage

Each successive UK Government has used schools and methods of education as a political football. Every time a new Minister for Education takes office there are new directives, often issued more for political point-scoring than genuine educational improvement, even though teachers themselves might assign an F-grade to the imposed reform. Parents typically do not see that the ills of the education system may arise from constant change in the sector and government demands rather than staff incompetence. Teachers have to record and analyse data, use new technologies and new resources – all of which increase their workloads. They often have to manage tight budgets and do more with less. Teachers are just an easy target for blame, so they become the scapegoats.

Having worked in UK schools, colleges and universities since 1982, my experience tells me that students – and their parents – are not what they used to be. I do not like to generalise, but I see that many parents' attitudes have changed since the long-ago days when I was a child at school (but of course my school days were in Bangalore, India). I was no stranger to disciplinary measures like having to stand on a chair facing the corner of the classroom, being thrown out of class, or getting a smack on the hand with a ruler. My parents did not defend my behaviour if my teachers complained that I was being a monkey in class. If you got a detention in school you usually got double trouble at home.

In England and Wales, caning in private schools was abolished in the 1990s, and in state schools in the 1980s. Fair enough, it is not a pleasant experience to smack or be smacked, and I don't advocate caning. But I've seen cases where regulations against touching a child have been taken to ridiculous limits. In 1987 I did a three-month placement in an East London secondary school. The teacher who first showed me round the premises gave me a brief introduction to the background of the children, thus: "This is a rough neighbourhood. A high percentage of ethnic minorities here suffer from deprivation; there are many single parent families, or both parents work long hours in poorly-paid jobs. So they have little time or patience for their children. Quite a few are alcoholics or druggies."

"Are the children well-behaved in class, though?" I ask, "Is it easy to maintain discipline?"

"Ha, not always!" he says. "I cannot even touch a child without exposing myself to the risk of getting blamed. It's particularly hard for male teachers. The other day a girl in my class was crying, she was too distressed to talk to me. But I can't touch anyone to comfort them when they are upset, nor to separate them physically when they might be locked in mortal combat with each other. And yet we are meant to keep them safe and happy – to be like social workers as well as teachers."

"It doesn't apply the other way," he continues, visibly distressed by the conversation we are having. "The children are allowed to be rude and aggressive!" He lifts his shirt and shows me an angry bruise on his torso, just beginning to turn from red to purple. "That's where a boy in my class punched me when I gave him a D-grade for his maths homework. How are we meant to improve their learning if they cannot accept feedback?"

"What about his parents?" I ask. "Aren't they concerned about his bad behaviour, and his education? Did you tell them about this at the parents' evening?"

"All I could do was hint at it, but when I met his parents I had the distinct feeling they wouldn't be on my side. Some parents are friendly and supportive, but a great many don't respect us and don't want to hear anything negative about their little darlings. They don't know what to do about it anyway – the children don't listen to them either. It's easier for them to blame teachers when their children misbehave."

I could see that teachers were almost powerless in matters of discipline. In that school they didn't want to risk facing aggressive parents who might assault them verbally – or even physically. The balance of power then clearly lies with students, and with parents who just want to believe their children are right. If some student accuses a teacher of bullying, physical or (worse still) sexual assault, the teacher may be immediately suspended from the job and even threatened with a lawsuit, subject to investigation. The regulations and attitudes of those in authority effectively treat teachers as if they are guilty before they can be proved innocent. Some teachers' careers and personal lives have been devastated by false accusations.

And now, on 12 May 2017, newspapers are reporting that 32 police forces across Britain have revealed a shocking increase in the numbers of children – some as young as 10 – who are carrying weapons into school. These are not sticks and stones but knives, air guns and even samurai swords. The police have to confiscate them and point out the horrific consequences of stabbing and shooting, but surely this situation would not arise at all if young people could trust that their schools (and neighbourhoods) were safe environments, free from any type of violence. Most carry weapons for self-defence. Having said that, I am reminded of the tragic death of Leeds teacher Ann Maguire: her 15-year-old student fatally stabbed her during a Spanish lesson in 2014.

Now if you are thinking that British schools are a veritable snake-pit, I hasten to add that violence and anti-social behaviours are not the norm everywhere here. The vast majority of youngsters are well behaved. Currently, in the school where I'm on the board of governors, I have seen close cooperation and excellent communications between parents and teachers. Most of the children are happily progressing, and each one is valued. Problems are dealt with discreetly through individual support, counselling and mentoring where needed. This is a well-resourced school in a relatively affluent area where parents are highly educated.

However, some perfectly polite parents in the real world can turn into The Incredible Hulk in the virtual world. E-mail and social media sites give them a platform to go on the e-rampage. Understandably, it's the bane of teachers' lives when these sorts of parents complain about anything and everything in ways they wouldn't do face to face. This sort of abuse seems to be on the increase. According to a 2015 survey by the NASUWT (the Teachers' Union),

60% of the 1,500 respondents said they were facing insulting, threatening and untruthful personal comments online. The survey highlighted that parents – rather than children – were responsible for the sharp rise in the number of posts on sites such as Facebook: 40% compared with 27% in the previous year.

More than a third of teachers had suddenly found videos or photos of themselves on Facebook, Instagram and Snapchat, with rude captions or comments, mocking them on their racial or sexual backgrounds, appearance and competence. This is particularly despicable; parents should be well aware of legal and ethical restrictions in the UK that are meant to prevent people from taking and publishing photos without the consent of the person. Far, far worse, some posts falsely accuse teachers of being paedophiles – an accusation which warrants police investigation and even arrest.

You would think effective action should be taken to stop this nasty stream of abuse. Most teachers did report it – to the school authorities, or to the police – and said that social media platforms must also take their fair share of responsibility for tracking and removing abusive content on their sites. For example, Twitter has 320 million users worldwide but employs only 100 people to deal with abuse. It would appear to be just skimming the surface on security issues.

So the NASUWT study found that little was done for teachers affected by online harassment. This may be due to the school's fear of further provoking the parents, or simply because freedom of speech is a human right: one head teacher explicitly stated that pupils and parents had a right to say what they liked about a teacher on e-media. And free education is also perceived as a human right in the UK. The result is a sense of entitlement – and this is not always balanced by a sense of duty and responsibility. Are parents not meant to be good role models for their children?! I fear this sad state of parental behaviours does not bode well for the future.

In comparison, my experience of recent research visits to schools and colleges in Bangalore tells me that education is taken seriously in India. It is valued because it is a privilege that typically has to be paid for. It is viewed as a passport to a better life-career. Teachers may not be paid high salaries, but the profession is respected and supported in its noble attempts to produce a future generation with the knowledge, skills and attributes of good citizens.

And here in the UK too there is good evidence that students' results show much better attainment and progression in schools where parents and teachers work together to educate and discipline children. After all, caning is not the best way to improve behaviour. What do children nowadays value most of all? Why, they value their e-media devices of course! It seems the greatest punishment nowadays is to confiscate their smartphones, tablets or X-box, and thus deprive them of access to social media or computer gaming – technologies to which they are addicted. In some schools parents cooperate with disciplinary measures, and ensure that this type of punishment is enforced at home and not only at school.

It was worth getting wet for

13 November 1966

On 3 November came a bit of news from Sao Paulo, Brazil, which at first sight appeared incredible. But it was not so incredible after all. It said:

"Businessmen inverted their umbrellas and shop assistants rushed into rain-swept streets here to catch a shower – of money.

Banknotes from 100 to 5,000 cruzeiros fluttered down with rain in the city's shopping centre. A first shower was mostly low denomination notes and people thought they were forgeries. But when the downpour really started with 5,000 (17 shillings) notes included, the cry went up, "It's not faked" – and pandemonium broke out.

No-one managed to find out where all the money came from but everybody agreed it was worth getting wet for." (source: Reuter)

****

On 3 November came another bit of news from Bangalore which at first sight appeared incredible. But it was not so incredible after all.

As the news spread of the inauguration of the Janata Bazaar, the shopkeepers in Bangalore inverted their umbrellas and collected the biggest bonanza of the year.

Shouted the bicycle shop owner, "Rama, Thimma, Govinda... run fast and tell all our relations and community men to stand in the queue at the opening of the Janata

Bazaar and buy up all the cycle tyres. Here, take this money."

Shouted the general merchant, "Kempi, Thimmi, Rami... run fast and tell your sisters, sisters-in-law and community women to stand in the queue at the opening of the Janata Bazaar and buy up all the baby food, Horlicks, Bournvita – anything and everything that is scarce. Here, take this money."

****

And thus, as the word went round that Rama, Thimma, Govinda, Kempi, Thimmi, and Rami... were queuing up to buy all the scarce commodities at the Janata Bazaar, notwithstanding the heavy rain, the entire community of businessmen repaired fast and queued up at the Janata Stores. And they all agreed it was worth getting wet for.

It was a matter of hours and the entire stock of bicycle tyres, baby foods, Horlicks, Bournvita – anything and everything that is scarce – was sold out. And the genteel men and women, the real consumers, un-accustomed to the pushing and elbowing of the bulls and bears, had to go home disappointed.

****

The next day the Janata Stores opened with their shelves denuded and with the announcement, "The sale of all scarce commodities like xxxx will be effected only on coupons to be obtained from the rationing officer."

On the other side, in the free market, Rama, Thimma and Govinda, with bicycle tyres slung round their necks, and Kempi, Thimmi, and Rami, with baby food in their baskets, vended them merrily at an atrocious premium.

The moral: Prices fall only when production outstrips demand and not by starting Janata Stores to vend scarce commodities.

Free Cash

According to a couple of press reports, ATMs have suddenly become generous and started handing out free cash. On one such occasion in November 2011, a cash machine attached to the Clydesdale Bank in Wishaw, Scotland, went haywire due to a technical fault, and spewed out double the money customers keyed in. I'm sure these customers thought Christmas had arrived early! Word spread quickly about this unexpected bonanza, and about 100 people queued up to take advantage of this ATM's generosity. However the fault was quickly rectified and explained.

A similar fault occurred in Dundee – once again, customers doubled their money. According to the reports, the Banks in question accepted it was their fault and didn't ask customers to return the extra money.

Now what would you do if you saw five £5 notes – £25 in total – attached to a board in your city centre? Would you be tempted to quietly pocket the cash? Or would you be suspicious – because you know that nothing in life is free? Maybe you're wary about being caught – on CCTV or someone's camera – if you do take the money.

This was actually a social experiment carried out in Manchester by The Lad Bible. They wanted to test just how honest and kind people might be. The £25 cash came with a message that read "This money is for people in need only." The experiment was filmed covertly and later uploaded on YouTube. The video shows many Manchester residents staring at the board, taking pictures of the sign, but not touching the free money.

At one point two women removed two of the £5 notes – not for themselves but only so they could give them to a homeless man who had been sitting there all day. He said he'd been too scared to take the money.

Then we see a man pinning an extra £5 note of his own to the board, and scribbling a message which says: "Take what you need, but don't be greedy."

Eventually the end of the video shows a woman confronting two men who simply go up and pocket the remaining £20. The men are undaunted - they merely laugh and walk off with their free cash.

Palmists, horologists, numerologists… and now futurologists!

26 May 1974

So far the world has known only tricksters, like astrologers, crystal-gazers, palmists, horologists, astro-numerologists and suchlike, who preyed on the gullibility of men and women by presuming to read the future. To this tribe is now added a new entity, which goes by the glorified name of futurologists. The astrologers and fortune-tellers cultivated an aura of mysticism to back them up, but the futurologists claim to predict the shape of things to come from unassailable data collected through scientific research. And, this being the age of science and technology, their prognostications are accepted by everyone as gospel truth.

It is in this setting that we viewed with considerable fear and trepidation the predictions of futurologists Dr P K Rohatgi and Dr B Bowonder about what would happen to India in the year 2000 AD. This, according to them, would be the scenario of India:

With compulsory birth control, the population of India would be stabilised around 900 million, but half the population would have no houses to live in, compelling them to dwell in kibbutz-type communes. Food will be scarce and protein malnutrition frightening. Surprisingly, however, a single food pill, supplied free by the Government, will meet the complete nutritional requirements of the people. A single concentrated 'energy pill' will provide the energy needed for a whole day. That would be Utopia indeed, with the gastric juices, liver bile, intestines, and all the rest, getting a complete holiday with no ailments. Dysentery and diarrhea will be banished forever.

Everything will be in short supply – sugar, pulses, fats, oils, meat, milk, fish, and whatever else you can think of in the domain of food. So also would be the supply of bismuth, lead, mercury, nickel, cobalt, molybdenum, platinum, silver, tin, tungsten, zinc – every conceivable metal and mineral. Gold, of course, would have escaped into space, becoming a universal myth. The energy position would be acute with the reserves of coal, petroleum and other fossil fuels exhausted.

As we thought about these fearsome things to come, barely 25 years from now, we said: What if! Indira has now got in her hands the nuclear bomb. That might also lead to Pakistan producing one. If it cannot, China will always give one to it. Then, Soviet Russia may move its entire nuclear stockpile into India, with the USA moving a bigger one into Pakistan. This shifting of nuclear pawns would doubtless culminate in an unprecedented holocaust, and who knows what would happen to the present 500 million people of India and the 3,000 million of the world! They might well get wiped out, leaving no food or pollution problems for anyone in the world to contend with.

As we cogitated on these prospects, we dozed off and dreamt one of the most fearsome dreams of our life. Toro, the mighty asteroid which is currently jitterbugging in the planetary system, finally decides to make a beeline towards our Earth. As it crashes on Earth, the cosmic impact is so great that the outer crust of our planet gets shifted: the North and South Poles shift onto the equator and the equator becomes the axis. Molten lava gushes out of the bowels of the earth, converting the oceans into super-heated steam and levelling the Himalayas. The controversial time-capsule, buried deep in the Red Fort, turns to ashes, and the mighty thousand-million-ton steel statue of Smt. Indira Gandhi, consisting of the entire steel production of India during 1974-2000, installed on top of the central dome of Parliament House, falls hundreds of fathoms deep into the newly created ocean – there perhaps to be detected by future archaeologists 100,000 years hence, leaving the world to wonder who this great woman was.

We wake up, shivering and sweating profusely, and say: "God's ways are inscrutable indeed! And so, why worry about 2000 AD?"

Photo by Ryan MCGuire (Gratisography)

Actually, are we not suffering today from surplus?

Photo by Jana Sabeth Schultz (unsplash)

Photo by Atharva Tulsi (unsplash)

Photo by Fancycrave (unsplash)

Are precise predictions prudent?

From my vantage point in the UK in 2018, the predictions of shortages made by these futurologists of yesteryear seem laughable. In the words of J K Galbraith, "Economic forecasting makes astrology look respectable." Of course one cannot treat the economy like a mechanistic model because humans do not behave like machines. Futurologists who used scientific formulae to predict the future could not have foreseen the extent of global connectivity that has been achieved by advancing technologies and free trade deals. Information and communication technologies radically remove some of the constraints of time and space. In our lifetime we've seen how the internet and email allow companies to work across geographical boundaries and to deliver their services and products to customers worldwide. And modern technologies have even changed who the workers, clients and customers of companies are.

It is self-evident now that every industry is being affected by amazing developments. We seem to be standing at the threshold of the 4th Industrial Revolution. Are we heading towards domination by robots? Dependence on artificial intelligence and self-driving cars? God forbid! Anyway, here I am going to steer clear of techie questions and predictions. I'm going to argue that much of the so-called 'developed world' today is suffering more from surplus than from the scarcities of food and energy that were predicted.

Even as far back as 1981, just about seven years after these predictions of great shortages were made, Richard Buckminster Fuller wrote "It is now highly feasible to take care of everybody on earth at a higher standard of living than any have ever known. It no longer has to be you or me. Selfishness is unnecessary and henceforth unrationalizable as mandated by survival… War is obsolete. It is a matter of converting high technology from weaponry to livingry."

----- R. Buckminster Fuller. *Critical Path,* 1981, Introduction, page xxv.

Fuller was idealistic about the future of humanity. Despite his concerns about the prevailing globally-dominant socio-economic system, he believed we humans would use our "technological ability to protect, nurture, support, and accommodate all growth needs of life." And he believed we would do this in inclusive ways that would generate wealth and create a utopia for everyone.

Gandhiji also famously said, "The world has enough for everyone's need but not enough for everyone's greed." The truth is we define 'greed' in different ways today. In the western world we have raised the stakes on our expectations and aspirations: what were once luxuries possessed by few are now thought of as necessities for all. And indeed it is true that more of us have television, cars, washing machines and other labour-saving devices. But we are not – by and large – willing to make sacrifices to create an equitable utopia for all.

To what extent has this situation made us happier? Even optimists admit that we may be suffering more from surplus than from shortages. I agree with Tom Waits when he says: "We are buried beneath the weight of information, which is being confused with knowledge. Quantity is being confused with abundance, and wealth with happiness. We are monkeys with money and guns."

Things like too many cars on the roads – are traffic jams not causing congestion and air-pollution? Making life more complex and difficult? For me, driving is no longer a pleasure but a necessary evil to get from A to B. Traffic analysts reported in February 2017 that Britain's roads are the most congested in Europe. Apparently we have 20,000 traffic hotspots – double the number in Germany and ten times more than in France. In these hot-spots pollution reaches high levels which can have serious health implications.

On average, a UK driver loses 32 hours and £968 a year from hold-ups in traffic jams. And Londoners suffer most of all, losing an average of £1,911. The national loss in productivity amounted to £31 billion in 2016, impacting businesses and consumers severely. Yet our love affair with the automobile continues unabated.

A survey by the British Parking Association shows that drivers lose an average of four days each year looking for parking spaces. 39% of people say that finding parking is a stressful experience. This is made worse because many types of cars are now manufactured wider and larger (probably to accommodate larger people!).

From time to time news bulletins in the UK remind us that the human race is undeniably getting larger. Obesity is increasing in all age groups. In December 2016, BBC Breakfast news reported research findings that showed people in the UK between the ages of 40 and 60 were in health crises due to diets full of fat and sugar calories. But no amount of advising, cajoling and scary advertising has really helped to reverse the obesity trend. We seem to be programmed to love foods that expand our waistlines and put us at risk of developing diabetes, cancer and heart disease.

Excessive alcohol consumption is also increasing health and social problems, and putting an increasing strain on the UK's National Health Service. The pressure on everyone to lose weight, look good and stay young, is weighing heavily on many people, especially on women. By all accounts it is stopping us from fully enjoying the great variety of delicious foods that are all too readily available.

But then again, do I really need to go into my local supermarket and be faced with a choice between 12 different types of yoghurts and 10 different types of bread? Call me old-fashioned, but faced with umpteen pizza and coffee choices I turn into a jellyfish with no decision-making ability. Standing in the queue for coffee I marvel at all the youngsters ahead of me who have no trouble defining their coffee identity: "I'm strictly a strong black espresso" or "I'm a skinny latte", or I'm a frothy Cappucino with chocolate flakes and marsh-mallows", or "I'm a large one with two sugars, weak and white, please." But me, do I really need to decide between Espresso, Americano, Macchiato, Cappuccino, Café Mocha – full fat milk, soya milk, etc.? Frankly I'd rather go to the peaceful, quiet café attached to the Baptist church, staffed by volunteers, and order the only coffee they have, served in a plain mug, reasonably priced and offered with milk, free refills and a smile.

It is a scandalous fact that many people (and particularly supermarkets and restaurants) in the UK throw out vast amounts of food which may be perfectly good for eating. The news in February 2017 presents another distressing statistic: 12 billion pounds-worth of food ends up in the bin each year.

The more affluent a country, the more waste it generates. People can afford to buy new goods so unwanted, unloved things get thrown away although they may be repaired or renovated. The UK generates 30 million tons of household waste each year, 10 million of which consists of packaging material that is not biodegradable.

Lots of us are guilty of environmentally unfriendly behaviours even though we should know the impact on global climate change and wildlife. Plastic is a particular problem. We use 35 million plastic bottles every day, about 16 million of which end up on our beaches, in landfill and in oceans. Greenpeace warns that about a truck-load of plastic is dumped into the oceans every minute. We know that turtles, whales, seals and seabirds can ingest plastic bags and particles and choke to death. Yet our use of plastic shopping bags in England only began to reduce in October 2015, when the government introduced a scheme that required large retailers to charge 5p for each plastic bag they issued.

Today the world is a utopia for some and hell on earth for others. There is another side to surplus – a hideous surplus of violence, oppression and suffering. We cannot ignore the hellish statistics emerging from the UNHCR: in the past couple of years some 69 million people have been displaced by war, persecution and conflict. The numbers of refugees seeking asylum, mainly from Syria, Afghanistan and Somalia, have hit an all-time high. Millions are starving in South Sudan, Ethiopia, Yemen and Somalia due to famine, caused by multiple factors: mismanagement of resources, bad government, war and climate change. Imagine the devastating impact on each personal life hidden behind such global statistics.

The UN High Commissioner for Refugees, Filippo Grandi, has voiced regret that affluent nations are reacting to this crisis by closing their borders. Instead of the political will to share the burden and fulfil the obligations of our common humanity, there is a sense of political paralysis and xenophobia. It is left to aid agencies, charities and humanitarian organisations to do what they can with limited budgets. And they are increasingly struggling to save lives and rehabilitate displaced people, especially the children who have become separated from their parents. Here is that horrendous statistic: children made up 51% of the total number of refugees in 2015.

We might ask ourselves, what is it all for in the end? Are we not suffering from surplus – in one way or another? Having much more than we need doesn't equate with being happy. Isn't it high time we tried to follow the example of the small Himalayan kingdom of Bhutan that officially measures prosperity not by GDP (Gross Domestic Product) but by GNH (Gross National Happiness). Happiness is decreed by its wise king as a goal for all its residents. What is it all for, in the end?

SECTION 3: POLITICS AND PERSONALITIES

My take on Politics is somewhat different from what you may expect. I am not by nature into Party Politics, so the views I express here are far-ranging comments about politics as life events in general. My parallel pieces to Dada's columns are grounded in what I read, hear and experience in the UK. In any case, political tectonic plates are heaving and shifting even as I write about them. So all I can capture is a snapshot in time: what I say today may be outdated tomorrow. Really, all one can say with any certainty nowadays is that political outcomes have become very uncertain. Recent election results show that all we can expect is to expect the unexpected.

The big difference since Dada's times is that political landscapes of the world we live in now have been transformed by social media. Opinions and debates are brought into the living rooms, bar rooms and board rooms of every citizen by multiple news reports, programmes and people's reactions to them. The 'opinion' floodgates on social media are open round the clock and pretty much round the world. Democracy now seems to consist of cumulative small mouse-clicks of participation. Everyone, anyone and their dog, can post something on Twitter and Facebook. It doesn't seem to matter if it's valid, relevant or malicious hoax. In this brave new world of super-complexity it is difficult to know what to believe.

In the past people could turn to responsible and ethical journalism as the repository of truth. But 'fake news' has become a new buzz phrase and phenomenon of our times. It parades as genuine news from a reliable source, creating confusion so that the truth is hard to find. It can be highly serious when it deliberately misinforms and influences the public in order to gain unfair financial or political advantage, or to damage a person or institution. I hope the pages that follow will encourage your own critical and creative thinking.

Are not the politicians supplementing their income by immoral means?

9 Jan. 1966

Having learnt that the cortege carrying the last remains of General Thimayya was to pass on Mahatma Gandhi Road at 12 noon, we stepped out of our office and stood on the pavement in the midst of a crowd that had collected there. As we were busy observing the general scene, a man wearing a *khaddar kurta, dhoti* and Gandhi cap, and looking very much like a politician, approached us with great warmth and wished us *Namasté*. On our reciprocating with equal warmth he started making kind enquiries about our family, our business and our newspaper.

Now, to be honest, we were quite surprised at his familiarity with our affairs, but much as we tried to place him, our memory would not respond, and we could not recollect who he was. However, courtesy demanded that we kept up the appearance of knowing him, and therefore we gave him polite but somewhat indifferent answers.

Having exhausted the usual trivialities, he commenced a lengthy narration about the greatness of the late General Thimayya and the loss the country had suffered in his passing away. We, on our part, kept on agreeing with him with our monosyllabic "Yesses" and "Nos".

Then the cortege having passed, we decided to walk back to our office, but our friend, the politician, detained us once again. He told us in confidence that he had picked up on the pavement a purse containing quite a bit of money, and that he was going straight to the police station to hand it over to the authorities so that the rightful owner got it. He further added that some time back he had picked up similarly a diamond necklace which he had promptly handed over to the police. For this act of good citizenship his Party had recommended his case to the President of India for the award of a *Padmashri* during the Republic Day Honours. But being a selfless worker, he had declined getting into the limelight by accepting so great an honour.

We were quite taken in by this great man, and expressed our admiration for his sterling qualities and selfless service. Finally, having shaken his hand profusely, we took leave of him and walked back to our office. A little later we went to the Parade Café shop to buy a few cigars and, as we put our hand into our hip pocket, we were greatly shocked. Our purse had gone.

We were rather intrigued to read some days ago a report in the paper praising the work of the Social Welfare Ministry and stating that prostitutes were no longer supplementing their income by immoral means. After the loss of our purse we exclaimed to ourself, "What about the politicians?"

Are not peers lording it in the House of Lords?

Yes – what about the politicians indeed! Corruption in politics – and in fact at all levels of society in India – seems to be endemic. Prime Minister Narendra Modi is attempting to eradicate it, but it's not going to happen unless everyone takes responsibility and develops a moral conscience.

In June 2013, I went to a Life Designing Conference in Padua. At the end of that event, I was free to enjoy my last day in Italy. I took the opportunity to take a ferry from Venice to explore the Biennale Architecture Festival in Giardini (one of the beautiful islands off Venice). The sun was uncomfortably hot and there was a lot of walking around between the various exhibits set up by different countries, but I persevered because everything was fascinating. I was however just about to succumb to the weather at the end of the afternoon, and catch the ferry back to the mainland, when an inscription on one of the exhibits attracted my attention – because it was about India.

This inscription on a pillar provided an interesting snippet of information about a non-governmental organization called the 5th Pillar: the NGO was campaigning against corruption and printing zero rupee notes in all the major Indian languages. The idea was to provide an easy way for ordinary citizens to say No to corruption. When they were faced with officials trying to bribe them for services which should legally be provided free of charge, they wouldn't have to say anything; they could simply take out and hand over a zero rupee note. While the note has no monetary value, it is a clear non-confrontational protest against those in positions of authority who try to misuse their power. The note was designed with an image of Mahatma Gandhi – that sends an anti-corruption message in itself.

It was strange to unearth this gem of information in a place so geographically remote from India. I did an internet search to find out more. But it is even more strange that my Indian family and friends (even those who live in India) look askance at me when I mention the zero rupee note. They know nothing about it. That's a pity because the note needs to be a weapon in everyone's battle against corruption.

Here, in the UK, the expenses claimed by peers in the House of Lords is a scandal that flares up in the media from time to time. The House of Lords is the upper chamber of Parliament, and its members are not elected but drawn from a vast range of occupations for their expertise. They are there to check and challenge the work of government, scrutinize and debate draft bills and policies. Peers are paid £40,000 per annum but they are not held to account for the work they should put in, and some do precious little or simply clock in to register for their £300 attendance fee without contributing to debates or votes.

In 2013 the *Mirror* newspaper first exposed this scandal; and now February 2017 brings fresh calls to sack all members of the House of Lords, and replace it with a fully elected chamber. The BBC has screened a damning new TV documentary entitled *Inside the Lords*, on which former Lords Speaker Baroness D'Souza reported that she saw a peer keeping his taxi engine running outside Parliament while he nipped in, just to clock in for his £300 daily allowance. She did not name and shame this peer, but said he wasn't the only one: there were numerous Lords who contributed zilch, yet claimed the perks of the position.

The TV programme also featured peers sipping champagne and showing off their country mansions. For instance, Lord Palmer inherited a £400 million Scottish mansion together with his seat, and was shown bragging about the solid silver staircase which, he proudly claimed, was the only one of its kind in the world. Others criticized the way the House allows its privileges to be abused, describing it as "the best elderly care home in London." Even the family members of Lords can drop in and take advantage of excellent service, subsidized meals and drinks, and the comfort of a lounge where they can have an afternoon siesta.

The worst of it is that much of what is happening is legally allowable. We tax payers have been through years of Tory austerity and are right to be disgusted by this type of immoral behaviour, especially as many peers are millionaires and these very same ministers are branding people claiming benefits as the "something for nothing" society. Double standards of the worst kind! Prime Minister Theresa May, please get your own House in order. Please deliver on your promise to reform the system. At the time of writing, many peers continue to claim income and expenses they haven't earned in all conscience.

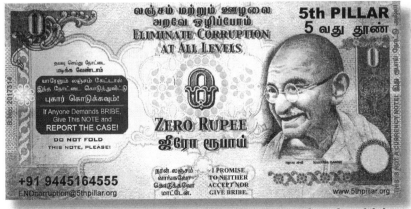

5th Pillar is an organisation fighting corruption, in which the zero rupee note is an important tool

Nanda's ticketless travail

22 March 1970

The railway minister, Mr G L Nanda, created history by travelling incognito in a third class compartment from Victoria Terminus to Kalyan, with the intention of studying for himself the hardships suffered by commuters in the suburban section of the Central Railway.

This was in the true style of the emperors of yore who used to disguise themselves as beggars and mendicants, and mix with the crowd to find out people's reactions to their rule. But Mr Nanda, with his Sadhu Samaj look, his characteristic drooping moustache, was easily spotted by the people in the compartment. The surprised commuters out of deference offered him a seat. Mr Nanda, however, waved them away saying: "I am a ticketless traveller; you have more right to sit and travel."

Now the snag is that Mr Nanda was a ticketless traveller. Could he not have purchased a 50-paise ticket to be on the right side, morally and legally? But that is the typical mentality of most of our Ministers, politicians and bureaucrats. Why pay when you can get something for nothing!

Politicians barge into a cinema with a dozen friends and the proprietor is there, cringing and fawning to receive you with garlands. You walk into a shop, make your purchases and fulfil the formality of asking for a bill. The shopkeeper is there with folded hands, assuring you the bill will be sent – and when it is not sent even after six months, you conveniently forget about it.

Rail, road and air travel is all free for you, as every journey is undertaken on State business, even if you are travelling to perform the marriage of your daughter.

If you are sitting upon a file involving an important decision, and if the victim concerned gets to know you like a Scotch whisky on the sly in a silver cup, then cases of Scotch whisky of the rarest vintage, along with dozens of silver cups, get into your house through the back door.

When an innocuous thing like a fruit basket is sent, you have only to part the cloth covering it and nod your approval after ensuring that half-a-dozen gold bars, more luscious than the fruit itself, are concealed within.

And so, what is ticketless travel between Victoria Terminus and Kalyan, a distance of only 45 kms, involving only 50 paise!

****

Our suggestion to Mr Nanda is to disguise himself as a *sadhu* to study the heck of a good time his compatriots in the Sadhu Samaj are having. In one evening his *brahmacharya* will disappear into thin air.

Corbyn's sit-down protest
on a Virgin train

Jeremy Corbyn, currently controversial and beleaguered leader of the UK Labour Party, was travelling on the morning train from London to Newcastle on 11 August 2016. He made quite an issue of not being able to find a seat on this Virgin train, which he described as "ram-packed". He claimed he wanted to sit next to his wife, Laura Alvarez, but couldn't find two empty, unreserved seats together.

In a video released the next day on social media, Mr Corbyn was seen sitting on the floor in the vestibule; and he was heard saying "This is a problem that many passengers face every day ... The reality is we need more trains. And they are very expensive. Isn't that a good case for public ownership?"

And in this way he politicised a personal experience into a generalised criticism of the rail system. Mr Corbyn's spokesman also made the same point connected with the Labour leader's wider transport policies: "Passengers across Britain will have been in similar situations on overcrowded, expensive trains," he said. "That is why our policy to bring the trains back into public ownership, as part of a plan to rebuild and transform Britain, is so popular with passengers and rail workers."

Jeremy Corbyn's sit-down protest turned into an extraordinary stand-up row with the rail operator, Virgin Trains. Sir Richard Branson, founder of the Virgin Group, felt the company had to take issue with Mr Corbyn's assertions. He endorsed the release of CCTV images showing Corbyn walking past unoccupied, unreserved seats before he sat on the floor. He apparently also later refused the offer from Virgin staff of a complimentary upgrade to first class.

Following this incident a number of images and messages were posted, debating the truth of Mr Corbyn's lament about the lack of seats. One big change since Dada's times is the technological advance that can audio-visually capture evidence and comment on people's public behaviours – almost any time, all the time.

What is evident in British politics is that politicians are not treated with the same deference and respect as they are in India. People in general, and journalists in particular, challenge and hold them accountable for their actions. You just have to watch TV programmes like *Breakfast News* every morning and *Andrew Marr on Sundays* to see that the BBC takes pride in exposing any kind of sleaze.

Isn't there Socialism in every act of the Government!

2 June 1974

About a couple of years ago, while we were driving down Mahatma Gandhi Road, we observed hectic activity: huge slabs of granite were being unloaded from lorries at the base of the green embankment, resulting in inconvenience to people wanting to park their cars there. The embankment itself was being dug in two places to a length of about 25 feet, and the excavated earth was heaped up in huge mounds, causing further inconvenience.

Some days later, a number of stone masons started dressing the stones with chisel and hammer, and the large part of the road they had occupied created quite a bottleneck in the traffic. We wondered what great project of beautification the City Fathers had in view that the Corporation had launched upon this frenzied activity. And so, curiosity getting the better part of consideration of important work, we stopped to enquire as to what the proposed construction was.

The workmen did not have a clear idea, but they said that, in its schemes for the beautification of Bangalore, the Corporation was constructing two cascades. Pointing to the granite steps that had been laid, a work-man said: "See those steps there – water is going to cascade over them 24 hours a day." And lo and behold! True enough, a network of pipelines had been fabricated

and a pump house was erected on top of the embankment.

A few days later the glorious project was complete. One evening, the Mayor, along with his retinue comprising the Deputy Mayor, brother Councillors and officials, inaugurated the cascades, or fountains, or whatever you call them, by switching on the pump, and water did start cascading merrily down the steps. By and by, a large crowd collected there, watching in stupefaction the spectacular beauty that the Mayor had brought to the city at a time when the water taps had gone dry. The Press, of course, came out with a glowing account of this achievement the next day.

The project, unfortunately, was short-lived, as the severest drought of the century hit the State, and no less the city of Bangalore. With no water, the pumphouse remained idle and the water-pipes rusted. Now, after two years, with the waters from the Cauvery having been brought to Bangalore, the waterless steps have become cascades again, and they are a sight for the gods to see. Especially at dawn, when some dozens of pavement-dwellers – men, women and urchins – use them for their morning ablutions, baths and laundry.

On enquiries made, a Government spokes-man said that the primary motive of the authorities in putting up the cascades was to provide this much-needed amenity to the poor. "How could a Socialist Government spend as much as two lakhs of rupees on waterfalls for the rich to feast their eyes on as they drive down Mahatma Gandhi Road? The real purpose was to provide the lowly pavement-dweller, who hasn't a water *chembu*, or the means to buy imported toilet paper, to clean himself up. Isn't there Socialism in every act of the Government!"

Socialism or commercialism?

43 years later, and the Congress government of Karnataka has dreamt up another project involving water – in Bengaluru, a city notorious for water shortages. *The Hindu* newspaper of 5 May 2017 reports that work is underway to construct a 2.5 acre sunken garden and a 100-foot high waterfall in an already marshy area of Lalbagh. The project aims to bring in something like 500 species of rare aquatic and marsh plants from other parts of India and from abroad. Of course it would be magical to see giant water lilies with seven-foot high leaves, without having to travel to the Amazon forest to see them. What a delight to see other exotic species too – water palms, hyacinths and different types of reeds and lotus, sourced from Africa, Europe and southern Asia.

The estimated cost of two crore rupees is partly being justified on the grounds that the exhibit will not only be an aesthetic tourist attraction, but will bring variety and added botanical interest to what Lalbagh already offers in the way of educational opportunities. The Department of Horticulture expects the wetlands feature to attract students of horticulture as well as environmental specialists and landscape architects. It says that plans for the waterfall are feasible because water will be diverted from Lalbagh's two existing lakes, to flow over the stone quarry behind them.

Now all of this sounds wonderfully aspirational and justifiable, on both social and commercial grounds. The thing is, I love every nook and cranny of Lalbagh from my childhood days. We used to live in Basvangudi and I walked our pet dogs there almost every evening, after school or college. I used to do my homework in a cave by the lotus pond, feed the deer, enjoy watching the rabbits in their round house. And I was always lost in wonderment at the fireflies in the bamboo grove. When monsoon rain bucketed down I'd shelter under one of the ginormous trees, trying to keep the dogs with me so they wouldn't run in the rain and get wet. Many a time I have walked on the bund beside the said lake, and felt a little scared by stories of ghosts under the tamarind tree.

So I'm sadly aware that Lalbagh's attractions haven't been well looked after. Where is the deer park today, and the enclosure for small animals? Are the lakes consistently cleared of algae and the nasty weed that used to accumulate and choke the health of the water? The Department of Horticulture would do well to ensure that everything nature offers in Lalbagh, in all its sheer beauty and abundance, is properly maintained. That would be better than dream schemes costing two crore rupees which are likely to run dry.

But of course the Lalbagh example is relatively minor compared with the numerous major conflicts in decision-making between socialism and commercialism. What about the decision for India to launch spacecraft while a large section of its population live from hand to mouth, struggling to make a basic decent living? But entering the space race does not even make sense in terms of commercialism. It's pure pie in the sky! There are people who believe that humankind will need to find another planet so that we can migrate and survive in future, because we will have destroyed our own Earth due to environmentally-destructive behaviours, causing catastrophic climate change.

In Britain, socialist values are severely under threat due to lack of money. Tory politicians are continually walking a tightrope, trying to balance the values of a welfare state system with the need for austerity to reduce the deficit and pay off the national debt. People here have become accustomed to free education and healthcare, and most are not willing to pay more taxes to support the ever-increasing need for more resources to provide these. More of that later, though...

A fable for Indira

17 Dec. 1967

Scene: A thatched hut in a slum area in one of the bigger cities of India. It is nightfall and quite dark. Swarms of mosquitoes are whining in the air, and the stench of stagnant sewers is unbearable. A cobbler and a tinker – inmates of the hut – walk in.

Tinker: "I sat in the marketplace the whole day and all I could get was 50 paise. How can I live on this, and what can I send to my wife and children in the village?"

Cobbler: "Huh! You are better off than me. I begged the whole day and no-one took the slightest pity on me. I am down to my last 10 paise."

Tinker: "Why did you beg, you rascal? Have you no self-respect?"

Cobbler: "To hell with self-respect. With all my implements pawned to pay for the funeral of my wife, what can I do – cobble with my teeth?"

Grave-digger (who walks in just then): "Will God have any mercy on me? Four days running and not a grave to dig! No-one ever dies – but sure enough I am dying of starvation."

The Goonda (a burly six-footer, all muscle and brawn, who has been slumbering in a corner of the hut, gets up rubbing his eyes, and shouts): "What the devil are you creating this racket for and disturbing my sleep? The same story the whole time – no money, no food, no money, no food. You are rightly paid for working. Why don't you be like me and do no work?"

The cobbler, tinker and grave-digger (all together): "Despite our hard work we are starving. What will happen to us if we don't?"

The Goonda: "Nonsense. You are all stupid fools. If all the working people like you stop working – do not lift their little finger – they can paralyse everything." He starts shrieking in a crescendo: "Stop working, stop working, stop working…" He pulls the cobbler, tinker and grave-digger out and orders: "Follow me."

The procession wends its way out of the slum with the Goonda leading and, in a little while, enters a toddy shop where the Goonda orders with great authority, "Four mugs of toddy."

The toddyshop-wallah, who has always been afraid of the Goonda, places four mugs on the table and meekly asks for the payment.

The Goonda: "Shut up, you widow's son! You have had plenty from me all these days for the putrid stuff you serve."

And thus from four mugs to four more mugs and four more… the company gets boisterous, and more boisterous, and still more boisterous. Just then a procession of 'Anti-Hindi' demonstrators is passing on the road. The Goonda picks this opportune moment to fling the last remnants of toddy on the face of the shop owner, makes a beeline for the procession with his inebriate colleagues, and starts howling in a crescendo, "Down with Hindi, up with Kannada; down with Kannada, up with Hindi."

A little later, sighting a heap of road metal, he picks up a handful, coins a new slogan, "Down with the police, up with the Goonda," and takes sharp aims at the skulls of one constable after another. Pandemonium breaks loose, street lights, shop windows, motorcar windscreens crack, a bus is set on fire, the processionists run helter-skelter, a *lathi* charge follows a cane charge, and finally gun-shots are heard.

****

The moral of the story is best related in the words of what Seneca said 2,000 years ago: "A hungry people listens not to reason, nor cares for justice, nor is bent by any prayers."

If you want the violence to die down, you must plan to give to the people a little rice to fill the cavity of their stomachs, a little clothing to hide their shame, a little roof to protect them from the inclemencies of the weather. You cannot do so, indeed you haven't succeeded in doing so, through your mighty Soviet-type Plans. The only way out, therefore, is to give the implements, the tools and the wherewithal to the crores of self-employed artisans – the peasants, cobblers, tinkers and grave-diggers of our nation – and with their instinct of self-preservation they will fend for themselves in no time. The surest path to disaster is to kill this instinct by making everyone lean on the State for everything.

Give a man a fish…

I see much evidence in India – at all levels of society – that the spirit of enterprise is alive and well. I've talked to homeless families living under flyovers in Mumbai about various articles they were making to sell. The children were weaving in and out of traffic stopped at traffic lights, taking risks to sell small items like these on the busy city roads. While they were forced to do this in order to survive, they were missing out on education. And in India there are clear links between unequal access to education and unequal access to work opportunities. Cycles of illiteracy, inequality and poverty continue from one generation to the next.

The Indian government does not provide free handouts. People are forced to work and earn. But there will always be debates about how much the state should provide and what exactly individuals can and should take responsibility for. There are some charities and non-governmental organisations (NGOs) that help, but there is no social welfare system of benefits for the poor. Self-help and community development have long been fundamental to our *Panchayat* system in India. Gandhiji strongly advocated that villages should be self-governing and not look to the centre for everything.

Mrs. Leela Chandrasekhar, an inspirational and very knowledgeable lady I met in Bangalore, had devoted much of her life to working with women in villages. Drawing on her extensive experience, she had this to say:

"Children studying in villages have brains but they lack opportunities… The background is different but the opportunities must be the same, and some extra special help we must give them, because they don't have the facilities that others have at home. The parents are illiterate, so when the children ask for help the mother may not be able to answer. But it will get better because educated mothers in the next generation will be able to help their children. But for now they need some special extra tutoring. Give them a lot more courage and self-confidence. Because that is lacking they cannot compete with others."

How best to break the cycles of inequality and poverty? For example, the Grameen Bank experiment has proved successful in enabling people to help themselves – not just short-term but in a sustainable, developmental way. This is best expressed in that well-known proverb *Give a man a fish and you feed him for a day. Teach a man to fish and you feed him for a lifetime.*

The Grameen Bank was founded by Muhammad Yunus in Bangladesh as a small-scale community development project. The plight of the villagers during the famine there in 1974 motivated Mr Yunus to help by providing micro-credit loans without collateral, initially to a group of 42 families. This social experiment proved itself over time as a profitable and humanitarian system, and has now spread to almost all the villages in Bangladesh.

Mrs Chandrasekhar described her involvement in a similar project which gave small start-up loans to women in a south Indian village: "What we saw in the village was that the women want to have a few more things – vegetables, a new dress for the children…. So we said, all right, we will give you 50 rupees each. And then you do whatever you want and let us know what is happening.

"So 50 rupees each for ten women – well, 500 rupees was not much for us. One woman with that 50 rupees bought a few vegetables, and had a little place, and said: "Whoever wants, I have already bought these, so you can buy from me". Then another one started making *idlis*. With 50 rupees she could make about a hundred *idlis*. She ground the rice flour. Then she said to the men going to the fields: *Breakfast is ready. I sell you the idlis. You take.*

"Like that they had small, small things, and they found at least the money was coming. They were really happy, and so at the end of the year they all came back and repaid that loan of 50, along with it they gave 5 rupees. They said: *One more lady can be helped, please.*

"So you see how it works, because too much money they cannot handle. Little, little sums they can handle. And they got this idea of repayment, you see! I have taken the money, *I must give back.* Then we told the banks they should come and open a branch. They said: *No, we cannot trust these people. They have no money, there's no guarantee. It won't come back.* We said: *Now look at this. The women have paid. We are going to open bank accounts in the women's names, and you loan the money. They will repay.*

"Then one bank came forward. They said yes. And it worked. They saw that the women always repaid because they felt better that way: *Oh, I must repay because I am going to tell my children this honesty, truth and all that.* So now they have started more branches – you see, one successful experiment and then they do more. After that we have continued for 15 years."

The Grameen Bank now has about 2,600 branches and nine million borrowers in more than 40 countries. The model has been adopted in similar projects even in some parts of the so-called developed world. For example, as of 2017, Grameen America has established 19 branches in 11 US cities. The World Bank is also financing schemes based on these principles of social justice, trust and regeneration. The vast majority of borrowers are women and the repayment rate is 99.6%. Similar schemes have been tried in Switzerland and Finland.

In the UK people expect the state to provide free education and healthcare for all, and at least basic benefits for those who are unemployed or homeless. Does this greater sense of entitlement foster a corresponding abdication of personal responsibility? One hears of families that have never worked. They survive on Welfare handouts like Incapacity and Housing Benefits and Jobseekers' Allowance – inheriting and perpetuating unemployment from one generation to the next.

In 2016 a rather extreme social experiment was conducted and televised by producers of Channel 5. They were interested in exploring the phenomenon of 'unconditional cash transfers' that had proven beneficial in places like India and Uganda. So they chose three long-term unemployed families in Hull and Merseyside, and gave them a cash handout of £26,000 in return for coming off benefits.

The first broadcast of *The Big Benefits Handout* showed a man simply turning up to knock on the door of a house, with a black briefcase stuffed with the cash. Initially the recipients of this unexpected windfall reacted by splashing the cash on luxuries they hadn't been able to afford. Viewers of the TV programme reacted angrily when they saw them opening bottles of champagne. One lady used the money to get botox injections instead of getting a job. Some got haircuts and driving lessons, but at least these turned out to be confidence-boosters which later gave them an edge in competing for jobs.

The producers knew that this social project posed a massive risk – there was no knowing what the families might do. But they felt it was high time for a more "grown-up debate on welfare" than the previous TV show called Benefits Street had provoked. They wanted to see what difference it might make if people were given the maximum total annual amount of benefits in one lump sum. Would it throw them a lifeline or set them up to fail for the sake of a dramatic tabloid TV programme?

So the producers took measures to deal with this project responsibly. Each of the chosen families was supported by a financial adviser, an economist and a psychologist. They had to allow their bank accounts to be monitored to ensure they were not squandering away the money. They were filmed over a period of four months, as they began to explore new learning and earning opportunities.

One enterprising young couple initially raised controversy by spending £950 on an inflatable slide and £460 on a raccoon. But one year on, they have turned these commodities into money-making assets: they use them in an established animal events business, entertaining children at parties with an owl, a 12-foot long python, spiders, iguanas, millipedes and other exotic creatures. They said they had learned to budget and would never go back on benefits.

An older couple with a 21-year-old son living at home also transformed their lives by using the cash to buy and sell goods at second hand on a market stall. The father is (for the first time) the proud owner of a van and a thriving business. The £26,000 has completely changed their attitudes and their circumstances.

So the big benefits handout seems to have been a positive experience, weaning the recipients off a life driven by state aid. On the other hand it still seems difficult for many people to economise, leave alone to save for a rainy day. It is said that a quarter of pensioners don't save – they rely on what the welfare state can provide. A worker from the Money Advice Unit said "People are ignorant about money, or they just don't care to live within their means. It's up to the government to teach financial management."

Heck, here goes reliance on the government again!

The Prime Minister needs due protection

12 April 1970

It looks as though indiscipline, turmoil and violence have taken possession of the whole world. With sons and daughters against parents, students against teachers, workers against entrepreneurs, peasants against landlords, the have-nots against the haves, the property-less against the propertied, the world appears to be in a perpetual state of anarchy. The racial issue between black and white is insoluble and, in the spectrum in between – the ebony, dark brown, light brown and yellow – there are bitter animosities.

The growing tendency towards escapism, the cult of the hippies, drug addiction and a large number of our young men and women gravitating towards animalism, are proofs of the fact that the world is once again going back to the dark ages. These things become obvious in the day-to-day news one receives from various parts of the world.

Of course, uncivilized and unparliamentary behaviour has become normal in the Indian State Legislatures and Parliament. Not a day passes when, in some State Legislature or other, the authority of the Speaker is challenged, or when members do not indulge in character assassination and abusive language. Indeed, in many places they come to fisticuffs with a free-for-all brawl, and the devil take the hindmost.

Now that is as far as India is concerned, but one would expect more civilized behavior in the Parliaments of advanced nations where they have a long tradition of democracy. It is in this light that the news from Ottawa, Canada, assumes some significance. It is reported that the Canadian Prime Minister, M. Pierre Trudeau, and M. Michel Chartrand, of the Quebec-based confederation of National Trade Unions, almost came to blows in a corridor in the Parliament building on 23 March. They glared at each other and exchanged abuse, M. Chartrand calling the Prime Minister "a Christ of a liar," and members of his government "goons" and "prostitutes". Other members present prevented what may have turned out to be an ugly situation with heads being broken.

****

This brings us to an interesting though alarming speculation. What would happen if a Naxalite or a Marxist or a Communist or a Shiv Sainik or a Kannada Chaluvaligar or a denizen who has escaped from one of the lunatic asylums manages to get himself elected as a member of Parliament? What if he were to treat our pretty Prime Minister like this? Our Indira Gandhi needs due protection, and a few crores ought to be voted in the present budget for this purpose.

The risks in politics

Dada could not have foreseen how prophetic his article turned out to be. He did not live to see that Indira Gandhi was assassinated at her own home in Delhi, on 31 October 1984. But it wasn't any of the denizens Dada anticipated as risks to her life – she was shot by her own Sikh bodyguards.

Politics is of course rife with power-play and conflict by its very nature. As so often happens, the risks to politicians come from somewhere closer to home than one might think. Our own Mahatma Gandhi was shot by a fellow Hindu, Nathuram Godse, who was a student turned social activist. He obviously resented Gandhiji's peace-making concessions to Muslims and to the newly-formed state of Pakistan. And, while Gandhiji was revered as Bapu, the father of the nation, his own sons did not respect him – they were a real thorn in his side.

Benazir Bhutto, a socialist democratic leader, likely would have achieved a great deal of good as Pakistan's elected female Prime Minister had she not been killed at the age of 54. She was shot in the neck and chest in 2007, as she was leaving a campaign rally of the Pakistan People's Party. She had stood up in her bullet-proof car, above the sun roof, to wave to the crowds. Al Queda later claimed responsibility for the attack, and even today a Taliban gang are suspects in the case. However there are still unanswered questions as to who was really responsible, and why she was targeted. The attacker couldn't be questioned because he detonated a suicide bomb just after using a handgun to shoot her.

Looking at the history of high-profile political assassinations, it would seem that it is good people trying to make good reforms who are particularly at risk. To pick out just a few of the many examples over the past several years, US President Abraham Lincoln was murdered in 1865, all because his assassin John Booth was vehemently opposed to the abolition of slavery. 'Honest Abe' was shot while he was watching a play in a Washington theatre.

Then in November 1963 everyone within living memory of John F Kennedy's assassination seems to remember the shock they felt when they heard the news that JFK had been gunned down while travelling in a motorcade. Again the assassin was a local man, Lee Harvey Oswald. Oswald was himself shot two days later by a Dallas nightclub owner.

Martin Luther King was influenced by Gandhiji and by his own Christian beliefs when he used non-violent methods in leading the struggle for civil rights in the USA. Aged only 39, he was shot by a fellow American, James Earl Ray.

In British politics, the unspeakably tragic stabbing of recent times was that of Jo Cox – a serving Member of Parliament aged only 41, and the mother of two young children. She had the most incredible energy, focused on bringing people in different communities together.

In this world of racial tensions and divisions she stood for integration: "We have far more in common with each other than things that divide us."

The shocking news that she had been shot three times and stabbed repeatedly reduced me to tears. The killer muttered 'Britain first' and 'keep Britain independent' – and these were the only clues to the fact that this was a politically-motivated murder. Jo was much loved in her Yorkshire constituency, in the Labour Party and in Parliament. But the EU referendum dredged up powerful emotions on both sides, and she appears to have paid the price for campaigning fearlessly to remain in the European Union.

Such a sad waste of young lives with so much potential for good!

Socialists and lunatics

20 Feb. 1966

Of the many tribulations of being an editor, the one we detest most heartily is the unceremonious barging in of people into our cubicle and haranguing us on the various topics of the day. From society belles, beauty queens, painters, dancers, musicians, politicians (of all hues), scholars, aspiring authors, poets down to rank lunatics and maniacs call on us. They might hand us either a bouquet or hurl a brickbat for what we had written the previous week. And, very deaf as we are, we sit patiently nodding assent to all they say, until the very imbecility of our nods tires and drives them away.

This morning we had a visit from a rare bird. As he walked in he announced that he was a famous scientist, and that he had made the most astounding discovery of the 20th Century. "See," he said, placing a diagram before us, "it all works this way. I am going to put a fan in front of my bicycle. When I start pedalling, the fan will start revolving and will in turn drive a small dynamo generating electricity, which will turn a motor. Then we come to the 'take-off' stage and the bicycle will run without any further pedalling or effort. It is so simple and yet so profound! I am amazed how in all these centuries nobody thought of this great idea."

Then he looked penetratingly at us so as to elicit an observation on his fantastic discovery, and for once we made a mistake.

Instead of nodding assent we said, "It will not work. You cannot produce energy out of nothing. It is a well-known principle of science."

Our visitor thundered in obvious rage, "What in hell do you mean by saying that it won't work – that energy cannot be created out of nothing? Are not our rulers doing that day in and day out? If you want the national wealth to go up, you simply print currency notes and put them in circulation. You want to increase the standard of living of the common man, you take the money of the rich and give it to him. Is not the nation going forward thus? And what about the Road Train? There was a time when one engine drove one bus, but now it is driving two buses and giving 200% efficiency. I am told they are shortly adding a third and a fourth bogey to it, thereby increasing the efficacy by 300, 400, 500%... and thus *ad infinitum*."

We said, "These are all Socialist myths. You cannot work such miracles in this mundane world. If you make an engine designed to run a single bus and then try to make it pull two buses, it simply gets overloaded, consumes more petrol, wears out faster and is probably working in the second instead of the top gear. What is gained is lost in wear and tear, higher upkeep and running costs. Not only that, it takes the toll of human life at every street corner, when it is turning. But under Socialism, the people are made to believe that such miracles are possible.

The myth, however, gets exploded sooner or later. Your great discovery is based on Socialist thinking."

Our visitor picked up his papers in great rage and walked out cursing us and saying that he was a fool to have expected a reactionary paper like *Mysindia* to give publicity to his fabulous discovery which would one day revolutionise all science.

We thought to ourself, "That is what the ruling party is saying about us all the time, and so what does it matter!"

Lunacy in a world of 21ˢᵗ century isms

Dada's articles about socialism bring home to me forcibly how politics has changed in the past four decades. 2016 in particular has been a dramatic – nay, a traumatic – year, when politics seems to have moved fast and furiously in a volatile and hostile world. The issues today are not debated using words like socialism, communism or capitalism; they are dominated by other isms: terrorism, fundamentalism, nationalism, protectionism, racism, populism, globalism… We are conflicted by a cold war of ideologies.

My diary entry, 22 June 2016:

Tomorrow the British electorate is to vote on what is proving to be a highly contentious issue: should the UK stay in or leave the European Union? The choice put to us is simple – Yes or No? Remain or Leave? And the issue is to be irreversibly decided by a simple majority. I wonder about the rationality of a Yes-No referendum in the highly complex world we are in. The many shades of grey have been simplified to a black-and-white question and decision, which surely is not taking account of the immensely entangled political, economic and social issues related to EU membership.

Some of these issues have been hotly debated for the past few months. Campaigners on both sides of the question were out in full force in the city centre of St Albans when I went shopping this morning. But today it was the sheer hostility of the Leavers that struck me. It was clear that they had reduced the argument to one of 'taking back control' of the UK border. It seems that this concept of taking back control is deluded; nevertheless it is paramount in the emotions of Leavers. This vote is all about stopping the influx of immigrants, who they scapegoat as competitors for jobs and spongers on the benefits system.

Since I am visibly an immigrant from an ethnic minority, some dagger looks from the Leave side were directed at me. I have never experienced this in St Albans and am surprised by how deeply unsettled I feel. I've studied, worked and raised my children here; I've felt this is my home away from home in Bangalore. I've put comfortable roots down, embedded in a community of friends from many different backgrounds. I've worked hard and received many awards, being recognised beyond my expectations for my professional contributions. I thought we had long since passed the point of explicit racism, but it seems to be back with a vengeance.

I still feel fairly confident that the rational facts and opinions of experts on the Remain side will beat the emotional populist arguments of the Leave campaigners. However the polls have been showing this is by no means certain. Umesh and I are determined to stay awake and watch the outcome on TV while the votes are being counted and the results reported during the night.

23 June 2016:

I fell asleep in front of the TV, despite my consternation as knife-edge votes were being counted last night. This morning I've woken up to shock horror news on the BBC: the knife has fallen and cut at the point of 52% in favour of leaving the EU, and 48% in favour of 'Stronger In'. Prime Minister David Cameron emerges from 10 Downing Street and announces he is stepping down. He was a staunch Remainer – so what else could he do? Boris Johnson, Nigel Farage, Michael Gove and other Leavers celebrate. Remainers suffer shockwaves and mourn.

I'm tearful about what is happening, and Umesh is also upset when he rings me to discuss things. He works in a legal capacity with financial services clients, and fears that the City of London will be much diminished as a result of leaving the EU. It will take years to disentangle the complex relationships Britain has built with the EU for more than 40 years. 53 direct trade deals, and many more deals that go through the EU to other parts of the world. Laws that have been unanimously passed with the European Court of Justice.

My thoughts turn to the many students from EU countries that I enjoyed teaching. They brought a serious study ethic to our university and raised standards. And I think of my staff colleagues too – from Poland, Czechoslovakia, Bulgaria, Greece… all with an excellent work ethic. They are bound to feel less welcome after this decision. And what about all the collaboration and funding that brings such wide benefits to research in the higher education sector? What about British students and workers who want to cross borders freely to study or work in EU countries?

It is hard to swallow this result. Did people really know what they were voting for – and against? The most incredible fact that emerges today (the day after the referendum) is this: a trending inquiry via Google search is "What does it mean to leave the EU?" And the second most often asked question is "What is the EU?"

Look at just some statistics and facts: 3.2 million EU nationals live in the UK. 9 million Brits live in EU countries. 71% of fruit farmers warned their productivity would suffer because they rely heavily on thousands of seasonal workers from Eastern Europe to pick strawberries and other summer fruit. They said that type of workforce was simply not available in the UK. The fact is that Britain depends on migrant labour – those who are willing and able to work hard for lower wages in unskilled or semi-skilled jobs that local people don't want to do. The hospitality industry warned they would face recruitment problems because EU staff are the majority workforce in hotels, restaurants, holiday camps and cruise ships. Several large and small construction projects would suffer from a lack of skilled builders.

Those who campaigned to leave claimed that Britain has such a strong economy and standing in the Commonwealth that it would benefit from the freedom to make its own trade deals with countries such as India, China and the USA. They conveniently forgot that these countries already trade with the EU, which just happens to be the UK's nearest and biggest trading partner.

The Leave campaign appealed to emotional nationalist and populist sentiments, while stoking up disdain for experts and evidence-based arguments. I realise that people reject the 'facts' presented by experts when those facts don't ring true within their own experience. Many people feel disenchanted by the established capitalist norms. They have not been listened to and feel left behind by the economic benefits created by globalism. So this referendum has given them a voice, and they have voted out of frustration and anger, choosing to believe slogans that were based on nothing more than false appeals. A big red bus in London sported largely: *We send the EU £350 million a week. Let's fund our NHS instead. Vote Leave. Let's take back control.*

23 June 2017:

A whole year after, Brexit has become a common buzz-word for Britain to exit from the EU. Article 50 has been triggered by Theresa May, our new Prime Minister. Never before have I heard so much forceful repetition in news reports as I hear now the phrase *Brexit means Brexit*. But what exactly does it mean?! We are in an era of political and economic turmoil. It has opened up a Pandora's box of tensions, not least in incidents of racist intolerance. Statistics released by the Home Office are scary: there was a 43% spike in hate crime the week after the referendum. Some doctors and nurses from the EU, feeling unwelcome after the result, have already packed up and gone. Can we afford to lose them at a time when the NHS needs all its human resources? So much for the *£350 million more for the NHS* slogan – where is it now?

Worst of all, the country is still just as divided between Leavers and Remainers. One cannot say anything without raising a storm of controversy somewhere. The energy and resources of the Government that are diverted by the Brexit effect should surely be focused on securing peace and delivering education, health and prosperity – two fundamental responsibilities of any government.

And see now, what with Brexit in the UK and Trump-ism in the USA, I fear Western democracies are running high on lunacy, fuelled by conflicting right-left populist ideologies with the centre ground of politics unable to offer a viable alternative.

Bhutto's nightmare

30 January 1972

"India recognizes Bangladesh" reads a headline in the morning paper, and as the eyes of Zulfikar Ali Bhutto fall on it, he gives the biggest holler of his life: "Damn these Hindu *kafirs.* They've gone and recognized Bangladesh! Snap all diplomatic relations with them."

A few days later, Bhutan follows suit and Bhutto gives another big holler: "Damnation! These Bhutani *bhooths*, these boot-licking stooges of India, have recognized Bangladesh! Snap all diplomatic relations with them."

A little later, the German Democratic Republic, Poland, Bulgaria and Mongolia all jointly announce their recognition of Bangladesh. As Bhutto learns of it, he starts beating his chest and tearing his hair – and performs the wildest and maddest fandango ever. "Snap all diplomatic relations with these perfidious crooks. I say, snap all relations: that is my order." And the orderlies run to cable instructions to the Pakistani Ambassadors in these countries to pack up their bags.

Thus it goes on, with country after country – Malaysia, Burma, Nepal – all recognizing Bangladesh. And, as the snapping and snipping of relations continues, Bhutto gets the most horrendous nightmare ever. With his erstwhile friends deserting him, and country after country recognizing Bangladesh, he finds he is standing all alone in the graveyard that Pakistan has become, isolated from the rest of the world. Cold sweat runs down his body. He exclaims: "*Ya Allah! Yeh kya ho gaya! Ya Allah, tu raham kar!* O Allah, have mercy on me! I am now prepared even to go to Tirupati to atone for my sins!"

The nightmare of political divisions and divorces

In our world, fraught with political power-play over the ages, history provides many examples of the rise and fall of empires; of the trauma experienced by populations displaced by conflict. We don't have to go far back in history to remember the chaos and bloodshed that ensued when India gained independence from the British Raj in 1947. The events of that time are vivid in the living memory of my mother's family. They were Hindus, caught on the wrong side of the line that Barrister Radcliff drew on the map of India: that fateful border line along the northwest which tragically divided the nation and brought into being the new State of Pakistan. And so it was that Lahore, where my mother's parents had raised their seven children, fell on the Pakistani side of that border.

Pithaji, my maternal grandfather, initially refused to believe that he and his family would be forced to flee as refugees, leaving behind their lands, homes and established lives. He was an eminently successful doctor in Lahore, with numerous Muslim patients and friends who begged him not to leave. But their attempts to reassure him came to nothing when he saw that Hindu homes were being looted and set on fire, people were being killed in cold blood, law and order had completely broken down. In broad daylight Muslim looters entered the family home and rode the horses away from their stables. That night the family left on foot under cover of darkness, carrying next to nothing. They walked the 60 kilometers to the Indian border, until they reached relative safety.

They were not alone in that nightmare: it is estimated that 17 million people were displaced by the partition. One million Hindus, Muslims and Sikhs lost their lives, so my family were relatively lucky to have survived. Pithaji had medical training and complete dedication to his profession, so he was eventually able to re-build a thriving practice in Delhi. However some of his cousins were landowners and farmers, so they lost the means of their livelihood and suffered severe breakdown in mental health from which they never recovered. What, for them, was the use of gaining national independence? They questioned the point of surviving partition when they had lost the point and purpose of their personal lives.

This tragedy was caused, not by some freak natural event like a tsunami or volcanic eruption, but by the flaws in our own human psychology. By at least a hundred years of British colonial Divide and Rule policies. By Mohammed Ali Jinnah arguing for a separate homeland for Muslims, while Mahatma Gandhi and Nehru were in favour of peace and a secular constitution within a united India that could value cultural and religious diversity.

Differences of opinion were also apparent on the British side. These divisions are evoked beautifully in a recent film, *The Viceroy's House*, directed by Gurinder Chadha, great grand-daughter of a family that survived partition. She is the only British-Indian woman director and author to address contentious topics. Her movie captures ambivalence: was Radcliff coerced into following the Mountbatten Plan? Was Lord Mountbatten himself manipulated and scapegoated? Who really knows? Critics will always interpret history through their own lens.

However certain facts and statistics provide indisputable evidence of the disastrous consequences of 'divide and rule.' The film is consistent with what my extended family and I know about the version of events that led up to the partition. In fact Dada had the rare privilege of

driving Lord Mountbatten around Bangalore in an open-top Cadillac, when he visited our city in 1946. I have a couple of photographs and a letter of thanks subsequently written and signed by Lord Mountbatten as evidence of this.

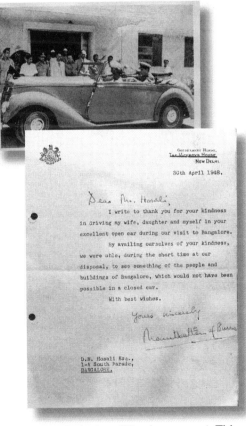

The partition of India did not resolve issues – far from it. Muslims were in a majority on two sides of northern India, so Pakistan was split into East and West Pakistan. A bitter war between these two halves led to East Pakistan breaking away to form Bangladesh in 1971 (leading to Dada's article, see *Bhutto's nightmare*). Conflict and tension between Pakistan and India have rumbled on and on down the years since independence.

August 2017 marks the 70th anniversary of Indian independence, and has led to a flurry of BBC and Open University documentaries reviewing the impact of partition. The TV programme entitled *Dangerous Borders* was made with two 'British Asian' journalists – one with origins in India and one from Pakistan. They presented themselves as typical second generation British Asians who are mostly unaware of what partition has meant. This may be because survivors found it too tragic and traumatic to talk about it – or because they were simply forced to focus on re-building their lives. And it is excluded from the normal history curriculum in schools and colleges.

So these two journalists travelled through the regions along each side of the 3323 km land border and talked to people who remembered the partition, and people currently still affected by it, in the states of Gujarat, Rajasthan, Punjab, Jammu and Kashmir. The programme was also visually fascinating as it showed the cultural and geographical diversity along the

Indo-Pakistan border: varied terrain ranging from desert areas and fertile agricultural lands to the snow-covered Himalayan mountain areas.

And now, the big question of our times: **is Britain broken by Brexit?** How did we in the UK become so polarized? Prime Minister David Cameron found himself hard pressed by UKIP opposition to prevailing conservative policies, and decided to let the electorate decide (via a referendum held on 23 June 2016) whether to stay in or leave the European Union. He was almost certain that the result of the referendum would favour his deeply-held beliefs and values: that the UK should Remain in the free trade zone offered by the single market and customs union. The shock result of the referendum showed that 48% of the electorate shared those views, but 52% voted to Leave the EU. This 52% majority contained some powerful campaigners and politicians who seemed to stop at nothing to make their hard Brexit voices heard (voices that spoke with lies and false statistics too!).

And so it is that Brexit will change the future of Britain and Europe irreversibly. We are constantly being told that "the people have decided" – but 'the people' have ostensibly not spoken with one voice. What about the 48% who passionately wish to Remain? However democracy demands that the UK government must carry out the wishes of the majority and prepare to leave the EU. In other words, we are going into a messy political and economic divorce, come what may.

Brexit has indeed become the new dividing line in UK politics. Wales surprisingly voted to leave, despite having received substantial benefits from EU grants. Substantial majorities in Scotland, London and Northern Ireland voted to remain in the EU, as did 96% of voters in Gibraltar. Nicola Sturgeon, leader of the Scottish National Party, wants Scotland to be recognized by the EU as separate from the rest of the UK, in its desire to Remain. She is claiming this is the desire of the Scottish majority and is in the best interests of the economy. So how democratic is the UK actually, when the government is going ahead without the consent of two of its member states?

The London mayor, Sadiq Khan, has also requested special consideration for London, and privileged access to the single market. He is warning that Londoners would suffer disproportionately from a hard Brexit. For example, the City of London is currently the financial capital of the world. It hosts a multicultural workforce full of younger professionals and global citizens. It is hardly surprising that many of them are distraught at the Leave result of the referendum. They fear that banks and financial services will move their headquarters to the European mainland – perhaps to Frankfurt, Paris or Luxembourg – in order to trade and move freely across mainland Europe. Added to the loss of business there is likely to be a substantial Brexit divorce bill running into millions.

And this difference between the generations is the other significant division brought to the fore by Brexit. The younger generation is predominantly in favour of Remain and often at odds with the older generation that voted to Leave. 70% of those between the ages of 18 and 24 voted to Remain. Many who are currently under-age to cast a vote will be the ones to bear the consequences of Brexit in future years. Have parents and grandparents betrayed the interests of their children and grandchildren?

The referendum has opened a Pandora's box of divisions and tensions along the lines of region, age and class. A section of society that has perhaps always been intolerant of people with different faiths and cultures seems to have discovered legitimacy for such views. Incidents of hate crime are reported every other day.

Conversely, I know of initiatives seeking to bring people and communities together, to break down barriers and challenge misconceptions and stereotypes. But even these groups are having to openly face the destabilising rage of populists from both left and right.

The ensuing confusion and polarization can rip at the very fabric of our society. Could Brexit cause the break-up of the UK? Only time will tell.

Our self-importance surely needs to be lowered to its proper place

15 Nov. 1970

Economically, notwithstanding our mighty Five Year Plans, India is still a backward country, with a standard of living about the lowest in the world. It is said that even Pakistan has fared better since Independence. Educationally, more than two-thirds of the population is still illiterate: in fact India enjoys the unique distinction of accounting for 350 million illiterates out of the 800 million in the world. Politically, she is the most unstable nation, with dozens of political parties believing in ideologies from the conservative Right to the ultra-Naxalites, all engaged in bitter strife, not only in the Legislatures and Parliament, but also in the streets of cities, towns and villages.

But when our self-appointed leaders come out with their orations in public, they needs must refer to our 5,000 year old civilisation, to our glorious heritage and culture, and endeavour to prove by quoting profusely from the *Gita* and the *Upanishads* what a great people we are even today.

And thus, if in any international forum our delegations are not accorded a place of honour, there is an immediate reaction, and much noise is made for a great nation having been insulted. Of course, if Ambassador Keating does not go to the Delhi airport to see Mrs Indira Gandhi off while she leaves for the USA, President Nixon himself gets a sock in the jaw.

A nonagenarian hobbled into his doctor's chambers and complained that his sex urge was very high and he wanted a medicine to lower it. The doctor, who was quite surprised at this, said: "You don't mean to tell me that you have any sex urge at your age!"

The old man replied, "Yes doctor, it is very much there, but all high up in the head. I want a medicine to lower it to its proper place."

Our nation's self-importance has gone to our head and needs to be lowered to its proper place.

The heights of self-importance!

One could argue that a nation needs to feel self-important, to have a sense of national pride. India does indeed need to remember its past glory and also celebrate its current successes, actually much more than it seems to do. Years of the British Raj have apparently robbed us Indians of pride in our own achievements and our authentic sense of national identity. All too often I encounter a sort of inferiority complex amongst us – else why do we typically value foreign products and ideas more than our own? Why do we get an Italian architect to design the updated Bengaluru airport, and make its interior décor look like an airport anywhere in the developed world?

Each of us as individuals need to have the type of self-importance that enables us to implement our best selves for our best purpose in life. Instead of engendering apathy, self-belief usually motivates people to strive for continual progress.

As for those in power and authority over us, we should be accustomed to self-important pronouncements from them as we hear these all the time on radio and TV. But there is a fine line between authentic self-esteem and arrogance, between confidence and complacency. That line has been crossed in spectacular fashion recently by some leaders in the USA and the UK. But judge for yourself – there is a joke currently circulating on the internet:

After passing on, George Bush, Barack Obama and Donald Trump are called up for a job interview with God.

God asks Bush, "What do you believe in?"

Bush replies: "I believe in a free economy, a strong America…"

God is impressed and tells Bush, "Great, come sit in the chair on my left."

God then interviews Obama and asks: "What do you believe in?"

Obama replies, "I believe in democracy, helping the poor, investing in health, world peace…"

God is really impressed by Obama and invites him to sit in the chair on his right.

Next God asks Trump: "What do you believe in?"

Trump replies, "I believe you're sitting in my chair."

Now this may be intended as satire or humour, but it is terrifying rather than funny because it's not far from Donald Trump's real self-concept. Now that he occupies the White House as the 45th President of the USA, he has the power to launch nuclear weapons, and he may have an itchy finger to press the red button at any time for any reason. At the time of writing, his fingers are mostly busy tweeting; and, while his delusional reasoning generates controversies daily, his status as King of Twitter is (so far) somewhat less scary than his war-mongering.

Throughout his depressing and gruelling election campaign he presented himself as the messiah who would restore America to its lost glory. But what sort of messiah could he be? He has achieved business success, no doubt, borne out by the grandiose Trump Towers that bear his name in super-sized gold letters. You only have to look at the golden Trump Tower in New York to see an iconic representation of his self-importance. But he has mocked women, insulted a disabled reporter, stoked Islamophobia and dismissed Hilary Clinton as if she was a washed-up candidate for prison rather than a genuine contender for the Presidency. How is it remotely possible for someone who is overtly sexist, Islamo-phobic, racist, bigoted and ignorant to ride a white horse (metaphorically speaking) to the White House.

At his inauguration on 20 January 2017 the media showed photos of vast empty areas where jubilant supporters should have been. We saw irrefutable visual evidence that the numbers attending were far fewer than at Obama's inauguration. And, on the other hand, we also saw vast numbers of protestors worried about the protection of women's rights and minority rights under his policies. Indeed the size of the protestors' crowd in Washington was so large that it filled the streets and couldn't even reach the White House. All this was accurately reported, yet The Donald claimed "I had the biggest inauguration audience that anyone has ever seen." He accused the media of lying and misinforming the public. He later called the Press "the enemy of the people." And any news which threatens him, or does not play to his grandiosity, is branded by him as 'fake news'.

His inauguration speech was belted out as if he had just won a boxing match. In the presence of former Presidents, he accused his predecessors of making false promises, and spoke of the incompetence of all earlier governments. He has continued to attack anyone and everyone who dares to oppose him, branding his opponents as weak, liars, losers and failures. Now, several weeks into his presidency, he is still riding roughshod over his own Intelligence Agencies and Press Corps.

The UK is not lagging far behind in its delusions of self-importance. Nowhere has this been more evident than during the campaign before the EU membership referendum. On 23 June 2016 the British electorate was given the opportunity to decide whether the UK should stay in or leave the European Union. Those who were in favour of leaving the EU used rhetoric full of self-important declarations about Great Britain being a great country with great connections around the world. Harking back to an imperial past, loud voices beset with ideas of supremacy touted delusions of grandeur, saying that the UK could call upon cooperation and trade with its friends in the Commonwealth, and therefore did not need its current relationship with the EU. Flying in the face of evidence, ignoring all the benefits we currently gain from collaboration with our largest and nearest trading partner, those in favour of Brexit insisted the UK could negotiate deals that would in effect allow us to have our cake and eat it!

So… while hell-bent on destroying the bridges we have with the EU, in a bid to build trade bridges and a special relationship with the USA, Theresa May invited Donald Trump to come to the UK on a State Visit in the summer of 2017. She was criticized for putting trade deals before human rights – of pandering to the President's colossal vanities. Of course he was happy to accept. He promptly announced that he wanted to play golf at Balmoral while the Queen watches him. The strange thing is that he ploughs on, regardless of mounting evidence that his executive orders are proving to be highly contentious – even immoral, unworkable and illegal in some cases. His skin is thick enough to make a hippo blush. He continues to act as if he can rule by divine dispensation.

Surely these cases of extreme and unjustified self-importance need to be lowered to their proper place.

Big cars make small difference

7 August 1966

If you have three yards of cloth you can make a coat and trousers with it, but if you have half that length of cloth you must be content with either a coat or trousers. With three quarter yard you may get a short pant, but with a strip four inches in width and three feet long, all you get is a Gandhian loincloth. If, however, the strip is two yards long, you may sport a necktie (a *kanth langoti*) on your bare body, and use the remaining portion as a *langoti* to hide your shame.

These are matters of common sense known even to the goofiest of goofs. But when Planning started some 15 years ago, such was the thinking put into vogue that people were made to believe that it was not the size of the cloth that mattered. The cloth could be stretched like India rubber to any size and, by the magic wand of the Planners, could be made to yield any number of suits. All that was necessary was a Plan under the aegis of the Government. The rest would take care of itself.

But the past 15 years have shown the confusion and chaos of this reasoning. We have a few full suits, some half, some a quarter, but the vast majority are loincloths. And quite rightly too, as Economics is a science and you cannot monkey with it.

****

At long last, however, sanity seems to be dawning on our rulers, and measures are afoot to curtail all expenditure – Plan and non-Plan. The axe is falling on many proliferations of the bureaucracy and even a department like the Council of Scientific and Industrial Research has had to retrench several hundreds of its research workers.

What is most heartening is the decision of the Prime Minister to make every Minister use a small car instead of the luxury cars they were accustomed to. Although the measure was laudable, the result has been ludicrous. Reads a press report: "A common sight at official functions is a small car followed by a big one, the first seating a Minister and the other the Secretary, or even the clerical staff." In sheer desperation Prime Minister Indira Gandhi remarked the other day, "The only difference now is that I am riding a small car and the Secretaries a big one."

We are a mere mortal and we do not presume to give advice to the demi-gods in the Government. But if we may have the temerity once, we would suggest to the Prime Minister that instead of just immobilizing the large fleet of luxury cars worth crores of rupees and just allowing them to rust, she should auction them publicly, with a minimum retention price of a few lakhs each, and with the proviso that no-one in the public sector should bid for them. Let those who have bloated on the fat of the land unearth their hoards and buy them.

Having done that she should retain just enough money to buy Indian cars at controlled prices and the balance of the currency she should burn publicly. The Indian cars so bought should once again be auctioned and the extra currency they fetch should once again be burnt.

If our Prime Minister were to repeat this a few times over, there would be no worry about future devaluation. In all likelihood the rupee may once again attain its previous status.

A smaller wall could make a bigger difference

One of US President Donald Trump's most contentious campaign promises was to build a wall along the US-Mexican border. He said it would prevent what he saw as "ruffians and rapists" from illegally entering the USA. Now that he has been elected, one of the first things he's done is to sign an executive order to deliver on this promise. The wall would extend about 1,933 miles and he vows to get Mexicans to pay for the ridiculous cost it would entail.

How feasible and effective might this be? Has Trump heard of tunnels and drones – things which can get under and over walls? Does he really know what he is dealing with when he insults his southern neighbour with inflammatory pronouncements: "We'll build a wall – and you'll damn well pay for it!" What is the cost in human terms? Since when has concrete created cooperation and goodwill? What would happen if Mexico retaliated by stopping its cooperation on issues like security and drug trafficking?

As any sensible person would expect, tension has rocketed between the two countries, even though Mexicans are temperamentally tolerant and laid back people. It is said that Mexican labour in the US tends to be exploited by Americans for their own advantage. Most of them are more baffled and hurt than angry. But their former President, Vicente Fox, has tweeted angrily, "We're not paying for no f***ing wall." He appears to have abandoned diplomatic protocol in response to Trump's own bad language.

Mexican President Enrique Peña Nieto cancelled a meeting with Trump over the standoff and has received immense public support for standing up to him. He is said to be capitalising on this surge of unity by urging people to buy products "Made in Mexico" – as a response to Trump's "America First". There is a newfound sense of national pride and unity amongst Mexicans, which may yet backfire on the Americans.

Mexican citizens have launched campaigns, using social media, to boycott all American goods and services. However many American companies that operate south of the border are in reality locally-owned franchises, employing Mexican staff – so such a boycott is not likely to improve matters. Trade between the two countries is immensely complicated and inter-dependent. Some six million jobs in the US depend on trade with Mexico. Many US companies outsource work, such as sending parts south of the border to be assembled more cheaply there.

All said and done, Trump's insistence on the wall, and the backlash from Mexico, can hurt both countries on both sides of the border. Yet he persists. He again more recently reiterated that the wall would be "tall, impenetrable, beautiful and powerful." He repeats and tweets endlessly so that people actually believe him.

Other Trump tactics since then have done nothing to endear him to the vast majority of people. Theresa May has been roundly criticised for issuing an invitation on behalf of the Queen, for Mr Trump to come on a state visit to the UK in the summer of 2017. Many ministers felt this compromised the Queen and put her in a difficult position. Nearly two million people in the UK signed a petition asking for this invitation to be withdrawn. A cartoon appeared in *The Times* edition of 31 January 2017, showing a distraught Queen saying: "One is suddenly tempted to build a wall." Even her corgi looks despondent in this graphic, and Prince Charles in the background is on his computer, no doubt adding his own signature to the petition. Prince Charles is particularly at odds with Trump on his refusal to collaborate on the vital issue of climate change.

Trump joined other world leaders at the G7 Summit in May 2017, in Sicily, where issues of common importance are discussed and agreed. But the first day of June 2017 is a sad day for our planet: Trump announced his decision to pull America out of the Paris climate agreement. After years of campaigning by Greenpeace, scientists and other responsible citizens, the Paris accord represents a significant step forward from the breakthrough achieved in 2015, when governments came together and agreed comprehensive planned action to limit global warming. Countries across the world have now signed up to this, including China and India. Trump, however, is putting 'America First' – prioritising jobs in places like Pittsburgh, where he wants to allow coal miners to dig up fossil fuels again. This at a time when the rest of the planet is envisioning a clean energy future. There is criticism from many EU leaders. Emmanuel Macron, newly-elected President of France, has implicitly destroyed any moral authority Trump may have had, in five simple words where he appealed for everyone to work together to "Make our planet great again."

Another cartoon that appeared on Facebook depicted a wall – not a prospective wall on the Mexican border, but a much smaller one that was built around Trump, with his face just visible, peeping over the top. Judging by the numbers of people who are signing petitions and marching in protest at his actions, the American President is going to need this protective wall – and a firewall denying him access to Twitter – in order to keep himself safe. Then surely this smaller wall will make a bigger difference.

What price appeasement?

11 January 1970

A meeting of the New Congress Party is about to begin. The petite Prime Minister of the most populous democracy in the world, Mrs. Indira Gandhi, walks in exuding the perfume of a rosebud and radiating the enthusiasm of her new dynamic policies. She is followed by her Harijan President and other admirers – pseudo-Socialists, the Young Turks, crypto-Communists, and a motley crowd of all those who have jumped on her bandwagon to achieve their own ends. In a corner of the lobby stand three young Harijans, tête-a-tête, hatching a conspiracy. The Prime Minister takes the chair of honour and, having banged the gavel on the table, says: "I call the meeting to order."

The first young Harijan jumps up and thunders: "Order, my foot! All this talk of Harijan uplift is so much stuff and nonsense."

The second young Harijan: "22 years have gone by since Independence and, leave aside any improvement in the status of Harijans, we are worse off than we were under the British."

The third young Harijan: "We want a time-bound programme for the uplift of Harijans to be completed during 1970."

The Prime Minister: "What is all this commotion about? What is your concrete proposal?"

The first Harijan: "This Jagjivan is no leader of ours. He is hobnobbing with Caste Hindus and has let down our case badly."

The second Harijan: "Considering that the Harijans form 40% of the population, we want 40% reservation of seats in all *panchayats*, local bodies, State Legislatures and Parliament."

The third Harijan "No, no, we don't want all that. We want the Constitution to be amended, making it compulsory for every young man from the Caste Hindus, especially Brahmins of the Kashmiri variety, to marry only Harijan girls; and conversely, for every young Caste Hindu girl, especially Brahmins, to marry only Harijan men. Prime Minister Indira Gandhi should set an example immediately. It is only thus that the social status of the Harijans can be improved. It must be done immediately, otherwise…"

The Prime Minister: "Otherwise what?"

The three Harijans in chorus: "We will walk over to the Syndicate camp and cook your goose."

Theresa the appeaser

The current UK Prime Minister Theresa May is being labelled *Theresa the appeaser* by some of her critics. In January 2017 she was all too quick to visit President Trump, just a week after his inauguration as President of the USA. During her visit, she officially invited Trump, on behalf of Her Majesty the Queen, to come on a State Visit to the UK later in the year. Trump accepted the invitation, although no specific date was fixed.

For a start, the premature timing of this invitation is unprecedented: no previous US President has been given this honour in his first presidential year. President Obama had to wait until he was half-way through his first term of office to be invited. So this move is being seen as a political attempt to rush into reinforcing the special relationship between the UK and the USA – essentially to put future trade deals on a secure footing, especially since the UK has voted to leave the EU. Following the Brexit vote, and the equally surprising results of the US election, the visit was supposed to pave the way for Britain and America to "lead together again" with renewed confidence, as Theresa May said.

But the invitation is proving highly controversial in the UK, where Trump's lack of basic human decency is provoking widespread condemnation. Theresa May seems ready to throw away years of special relationships with our European partners in favour of building a business relationship with a President whose bullying tactics fly in the face of traditional British values and human rights. Former SNP Leader Alex Salmond accused Mrs May of "showing desperation".

The worst of it is that – almost the day after Theresa May's visit – Trump issued his most bigoted executive order, banning refugees and citizens of seven mainly Muslim-majority countries from entering the US. He said this was necessary on security grounds. The agencies tasked with enforcing this ban were not consulted or forewarned. As you may imagine, total chaos ensued at airports around the world where hundreds of people were suddenly left stranded. Some of those affected were permanent US citizens who had legitimate visas and were trying to return home from trips abroad. All media channels had a field day interviewing and showing pictures of the disruption to people's travel plans and the difficulties of enforcing the ban. American courts ruled that it was unlawful.

In effect Trump was suddenly tarring all Muslims as terrorists: citizens from Iraq, Iran, Syria, Somalia, Libya, Yemen and Sudan. One Mr Jones wrote on Facebook's events page that day: "That includes people who helped the US army. That includes people on holiday trying to get home via the United States. That includes people trying to be reunited with their dying parents… Let's stand in solidarity with those targeted by Trump's hateful government."

In several towns and cities across Britain this news brought thousands of people onto the streets in protest against both Trump and May. In London a large crowd of protestors marched to Downing Street, chanting slogans and holding large placards which clearly wanted to show disgust at a racist, sexist President, and also at Mrs May for refusing to condemn his crackdown on Muslims. Surely his demonization of the whole integral Muslim section of society is a serious matter that should be condemned.

Trump – Special Relationship? Just Say No!

Where's your moral compass, Mrs. May? Dump Trump

Refugees are welcome here. Trump is not

Scotland against Trump

A lady in Glasgow with a head-dress depicting the statue of liberty held the torch of justice in one hand and a placard reading *Lady Liberty Weeps*. She told a reporter that she was from the US – supposedly 'the land of the brave and the free' – but here she was now, ashamed of Trump's policy on immigration.

A young Jewish lady held a placard which read: "Anne Frank could have been an 87-year-old living in Boston today but she was denied a visa."

MPs held an emergency debate on the implications for immigration. Then a petition calling for the State Visit to be withdrawn was started online and reached two million signatures. The strength of public feeling forced Parliament to debate the issue in depth. A crowd of protestors demonstrated again outside Westminster Hall as the debate took place. Labour politicians including Shadow Home Secretary Diane Abbott and Shadow Attorney General Shami Chakrabarti addressed the crowd. Shami said, "The world is in a precarious position. The State Visit is an act of appeasement. We will not make the world a safer or fairer place by appeasing bullies like Donald Trump." She urged Theresa May to think again. But a few other MPs felt that withdrawing the invitation would snub the US President, embarrass the Queen and put post-Brexit trade deals in danger.

Despite the opposition, Theresa May has refused to back down and the invitation still stands. What price appeasement: putting the need to secure trade deals before the morality of supporting human rights!

SECTION 4: GENDER MIND-BENDERS

Boys will be girls and girls will be boys

19 September 1971

In our times – and by that we mean the twenties of this century – boys were brought up like boys, to grow into men. Now and then some doting mother did make the mistake of letting her son's hair grow into long curls and put a frock on him. But that was only when he was a little babe. But when the boy was a little older and a mother committed the error of putting on him a brightly coloured shirt, or one with flowery prints – anything smacking of femininity – the other boys took care to see that such a folly was never committed again by knocking hell out of the offender.

In the half century that has gone by since, the situation has changed considerably. The attire of our boys and girls has got so different that sometimes one does not know whether a teenager is a boy or a girl. This type of transformation seems to have taken place worldwide, the West being affected more by it. Fortunately our country, except for the upper echelons of society, remains comparatively free from this trend.

It's a common sight in England to see teenagers, boys and girls, in the tube and on buses, cinemas and theatres, sitting huddled together, cheek to cheek, the hair of both worn in the same long hippie fashion, the same slacks, the same pointed shoes, the same overcoats, the same rosy cheeks and lips, the only characteristic differentiating the boy from the girl being a few unshaven whiskers here and there. But, surprisingly, many a girl has also a downy growth on her upper lip so that it is a baffling problem to tell which is the boy and which the girl.

While in the United States some years ago, one of our confreres, a scribe, a brother in the same profession, a correspondent of the *New York Times*, Santesson by name, volunteered to show us a bit of life not commonly seen by the average run of tourists. He took us to a number of joints in Greenwich Village, one of which was the Pseudo-intellectuals Club, as he termed it. This indeed was a rum joint, full of rum guys, a sort of beer salon reeking of tobacco.

Santesson introduced us to some of them and, after a few glasses of beer, everybody became very chummy. We particularly remember an attractive chap in slacks and an open-neck shirt with a hairdo which was a cross between the shingle and the bob. We do not know how, but we became specially chummy with this fellow. With our arm around his shoulder we were telling him about life in Bangalore, when we were joined by his attractive girlfriend. We gave him a whack on the back and told him he was a lucky dog. Santesson intervened to say, "He is a she, and you may replace the word 'dog' by 'bitch'!"

Then it dawned on us with a shock that the person we were taking liberties with was not a boy but a girl. And now, when we find this disease spreading to India that was once Bharat, and our boys strutting about with long hair like the hippies, pointed shoes, girls' blouses and stretch slacks with their buttocks popping out of them, we are seized with a mad desire to administer a running kick to them in the exact same spot.

The shift towards gender neutrality

When Dada wrote this column in 1971, only two sexes were officially recognised, male or female, determined at birth by biology. Since then, new options have appeared on most official forms in Britain, allowing respondents the choice of stating not only if they are Male or Female but something 'Other' or 'Prefer not to say'.

Gender however is a social construct, based on the subjective way in which people perceive themselves and others in relation to behaviours, roles and preferences. Defined gender perceptions were much more prevalent in Dada's days, and I think we children were socialised into 'pink or blue stereotypes'.

The trend towards gender neutrality has gathered momentum in the years since, especially in the Western world. Here it is common for boys and girls, men and women from all walks of life to adopt denim jeans and shirts – almost like a uniform for leisurewear. The distinct lines between gender-specific behaviours and roles have become blurred, and stereotyping is much less common.

This trend is in many ways of advantage, especially to girls who are liberated to choose from a wider variety of occupations. In my childhood I used to hang out with my young uncle Bachu, who was in engineering college at the time. I was fascinated by the flying models of aircraft he used to make. "I'm going to be a pilot when I grow up", I told him with utmost confidence. But that aspiration was quickly dismissed as pie in the sky: "Girls can't be pilots" he said. And so it transpired in the fullness of time. He became a pilot with Air India and I joined later as an air hostess.

Strangely enough nowadays in the UK, more and more young people seem to be confused about their gender identity, feeling that they are born in the wrong body and should actually be the opposite sex. This extreme distress has increased to the point where it is now officially recognised and diagnosed as a psychological disorder known as gender dysphoria. Hormone treatment and/or surgery may be the only way to alleviate that distress.

A news report in 2017 stated that the numbers of children being referred to gender identity clinics had quadrupled in the past five years. As far as I'm aware, the National Health Service's only facility for this is based at the Tavistock Centre in North London. 84 children as young as three to seven years old were referred in 2016, compared to 20 in the year 2012-13.

What could possibly be causing this spike? Could it be that the introduction of gender identity teaching in schools has planted seeds of confusion in young minds? Schools have been under increasing pressure to create a safe and inclusive learning environment where everyone is accepted, even if they do not conform to the normal stereotypes. Some schools have deliberately changed to mixed-sex toilets and changing rooms.

Why can't we just leave our young people to explore and develop their identities in their own time, without imposing adult concerns and concepts on them at an impressionable age? Looking back, I recall I was a terrible tomboy until about age ten, but my parents were not judgemental about my preference for playing rough and tumble with the boys, or pretending to be a wild man in a jungle when I built a little hut in the corner of the garden, with a thatched roof plaited out of large coconut palm leaves. I'd fashioned a bow and arrow from pieces of wood, and the centres of our wild figs were perfect targets for my shooting practice.

But it is now acceptable – even preferable – to declare one's sexual identity publicly, whereas homosexuality was not so long ago considered to be a perverse deviance from the social norm and a punishable crime. Sadly many gay men were driven to suicide.

Recently in London, many people gave creative expression to their feelings and views during LGBT / Pride Month, when their Lesbian, Gay, Bisexual or Transgender identities were publicly celebrated. Quotes such as the following sought to silence doubting and biased voices:

"You don't fall in love with the gender. You fall in love with the person."

"Love is too beautiful to be hidden in the closet."

"Homosexuality is found in over 450 species. Homophobia is found in only one. Now which seems more unnatural?"

Even Mynah birds use the unmentionable four-letter word

28 June 1970

The following amusing report appeared in the press recently:

CHICAGO, June 22:   Residents called police yesterday when they heard repeated cries of "Help me, help me, please help me" from a nearby school.

Policeman William Diaz climbed an eight-metre fence and traced the sound to the school's basement. He smashed a window and dropped down to the basement floor.

The cry was coming from a locked store-room. "Come to the door," the policeman shouted, "nobody will hurt you; you are safe."

But no-one came. So Mr Diaz broke down the door and came face to face with a Mynah. Mr Diaz said the bird – a pet of the school janitor – seemed angry at being found. It switched from "help" to another four-letter word.

The years 1941-42 were very interesting in India. Britain was engaged in an all-out war, and the colossal expenditure of hundreds of crores on the war effort had, after years of depression, created unprecedented employment opportunities. A very large number of young men had obtained emergency commissions in the Army, Navy and Air Force, and there was great prosperity all round.

One such army officer had got married to a very pretty but not so well educated girl who, nevertheless, in the company of other ladies, had learnt a smattering of English and had started speaking it in great style.

At a party one day the said young lady reported: "Last evening I went for a walk on Queen's Road and a Tommy accosted me and started pestering me." Someone intervened to ask, "Then what happened?"

The young lady who, like the Mynah, was ignorant of the meaning of the four-letter English word, said "I asked him to f… off and he f…ed off."

Everyone in the company was aghast at such an appalling expression coming from a girl. But a few moments later, when the shock had died down, someone pointed out to her that the expression she used was quite indecent, and no lady should use it, etc., etc. At which the young lady remarked: "I am so awfully sorry, but that bugger, my husband, uses it in every other sentence!"

Even a presidential candidate uses unmentionable language

"Lock her up... Jail the b..ch... Grab her by the p..sy."

Who do you expect was caught using this vulgar language? Was it a drunk and disorderly lout with an ASBO – an Anti-Social Behaviour Order? Normally such language is too unacceptable to be printed or reported – but, incredibly, these were just a few of the soundbites emanating from Donald Trump while he was on the campaign trail, vying for presidency in the USA. When he was caught on video using these words with reference to women, his supporters passed them off as normal locker-room banter.

But isn't it true that the words one uses in unguarded moments reveal one's real thoughts and attitudes? So in 'the land of the brave and the free' Mr Trump has repeatedly used his freedom of speech to shock, insult, complain – and inflame the worst emotions of voters rather than appeal to their intellects. Eventually the strange question blowing in the wind is this: has he gained entry to the top job in the most powerful country in the world despite his use of language, or because of it?!

Social and mainstream media have had a dramatic year, seizing on his electoral pummeling, the likes of which has never been seen before. The press reported with gusto his despicable attacks on his opposing democratic candidates – "crooked Hilary" as he vengefully called Hilary Clinton – and "Lyin Ted" as he branded Senator Ted Cruz. In fact anything he disliked and anyone who opposed him was fair game. Twitter afforded him an internet platform for constant verbal sparring – punch and jab tactics he used even against the US intelligence agencies and the press. Very largely, however, I think he owes much of his electoral success to the press reports and digital media which gave him the oxygen of publicity. The media didn't do half as much for Hilary Clinton.

It is incredible though that he attracted supporters – even vast numbers of women – who seemed to swallow wholesale his lies and half-truths – to become ever more excited by the vulgar slander and defamation that became the norm in his campaign. "When somebody screws you, you screw them back in spades" he wrote in 2007, with reference to business deals. Voters in the US seem to have trusted his business acumen in making deals that would put 'America First' and advance their economy, but even here intelligent policy discourse has been conspicuous by its absence.

I am not an American citizen, but several of my 'summer cousins' live in various parts of the

USA. My young cousin Mita, who has worked in the United Nations in New York for several years, posted on facebook thus:

"I find it despicable to see the kind of attacks against women that have passed for acceptable language. This is something driven by deep disrespect, misogyny and lack of education, in a country that should be leading on all fronts. Young men and women should take back this space by refusing to let the 'angry, anti-establishment electorate' be an excuse for gutter-level conversations about race, gender and human rights.

"The fetishization of wealth and celebrity status is what is driving so much of this narrative. Hopefully there is a generation out there that will see through the cravenness of a life measured in gold cufflinks, gilded toilet seats and trust funds. And in my view, a life of public service is still more honourable than a life spent replenishing your coffers and avoiding taxes. Really, is this what the marginalized millions see as 'leadership'?"

And later, Mita went on to post this comment:

"I don't understand. If I used Twitter to make unsubstantiated charges and baseless smears against an important public figure, like a Head of State or Government, or to have a public raging session, would that not constitute improper use of the platform? Wouldn't my account be shut down and a defamation / slander suit be initiated? Oh wait, it happens all the time against certain countries and people. I'm just trying to fathom how the rules are different, depending on who you are. Orwellian!"

Good on you, Mita – for voicing these thoughts so eloquently. Personally I think Trump's attitude to women and minorities – in fact this whole situation – is completely bonkers. Oh, hang on a minute – I'm not sure if 'bonkers' is a rude word… but people around here say it all the time.

It is an unequal world indeed

12 July 1970

Notwithstanding the great heights which our civilization has reached, this is still an unequal world. Man calls the female sex the Better Half, and yet practices bitter discrimination against her. He calls her the Fair Sex and metes out unfair treatment. And especially in the western world, where they talk so much about equality, such discrimination is rampant.

There they dote on women, put them on a pedestal and worship them, shower upon them all sorts of luxuries – glittering diamonds, expensive mink coats, fine silks, exotic perfumes and what-not – but deny them equal rights. And in a large part of the world, even today, the right to vote is denied to them.

It is only in the enlightened Communist world that women get a fair deal. There they can easily become tractor drivers or machinists or workers in heavy construction, or even trench diggers. But this is an unequal world nevertheless.

The King's wife becomes a Queen in her own right. The Minister's wife gets her own equal status and social standing. The Rotarian's wife becomes a Rotaryann. But reverse the situation: the Queen's husband becomes at best a Duke, following her meekly like a pageboy. The lady Minister's husband, if he accompanies her at all, is put down as a Secretary; and if he is not well-dressed enough, he is put down as a chauffeur. The husband of an Inner Wheeler merely becomes an Outer Wheeler. And Sita Hosali's husband is referred to disparagingly as "Oh, he is Sita Hosali's husband." Isn't this an unequal world?

Was it not the fair face of Helen of Troy that 'launched a thousand ships' and 'burnt the topless towers of Ilium'? Is not our charming Prime Minister leading the country towards the Holy Grail of Socialism? Isn't she leading all the great leaders of the Congress Party by the nose – favouring or disfavouring one or the other, dismissing, demoting and installing them as Minsters, one by one? Don't you call this an unequal world, where power and authority resides in the *sari* rather than in the *dhoti.*

Inequalities in a High Flying World

"What would you like for lunch?" I ask the captain, co-pilot, navigator and flight engineer, each in turn. "We have the usual Indian vegetarian option, we have chicken – cooked Western style – and lamb curry. Also today I can add fresh mango slices to your choice of dessert."

I take their meal choices to Robin, the steward who is working with me in First Class on this flight. He says, "So you've already promised them mango – now there will be none left for you and me!" He dramatically raises his eyebrows. "I shudder to think what else you have promised them." He flaps his hand and winks, a grin slowly widening across his face. He is full of banter and a slightly flirtatious attitude. I laugh. I like the way he teases me, as if I'm his younger sister. (I am naïve at the time about gay guys.)

So in 1968, after five months of working as an air hostess on long-haul Air India flights, I am equally comfortable serving meals to the cockpit crew and to passengers in first and economy class. I've learned in training to offer cheeses, wines and champagne I'd never heard of before: Stilton, St Emilion and Veuve Cliquot have moved from the realms of the exotic to the commonplace. We are proud that menus and standards of service are unique selling points on our flights. No plastic at all – passengers get stainless steel cutlery, ceramic dishes and cups.

Stewards do most of the prepping in the galley. So Robin heats up dishes and lays them out on trays according to my orders. There are no trolleys – I have to treat each passenger like a special guest so I take out and deliver two trays at a time. Someone has used a pedometer to calculate the average distance we air hostesses walk on typical long-haul flights: it amounts to 7.2 miles. Because 'the customer is always right', my face aches with the smile I keep plastered on it at all times. And because we hostesses are the frontline face of Air India we've had advice on skincare and makeup from Elizabeth Arden herself. All this has become the new normal for me. Beyond the glamour... well, I'm aware that a couple of my colleagues have been grounded for putting on weight, and one has been sacked for repeated outbreaks of acne. It isn't in the least bit glamorous when we have to balance heavy trays and carry on with service even in turbulent weather.

Stewards have their own challenges. They do much of the heavy lifting. Robin is also in charge of keeping financial accounts for the optional alcoholic drinks that passengers have to pay for. He converts the different currencies we accept on board and deals with any issues the passengers raise. We accept this as the natural order of things. Why shouldn't stewards use their typically extra height and strength to help place baggage in the overhead cabins? And to open and close the heavy doors ready for take-off and landing? It doesn't strike any of us to query our gender-based job titles, roles and tasks. After all, foreign travel, sight-seeing, staying in 5-star hotels is only possible for the privileged few. Most of us feel like fat cats that have all the cream, despite a modest basic salary and an out-station allowance of £3.10 per day.

Anyway, I'm happily putting down trays in front of the cockpit crew on this flight from Singapore to Kuala Lumpur – until suddenly we hit an air pocket or something that causes the plane to lurch. The hot lamb curry I'm serving the navigator jumps off the tray and lands in his lap. Oh. My. God! Butterflies suddenly fill my stomach. I run and pick up a bunch of hot towels that Robin is prepping for passengers, run back with the instinct to mop up – but stop! I have to just drop them in his lap and let him mop before the evil stains of turmeric can begin to spread on his trousers.

Would the navigator report me? Would I get the sack? Well, the incident went almost without comment. The navigator, bless him, was kindness and politeness personified. He only said with a glint in his eye, "Just don't spill hot coffee on that part of my anatomy."

On the second leg of this flight, from Kuala Lumpur to Madras (now Chennai), we run into turbulence that drives our stomachs up into our throats. Even all the cabin crew are strictly strapped in while the aircraft lurches through wicked black storm clouds and lightning that can be seen repeatedly snaking past the windows. I strap myself into the only empty seat I can find amongst passengers in economy class. Many are visibly terrified. The lady across the aisle from me makes signs of the cross and mutters prayers. Some make signs of the 'very cross' - they curse, moan, groan and muffle their screams. Others are calling upon whatever god they believe in to save their souls. I say to those within earshot, "We are going to be fine. I've flown through storms like this before."

I look back and see that Akilya, my colleague, is sitting on the jump seat with Robin, clutching at him and screaming loudly every time the aircraft does strange gymnastics. I am actually appalled at her behaviour as we've been trained in emergency procedures to keep calm and put passengers first – always. But did her behaviour result in any disciplinary action? Not that I know of.

Fast forward to August 1970 – two years later, when I'm posted in London, UK. I've been feeling feverish for days but I've tried to carry on with my job as I still love flying. But, silly me, I nearly collapsed on my flight from Beirut. I finally had to see a doctor and report sick.

****

I sit up in my hospital bed, electrified and bemused, as Jimmy Naigamwala, the Air India Chief of Staff, suddenly appears at my bedside together with one of the senior air hostesses. I only know Mr Naigamwala as someone who schedules our flights to and from Heathrow Airport. I could thank him for sending me to some wonderful destinations, but I could also blame him for messing up my body clock and sleep cycles. I cannot imagine he's come on a friendly visit to wish me well. Since I've been in Colindale Hospital for two weeks by this time, I assume he must have decided to see for himself that I'm not just pulling a sickie.

"We had a spot of bother finding you in this ward," he says. "Why are you registered here as Arti Kumar and not Arti Hosali?"

I am taken by surprise and feel the heat rising in my face. I can only stutter, "Kumar is my fiance's surname; he must have admitted me by that name because we've been engaged for a while now."

The two of them say no more about this, but they leave me with more suspicion than sympathy in their eyes. When I am back home from hospital, just about well enough to report back for work, a letter lands on the doormat. I see that it's official, with the airline's logo on the envelope, and my hands tremble as I open it. The letter baldly states that I'm fired as of the day of my marriage, and I will not receive any payments due for work carried out after that date.

The knot which has started to form in my belly rises to constrict my throat as I realise that Mr Naigamwala had duly proceeded to check out marriage registration documents held in Somerset House, and discovered my guilty secret. It's only guilty because it's against the regulations for air hostesses. When I accepted the job I'd had to sign a contract that contained the clause: "You will switch to a ground job or resign if you get married, or when you reach the age of 30, whichever comes first."

No such clause existed for stewards. And the law protecting me against gender discrimination did not exist at the time. So it happened that my decision to quietly put my private love-life on a moral and legal footing became a sackable offence.

****

But let me fast forward several years to 8 March 2017 – the date when International Women's Day is celebrated as an annual event. Air India marked the occasion this year by setting a world record, for the second time. They staffed a return flight from New Delhi to San Francisco with an all-female crew. Everyone involved in every aspect of the round-the-world flight was a woman. Everyone! Not only the cabin crew but also the cockpit crew – the captains flying the Boeing 777 – the engineers, the check-in ground staff and the air traffic controllers who cleared the flight for take-off and landing.

Ah, well! That is a far cry from my own experience some 50 years ago!

Confusion worse confounded

August 1965

The worst of having a wife who is a keen newspaper reader is that she suddenly flings a question at you about this or that news item in the morning paper. Engrossed as we are with the several preoccupations of running our own magazine in this 'licence-permit Raj', we barely get time in the mornings to scrutinize the headlines. We leave the serious reading to the afternoons when we have comparative leisure. At breakfast this morning, therefore, as we were revolving over the problems of the day, she confronted us with the question, "Have you seen this news item about 14 crores being spent on food research?"

Being taken unawares we said, "What? What 14 crores?" She answered, "They are going to spend 14 crores on food research. God help us!"

Not having read the particular news item and feeling ashamed for not having done so, we answered her question by asking another: "Have you seen the one about donkey's and camel's milk replacing cow's milk?"

Our wife interjected with some irritation, "Yes, I have seen some Central Committee on Food Standards making the stupid suggestion that we take to donkey's milk, to make good the shortage in cow's milk. But camels are few and far between – even in the Rajasthan desert – and the donkeys are a disappearing tribe except for those

in politics. But what has happened to the crores that have been spent on our modern dairies? They don't seem to be yielding any milk so far." She added, "In any case, there is nothing new about donkey's milk. For thousands of years our village mothers have used it in the belief that it guards against stomach complaints. Your own mother informs me that you were fed a few teaspoonfuls of it during the first fortnight after your birth. Now that I come to think of it, your cast-iron stomach as well as the assinine streaks in your character are both due to it."

Being a bit embarrassed by this analysis we decided to break her train of thought by asking "What about the 14 crores?"

She entered into a lengthy diatribe on the Government's suggestion to spend 14 crores on research to prevent the loss of foodstuffs during storage, handling and transport: "They have suddenly become aware of the fact that 24 million tons of food-grains are destroyed every year due to these causes. Where is the need for research on this matter when all advanced countries possess the most scientific knowledge to control weasels, rodents and other pests which cause such damage? Any enlightened country could share this knowledge and help us.

"But they appear to have taken leave of their senses. We must further multiply bureaucracy, engage a team of lazy sluggards – from secretaries, scientists, clerks, stenographers and, last but not least, that much patronized entity of peons – spend 14 crores, and the result will be much like our Bangalore Dairy: fine buildings, glittering machinery (at a standstill), an army of men (busy doing nothing) and no milk.

"And what about the rodents and monkeys who destroy one-fifth of our crops? It appears our Corporation has already spent Rs. 25/- per rat during their 'special drive' to destroy rodents in Bangalore. Isn't that efficiency par excellence? The figures for monkeys are not available but they will surely be ten times more than those for rats."

After a quiet of a few moments she said, "And look at this report about Andhra Pradesh serving a notice on the Centre, telling them that as only 82,000 tons of fertilizers have been supplied to them as against their requirement of 2,25,000 tons, they would not be in a position to supply any food-grains next year to other States. This surely is planning run amuck. Why don't they spend the 14 crores on fertilizers so that, with their natural advantages, Andhra Pradesh can increase their food production and feed other States. I have decided to lead a delegation of all the housewives of Basvangudi to the Vidhan Soudha so as to make the ministers see what appears to be obvious to everyone."

In some consternation we exclaimed, "No, no, please don't do that." Even as a news-paper- man we are not free to give such democratic expressions to our feelings. After all, we have a newsprint license and, if it is cancelled, on what shall we print this weekly essay of ours?

Ability in search of opportunity

The article above is one of the few where Dada writes about my mother. My sister Rani and I called our mother Bhabi, even though the word means sister-in-law in Hindi. Well, that's what she was called in our extended family, and even by some friends, so we just followed suit and were never told any different! I suppose, what's in a name? She was our beloved mother all the same.

As is evident in Dada's article, Bhabi was an avid newspaper reader and formed her own intelligent opinions about what she read and discussed. Looking back at her life now, I'd say she had skills and attributes that could have found expression in a rewarding career. But most women of her generation were expected to be full-time housewives and mothers, with limited opportunities to engage with the external world of work. So much talent fell on infertile ground! But of course women also need to have aspirations aligned with the right combination of knowledge and skills for a profession. Bhabi was content to flower gracefully in her home bower. Her gentle, passive nature would have struggled to flourish in the type of competitive work environment both Rani and I found ourselves in as adults.

Bhabi did have the advantage of a liberal education. Her father believed in equality for men and women, and ensured all his sons and daughters could realise their potential. He spotted Bhabi's creative interests and arranged for her to study at Shantiniketan, a school near Calcutta shaped by the vision of national poet Rabindranath Tagore. Tagore had developed a flexible curriculum that encouraged student affinity with the natural environment. Bhabi spoke of her time at Shantiniketan with nostalgia and affection. She clearly found the freedom there to develop her unique personality in an atmosphere of spiritual peace. She described meeting people of different cultures, and the experience of integrating disciplines that are normally seen as separate.

Shantiniketan fostered Bhabi's creative talents. As a child I loved to explore and admire her artwork, and she always encouraged my own creativity. She stitched and embroidered clothes for Rani and me, and knitted our woollies. She really was quite a knitaholic: "I don't know what to do with my hands if I'm not holding knitting needles," she was apt to say. All of us in the family, and even neighbours and friends, ended up owning a jumper or shawl knitted by her. I still treasure these garments. But in her lifetime she wasn't given the credit she richly deserved.

Looking back I'm contemplating how the world of opportunity has changed for women since those times. It is but one of those many Indian contradictions that the nation is ranked 134th in gender equality, yet influential, inspirational, highly successful women are to be found in all walks of life. At the time of writing, India has six senior-ranking cabinet women ministers out of 27. This is the highest number in more than a decade. And in a recent

cabinet reshuffle, Prime Minister Modi appointed Ms Nirmala Sitharaman as India's first full-time woman defence minister. She was previously a minister of state for commerce and industry and has also been an effective spokesperson for India's ruling Bharatiya Janata Party (BJP). Her appointment has been widely welcomed, and described as a reflection of the growing status of women in Indian society.

As with all socio-political matters though, her promotion was not without controversy and criticism. Currently women in the armed forces comprise just 2.5 %, working mostly in non-combat roles. But since February 2016 they have been allowed to work in all roles on par with men. As I write, my armchair travels round the internet tell me that three intrepid Indian women are shortly to become fully operational MIG-21 fighter pilots. These pilots are trained in air-to-air combat, which demands a very high level of mental alertness. They have already flown solo sorties in fighter aircraft, and are now breaking new ground, as the saying goes. Or rather, they have broken into airspace that was previously the preserve of men in the Indian Air Force. Ms Sitharaman will however face the considerable challenges of implementing new policies, plans and investment to modernize the armed forces.

The majority of Chief Executive Officers in Indian banks are women, even though banking is notorious worldwide for being the most misogynist of industries. Here in the UK, women at the Bank of England typically earn 26% less than their male colleagues. Figures released under the Freedom of Information Act indicate that the median salary for its women workers was £41,082, compared with £55,828 for men. This is strangely incongruent with the Bank's decision to replace the image of Charles Darwin with Jane Austen on the £10 note. So is this just a token gesture towards valuing women?

In the UK we have had years of demands for workplace diversity and equality. Yet an investigation by the Sunday Times newspaper found that the pay gap between men and women working in the public sector is still widely prevalent. The divergence is greatest at the higher end of salary scales. It is typical that far fewer women reach senior positions in almost any industry sector. Girls perform equally well if not better than boys at school; women get more degrees than men, and have the requisite leadership skills, yet they comprise only 15% of corporate boards. ('Women on Corporate Boards Globally' in *The Catalyst*, March 2017).

There are many complex reasons why this might be. Behind every statistic there is a personal story, and a comparison of figures only gives us a helicopter view. Men have their own pressures – society expects them to be principal providers for their families. They may feel their responsibilities heavily but they seek counselling and healthcare less than women, despite needing it just as much – or more. Striving to be strong, keep a stiff upper lip and just get on with things does not allow them to process any trauma or anger they may experience, and this can lead to mental health issues.

Again, statistics paint a bleak picture: suicide is the number one cause of death amongst men under the age of 50. And after divorce, three times more men than women commit suicide, often because they typically have to cope with the loss of family relationships while also having to pay alimony. They are far more likely to become homeless and depressed and end up in prison.

When I drive past roadworks or walk past a construction site in the UK there only seem to be men doing heavy or risky work, shivering in minus degree temperatures. I don't ever see a woman pulling heavy bins to empty into the bin lorry.

What about standing back and looking at 'gender equality' more objectively, in context? We need to deconstruct gender issues and remember they are compounded by class, race and other factors. Individual choice is determined not only by gender but by biology, peer pressure, personality, interests and abilities – factors that are often independent of the stereotypes.

How will the Speaker hold her tongue?

26 March 1972

It is said that the female of the species known as Homo sapiens is more talkative than the male.

The baby girl starts talking earlier than the boy, and her chatter continues right through life. Observe a group of college girls and their talk is unending. If there is a boy in their midst, he cannot even get a word in edgeways. At cocktail parties it is the women who lead the conversation; the men merely make grimaces and listen. It is the female cuckoo that coos, not the male. That seems to be the law of creation.

It is therefore in the fitness of things that Smt. Nagarathnamma has been elected Speaker of the Mysore State Assembly. Now the Speaker will speak endlessly. But, according to tradition, the Speaker is not expected to speak. How will, then, Smt. Nagarathnamma hold her tongue?

An old couple quarreled for fifty years of their married life and, as the golden jubilee arrived, the wife, in great endearment, asked: "How shall we celebrate our golden anniversary, darling?"

The man paused only for a moment and said, "How about observing a minute's silence?"

Let us instead give a full five minutes ovation to Smt. Nagarathnamma on her election as the Speaker of the Mysore State Assembly. Let us hope that, in the true parliamentary tradition, she will hold her tongue and speak the least.

_____

How will women's voices be heard?

It seems to be a common stereotype that women talk more than men. There is a Chinese saying: "A woman's tongue is her sword, and she never lets it get rusty." Dada's column may well ring true of women in domestic settings and informal social groups. My experience however tells me that men usually speak more freely, and with greater authority and confidence, in the large professional groups where discussion is important. After a presentation, for example, when questions are thrown open to the audience, perhaps 9 times out of 10, a man is more likely to raise his hand and ask the first question.

Back in the day when I was growing up, typically men were the doctors and women were the nurses; men were chief executives and women were secretaries; men were retail managers and women were on the shop floor. Gender imbalances and inequalities are shifting in present times, but women still feel they have to work harder to make their voices heard – and valued. In September 2016 I began to come across 'the shine theory' emanating from the team of women in President Obama's cabinet. When Obama took office in the White House, two-thirds of his senior staff were men who had worked on his campaign. The cabinet office was a tough male-dominated inner circle for women to break into. They complained they were not invited to key meetings. How could they contribute if they were not even in the room?

Even when female staff did manage to gain access to meetings, they found their voices were being ignored. So they collaborated and started using a system to amplify and 'shine a light' on each other's views and ideas. When a woman expressed an idea other women would repeat it, naming and giving credit to its author. This method of consistently shining a light on both the idea and its originator forced men to acknowledge the contribution and give credibility to the woman who had expressed it.

So, did the shine theory actually achieve its purpose? It is reported that Obama noticed, and started to consult more with women on his team, and with junior aides. By his second term of office half of all White House departments were headed by women. How did this more even gender balance among his top aides come about? To quote Valerie Jarrett, his senior adviser: "I think having a critical mass made a difference. It's fair to say that there was a lot of testosterone flowing in those early days. Now we have a little more oestrogen; that provides a counterbalance."

2017 will also go down as the year when women joined together to make their collective voices heard against sexual harassment. Men in high official positions have been accused and brought down as never before. The most high-profile case as I write is that of Harvey

Weinstein, who appears to have got away with some serious assault and rape incidents stretching back over a period of three decades. The women who had tried to complain about his predatory behaviour in the past were not believed or listened to. He exploited his power as a Hollywood producer and threatened to damage their careers if they didn't comply. But now, more than 60 A-lister celebrities have made specific allegations, including Gwyneth Paltrow, Salma Hayek and Angelina Jolie (to name but a few).

Then many more people in the entertainment industry denounced his disgusting abuse of power, including Meryl Streep, Dame Judi Dench and George Clooney. In the wake of the Weinstein allegations, the power of social media was harnessed by Alyssa Milano, an American activist and actress, to tweet the message "If you've been sexually harassed or assaulted write 'me too' as a reply to this tweet."

The #MeToo hashtag campaign spread virally, gathering momentum across many countries. It gained credibility with local alternatives in other languages too. It is said to have prompted 55,000 replies in the first 12 hours alone. Women everywhere were given this online platform to voice their experiences and denounce abuse which they had hitherto often suffered in isolation and silence.

Personally I was amazed at the widespread nature of this reaction. I asked a friend what she thought about the magnitude of the problem that was emerging. We wondered how sexual misconduct was being construed. Some women were accusing their male colleagues of what seemed like harmless flirting: an arm around a shoulder, a hand brushed against a knee, a compliment on how they looked… "I'm slightly worried about this trend," my friend says. "I have sons, and you know, Richard in particular is single. He is pretty much married to his high-flying job in the city. I have met some of his friends and I know he can maintain platonic friendships with women colleagues – he works hard but also plays hard – and he could be at risk in this current climate of accusations."

I tend to agree with her. The #MeToo movement has extended into the #TimesUp campaign (time's up for sexual abuse). It seems that everything that is remotely sexual has become suspect: men in Hollywood and Westminster are being named and shamed with zero context, explanation or evidence. If those who are guilty of serious problems are placed on par with relatively minor indiscretions, this weakens the message by focusing on trivia.

If women want our voices to move from the virtual world into the real world and our lived experiences, we must use our newfound collective power with the greatest of responsibility and truth in matters that can actually destroy the lives and careers of men. It is just going to damage the cause of justice, equality and sexual freedom for women if these tweets are fuelled by a general hatred of men, or deliberate misjudgement of behaviours. While it is good that this show of female solidarity against sexual harassment may be a defining watershed in our times, social media campaigns must lead to fair and genuine social change for everyone.

Sure enough, the #MeToo movement has provoked a backlash. In France 100 women signed a manifesto in *Le Monde*, deploring the puritan nature of the allegations against men who might, in some cases, only have been making a clumsy attempt towards a romantic relationship. This group of eminent women (actresses, authors, intellectuals, psychiatrists and journalists) denounced #MeToo and #TimesUp as a witch hunt that has gone too far. They also felt that these movements carry the taint of presenting women as powerless victims of male oppression. Many Hollywood stars who protested have benefited from projecting themselves as sexy women; they are proud of this image in the public eye.

Post Weinstein, a debate was aired on the BBC Sunday morning programme, *The Big Questions*, on the topic *Is time up for flirting at work?* Where do we draw the line between flirting and harassment? For one man the line was clear: he described it as the difference between a game of ping-pong and rugby football! Many voiced the opinion that flirting should not be conflated with criminal rape and serious sexual abuse. They felt that flirting is a playful, healthy, natural dynamic that makes the workplace more enjoyable and stimulating. It is human instinct to be attracted to the opposite sex (or to a person of the same sex), and romantic advances are a healthy way to establish a relationship. 14% of people get married as a result of meeting in the workplace.

But then again, in a culture that allows considerable sexual freedom and equality, it may be more difficult to establish the boundaries between flirting and predatory sexual behaviours. One woman on the programme said she worked with a cohort of young women who flaunted their 'physical assets' and actively invited attention from men. And when men misinterpret the signals because the old norms have changed, women accuse them of disrespect and misconduct.

Women should indeed be wary of putting Victorian double standards into reverse – in effect turning the patriarchal boot into a vengeful stiletto. Fundamental feminists will not even allow anyone to mention that some irresponsible women drink so heavily that they cannot remember what transpired, so there is lack of credible evidence when they accuse a man of rape. This is indeed difficult territory – and it can be subjective and ambiguous in each specific case.

Photo by Samantha Hurley (Burst)

On choosing a beauty queen

6 June 1965

Bangalore: The other day we went to see the Chesebrough Pond-Femina Beauty Contest. As we walked into the Ravindra Kalakshetra we found ourselves transported into a strange world reminiscent of the fashionable theatres of London, Paris and New York. Our nostrils were filled with exotic French perfumes, and we wondered how, notwithstanding all the import restrictions, so much of it had found its way into Bangalore. And wherever our casual eyes were cast we sighted beautiful women clad in gorgeous silks, with make-up and hairdos from Ajanta to Faradiba, bouffant and what-not. It looked as though they were all vying for the honour of the Beauty Queen; certainly many of them deserved it. And as we relaxed in this gracious atmosphere of beauty, the contest commenced.

About 30 of the Bangalore belles who were competing in the contest appeared on the stage. As girl after girl passed on the dais we vainly searched for the beauty to be crowned, but even after the first round was over we could not spot the one we had envisioned as 'Miss Angel Face'. We looked into the hall, at the many usherettes and volunteers, and felt that many of them ought to have been in the contest with a better chance of success. And so we sighed: what a travesty of reality that they were not there. In this mood we started cogitating over what our concept of beauty was: what

Indian beauty was in contradistinction to European, Nordic, Latin, Japanese, Chinese or Negroid beauty.

The other day, as we had stopped our car in a traffic jam, we looked at the adjoining bus stand and a beautiful girl gave us a *respondez s'il vous plait* look which made our heart skip a beat. We did respond and gave her a lift to Mahatma Gandhi Road. That girl we thought was truly the 'Miss Angel Face'. Raven-haired, dove-eyed, slender in the right places, neither too tall nor too short, with that pre-dawn twilight complexion where the night meets the day – a real Usha, the colour of honey and cream – in fact everything that our ancients have chiseled in stone: that is what this girl was. What is more, she was utterly feminine with that undefinable something which makes the hearts of men miss a beat – a quality with which, we thought, *Femina* ought to be concerned. She was not aided by 'Hakobas' or 'Khatau Voiles', neither had Chesebrough Pond touched her skin, but it was petal-soft. (We did not feel it, we only saw it!) We do not know what her vital statistics were, but they were truly vital.

With such *femmes fatale* to be found on the roadside, we thought it was a real parody that Bangalore had produced for this beauty contest dozens of highly anglicized girls who, with their western hair-dos and cosmetics and Indian *sarees*, looked strange indeed.

Now as we sat in the show we argued with ourself about the why and wherefore of this strange paradox. An ancient scene from our memory flashed across our mind. In 1949, in the balmy and irresponsible days of our youth, a strange wanderlust took possession of us, and we found ourself in Cairo – not the Cairo of socialist Nasser but of despotic Farouk. Wasn't Cairo gay and wicked then! Amongst the shows we saw there was a fashion parade in which the fashions were missing and all the models were in nature's garb itself. After the many European models had stolen the hearts of the audience, there appeared a divinely proportioned, raven-haired black beauty of nondescript origin – but very much like an Indian girl. The most thunderous applause was hers, and everyone was raving mad about her.

What was the explanation behind this selection of a black beauty by a predominantly white audience? A question of polarity, we thought: the white liking the black and the black liking the white? And that might explain the reason why a black country like ours chooses an anglicized girl as a beauty queen. It must be conceded, however, that the one eventually chosen as 'Miss Angel Face' did have the best claim among those who contested.

Diverse Indian concepts of beauty

Photo by Kevin Grieve (unsplash)

Photo by Avnish Choudhary (unsplash)

Photo by Loren Joseph (unsplash)

Beauty – a contestable quality?

Beauty contests are controversial. Some feminists argue that they demean women by reducing them to certain physical qualities that can be strutted on a platform and judged by a panel. The judges eventually have to choose one beauty in order to crown her Miss World or Miss Universe – or Miss Angel Face. I wonder what criteria they agree on when they narrow down this choice. (You can see I don't know much about beauty contests.)

Generally speaking, we humans seem biologically wired to equate beauty with good health and youth. That's hardly surprising. But I recall playing with the folds of skin on my grandmother's neck when she held me as a baby, finding beauty in her dark, lined and stern face, where her long-life story was finely etched. And my mother had the beauty of serenity and grace that shone from within as well as without. Her comment about old age was typical of her wisdom: "when eyesight begins to dim, it's time to look inwards."

The idea of going to a beauty parlour had never occurred to my grandmother and mother. Natural beauty was much admired while the use of cosmetics was frowned on in my growing up years. But when most Indians are naturally dark, why do so many equate beauty with a fair complexion? Marriage ads frequently seek 'fair brides' and sales of Fair & Lovely creams by far exceed any other skin cream.

It has now become commonplace for women to visit beauty parlours, aspiring to achieve the type of appearance and glamour that is perpetuated by the media. Once rare, there are now more than 5,000 beauty salons in Delhi, Mumbai and Chennai, with Kolkata not far behind. Even small town and village salons are obviously influenced by images that cater to a westernised concept of beauty.

Even so, I do believe that beauty is indefinable and subjective: *beauty lies in the eye of the beholder*. But now, in our digital age, beauty lies in the hands of the skilled photoshopper. Perfection is portrayed via airbrushed images in the media, and the pressure to look good can have a devastating effect, especially on vulnerable young people. It can be a major cause of self-harming, which has risen between 2013 and 2016 by 70% among girls in the age group 13-16.

The practice in some countries to formally judge people according to how society thinks they should look is particularly deplorable. For instance, in South Korea employers require job applicants to include a recent photo on their CV. This implies they are going to screen and discriminate amongst applicants using appearance as a selection criterion. It is said that 60% of applicants are rejected because they do not conform to the prevailing standards and concept of beauty. This isn't just morally unacceptable – it doesn't even make good business sense.

It would simply do all of us a power of good to be mindful of the beauty that surrounds us every day. What do we really, really look at in our humdrum lives? Do we look skyward and notice the changing formations of clouds? Do we only notice a spectacular sky when the sun rises or sets? I was once so thrilled to see a complete half-circle rainbow when I was travelling by bus in Hyderabad that I felt compelled to call out and draw attention to it; but my fellow travellers didn't seem to share my excitement. Anyway, here's my attempt to express my sense of beauty in the colours of everyday things.

Shades of Perfection

A spectacular orange sky at sunrise
A splash of cream in my first cup of coffee
Cherry-red tomatoes, green olives, brown bread
Dappled gold sun pooling into grey shadows.
Eddies and swirls in a sea of blue-green
Glints of bright emerald, shades of cool jade
Pale gold beach sand under bare feet
The perfect colours of a perfect morning.

The 'lowdown' and the 'high-up' of the mini-sari

4 Dec. 1966

Some years ago we were privileged to be on the Brains Trust of a Rotary meeting. As the proceedings were jogging along, someone from the audience asked the question: "What is the best style in women's clothes?" The Master of Ceremonies looked at us and said, "Mr Debu Hosali will answer that question."

We said, "The necklines are plunging and the hemlines are rising. Where the twain meet will be the best style for women."

A girl from the audience got up and said, "That is shocking. Do you suggest that such a thing would happen to Indian women?"

We said, "Notwithstanding the fanatical orthodoxy of Morarjis and Nandajis, there is no reason why the Indian girl should be any different from her Western sister."

The girl came out with the rejoinder: "The hemlines of the skirts may go up but those of the sari would remain very much where they are today."

****

During the last racing season in Bangalore, when the city was invaded by pretty girls from Bombay and Calcutta, we made our first acquaintance with what is now known as the 'lowdown'. An exceptionally good-looking girl was walking past in the members' stand, and as we looked at her closely we were shocked to find that her sari had slipped down 8 to 10 inches below the normal position in which it is worn. For a few moments our dimming eyes could not take in the whole spectacle. We nearly came to the conclusion that, due to some accident, the garment was slipping down and, unless we helped her to retain it in place, it may well fall to the ground. But the *sang froid* with which the girl walked was such that it was no accident that the garment was where it was, but had been deliberately put there. And then it flashed across our mind – it was the latest style, the famous 'lowdown'.

But wasn't it a great sight! With the neckline plunging precipitately down and the waistline precipitately following suit, with the 'lowdown' going as low as it could go, here was a sight for the *rishis* to behold – surely one which cannot be paralleled anywhere in the West, except at swimming pools or beaches. At least in this the Indian girl had gone one better than her Western sisters.

****

Now comes news from Bombay. Some fashion model said the other day: "In England they are wearing mini-skirts, eh? In India we will have the mini-sari, both the 'lowdown' and the 'high-up'." And she did

Some tradition-al styles are mini-saris.

appear in public in her mini-sari, a foot wide pleated ribbon of cloth wrapped round her waist, with the pallau flowing behind her like a big tail. Wasn't it both low down and high up?

As the model appeared on the pavement in this newest of the new styles, there was first stunned silence followed quickly by cat-calls and wolf-whistles from all and sundry. A venerable Congress-man wearing quarter inch thick glasses, having got bemused, focused his eyes on this strange sight and

refused to take them off. A septuagenarian grandmother beat her head in despair and exclaimed that *Kaliyug* was already here. A college student fell flat on the pavement, in a swoon it appeared, but presumably to obtain a worm's eye view; and a four year old child, tagging behind its mother, said "Mummy, look – that girl has forgotten to put her skirt on."

****

It is rumoured that an extraordinary session of the All India Congress Committee has been summoned to discuss and report on the corrupting influences of fashions emanating from the West, and to recommend to the Planning Commission to allocate five crores in the Fourth Plan on projects to wean our youth from such influences.

The politics and profanities of hemlines!

Photo by Joshua Rawson Harris (unsplash)

Photo by Jyotirmoy Gupta (unsplash)

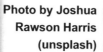

Photo by Saksham Gangwar (unsplash)

Fashion worse confounded

"My son puts on any old shirt and shorts and runs out the door," a lady in my knitting group says. "My teenage daughter spends at least half an hour in front of the mirror." Her remark starts a discussion amongst us. Most of us agree that girls at an impressionable age experience peer pressure to use make-up, look attractive and conform with prevailing fashion trends. Posting selfies on facebook and judging their self-worth according to the number of 'likes' they get from their friends is a pernicious trend. We, of a previous generation, recall a more carefree childhood, free from the tyrannies of social media.

Women seem to worry about their appearance to an extent that might restrict their lives and achievements. BBC Breakfast news on 16 January 2017 drew attention to the particular pressure on women to lose weight, resist wrinkles, try and look as perfect as the celebrities whose images in magazines are photoshopped and airbrushed by computers. It is difficult to resist this pressure, especially for those in the public eye, when the media spotlights what they wear and how they look.

To give just one recent example, the *Daily Mail* reported on a meeting between Prime Minister Theresa May and Scotland's First Minister, Nicola Sturgeon: instead of keeping the report focused on Brexit, which was the subject of their discussion, they showed a photo focusing on their legs. The headline read *Never mind Brexit – who won Legs-it*!

And then how's this for making a mockery of laws against gender discrimination: My friend Deepa, who is a receptionist at an advertising agency, tells me her boss pulled her up the other day for wearing flat shoes to work. The dress code in some companies dictates that women in customer-facing jobs must wear make-up and high heels. This despite the fact that high heels carry increased risks of falls, twisted ankles, even fractures and other negative health outcomes.

The fashion industry has been under pressure for quite awhile to stop favouring skinny models who strut down catwalks, the latest fashions draped on their starved frames. But now they want to clamp trademarks on glamour for top models like Naomi Campbell; so woe betide others on the catwalk who attempt to copy the unique way she struts, pouts, flicks her hair…! Has the world gone mad?!

At least the industry is trying to project more normal images of women. But what might we consider 'normal'? The average weight of an adult in the UK is now said to be in the over-weight range, but many are unaware they are in that unhealthy bracket. The call for 'body positivity', regardless of weight and shape, has led some in the world of fashion to employ super-sized models. However even that move has provoked the outcry that super-sized models are changing the public perception of obesity and thus normalising unhealthy lifestyles.

Taryn Brumfitt, Founder of the *Body Image Movement,* wants women to accept and embrace their natural appearance. She was interviewed about the documentary she is making entitled *Embrace*. Her research revealed that poor body image has become a global epidemic. With rising levels of obesity, 91% of women say they hate their bodies and describe them as "disgusting". Far from enjoying more and better health-giving nutrition, constant battles of the bulge are weighing us down with negative thoughts.

The magazine *Attitude* featured an article showing that men seem to be almost equally concerned about body image. 89% said they thought it was important and 54% were unhappy with the way they looked. Well yes, deeply ingrained in the male psyche too there is no dearth of vanity and ego, pure and simple. At the first signs of a receding hairline or follicles refusing to obey their current hairstyle, men are not immune to panic – but to panic silently in most cases. Because the public image that most men want to portray is that they have little or no concern about their appearance. Most do manage to separate their real lives from the images of fashion-conscious, impeccably groomed, impossibly fit and attractive male models who advertise high-end style.

Yes, I say, let's all do that. The quest to look fit, young, perfect – well there's a wonderful real world where that ridiculous quest should not dominate our lives. Let's also remember the high environmental price we pay for our fashion habits. How many of us are aware that fashion is the second largest polluter on our planet, after oil and coal? Many developing countries use massive amounts of their water resources to produce cotton crops for our denim jeans, to an extent where rivers have run dry and once-lush fields have turned to arid deserts. And the monetary cost – well blow me down with a feather, I see that the denim market is estimated at £1.5 billion in the UK alone. Even more mind-boggling is the trend in ripped jeans and the difference in price: you could pay £725 a pair for Gucci ripped jeans at a high end UK store like Harrods, or just £7.99 at good old Lidl's.

Photo by Arun Sharma (unsplash)

Metal magnetism or feminine magnetism?

4 October 1970

An interesting report, emanating from the Associated Press, says that Miss Katie Boyle, a well-known television personality, had to strip at Geneva airport as the anti-skyjack special electronic device installed to detect the presence of metal, or rather guns and grenades, gave the signal that Miss Boyle was carrying something dangerous. The dials of the machine started trembling, blue and red lights flashed, and Miss Boyle was hauled up on suspicion.

She had laid aside every metal object she was carrying, but the Swiss security agents were not satisfied: the machine insisted that she was carrying guns and grenades.

Eventually, Miss Boyle had to fling away garment after garment, in the style of a strip-tease dancer, and stand in the altogether. But the machine still gave a positive result and insisted that she was carrying metal. At long last, the security guards concluded that a magnetic attraction inherent in her body was affecting the detector. They issued her a printed card explaining the phenomenon, exempting her from undergoing the ordeal of stripping every time she travelled by air.

****

Now this sure is a young lady with the Midas touch. She must have a heart of gold, a brain of uranium or a will of steel like our Prime Minister – surely a lady worth her weight in platinum!

But what the Swiss authorities did not realise was that by issuing a certificate to her, they have offered her complete immunity now to transport any amount of gold, or even obtain an assignment as a top agent of skyjackers. She can now give up her television job and take to any of these lucrative pursuits for the Palestinian guerrillas.

And what if the Midas touch really affects her, and all her vital attributes get frozen into yellow metal! She certainly is confronted with a choice between radiating metal magnetism or feminine magnetism!

Some observations on 'feminine magnetism'

Women are supposed to be 'the fair sex' – dutiful daughters and wives, nurturing mothers, caring sisters and friends… Not always of course! In contemporary times it could be especially fatal to trust a woman just because she's a woman, or to grant a woman exemption from going through airport security. Did you see the 1998 Bollywood movie *Dil Se*? Manisha Koirala is brilliant in her role as a female terrorist, and Shah Rukh Khan intelligently portrays the psychological development of his character as he deals with the conflicting emotions that draw him towards her powerful feminine magnetism.

In the past couple of years some instances have emerged of women being complicit in terrorist incidents, defecting from the UK to Syria, and becoming terrorists in their own right. 12 May 2017 brings news that three Muslim women are accused of conspiring to murder, plotting a knife attack on members of the public in London. They are said to be Britain's first all-female terror gang. One member of the gang was shot when her house was stormed – the first woman to be shot by counter-terrorism forces in the UK. Two of the gang are mother and daughter; both wore full face veils at the Westminster magistrates' court, and were asked to lift at least part of their veils so that their eyes were visible.

The wider implications of allowing full *burkhas* in public and professional spaces is currently the subject of debate in the UK. Should women be allowed to hide behind such attire? It is widely felt that body language and non-verbal communications are a vital part of human interaction, so effective interactions are difficult if not impossible where a person's face is invisible. Whenever this topic is aired in the media, however, opinions seem to be divided. The jury is still out and no formal action has been taken so far to ban the *burkha* in the UK.

Some comic interludes in our life

28 May 1967

What is it that a young girl cannot get a man to do, especially when she has all the attributes of beauty? Confronted with a being like that, even a staid, sober and prosaic person like Deputy Prime Minister Morarji would relent and start dancing attendance on her. No wonder then that, at the London airport in August 1949, when we were taking an Air India flight to Bombay on our return journey from the USA, we found ourself in a similar circumstance.

At the airport lounge we sighted an Indian girl with a divine figure, perfect features, long black tresses, complexion like milk and honey and a smile like that of Usha – the glory of the dawn – truly a person capable of launching not merely a thousand ships but all the nuclear armoury of the world. After months of seeing American and European women, this Indian girl cast an indefinable spell on us. As we were drinking in her beauty and getting intoxicated, the departure of the plane was announced. We picked up our bags and made for the queue, to find that this dream damsel was right in front of us and was in real distress with the load of baggage she was carrying – two handbags and a heavy overcoat in one hand, a huge paper bag bursting its seams in the other, and a camera slung over one shoulder.

At this point the damsel in distress looked back, switched on her bewitching smile and gave us the RSVP look. Our chivalry now rose to a fever pitch; we readily agreed to relieve her of a part of her burden and were favoured with the huge paper bag.

As we were trudging along, we were shocked to find that the paper bag, having burst its seams, was discharging its miscellaneous contents on the tarmac – two pairs of high-heeled shoes, several pairs of sandals, bras, panties, blouses and petticoats, some washed and some unwashed. We glanced back to find that we were the last passenger on the tarmac, with no-one to help us, and were truly impaled on the horns of a dilemma. Beads of perspiration appeared on our forehead. In the meanwhile, the damsel whose property we were carrying was 50 yards ahead of us and, although we yelled at the top of our voice, "Miss, Mademoiselle, Madame, *Shrimatiji*, hey you, girl!" it was of no avail. The roar of the aeroplane engines completely drowned our yells. Therefore there was no option but to pick up all the sundry items – bras, panties and what not – and to push them in all our pockets. And with the shoes and sandals slung on our shoulders we ran to the aeroplane.

The damsel had now stopped on the gangway, obviously to find out where the man with her paper bag had disappeared and, as we approached, the smile of the dawn yielded place to the frown of the noonday sun. She said: "You naughty man! What have you done with my paper bag?"

We said, "It has burst." "And where is all my stuff?" Without bothering to answer her we climbed the steps of the gangway and unloaded all the miscellaneous wares onto the first vacant seat, with all the air hostesses and passengers roaring with laughter.

****

Now you may think that we were made a proper monkey of, but every cloud has a silver lining. What greater intimacy do you want with a girl than having carried her unmentionables in your pocket? And that gave rise to a tantalizing, although mild, flirtation throughout our journey to Bombay – a fact we have concealed all these years from Sita. But now that we are old, the punishment is not likely to be greater than a frown or the appearance of hurt pride.

The bare necessities

It strikes me that attitudes to 'unmentionable undergarments' have changed considerably over the years. At least I'd say that Western attitudes are more liberal in showing the human form in all its bare necessities – as evidenced all about us here in the UK, in advertisements and films.

I'm reminded of a comic interlude that occurred when I took time out from a conference I was attending in Sydney, Australia. I felt I had to take advantage of being outdoors in the sun, and thought it would be ideal to explore the vast stretches of sandstone clifftop trails that are an attractive feature of the city. I had heard particularly good things about the Federation cliff walk, which is about five kilometres long and offers panoramic views of the Pacific Ocean. Sure enough, I was not disappointed. The clifftop path also meandered through pleasant parks, and I came upon a lighthouse at one stage.

I had not counted on the strength of the sun, though – beating mercilessly down on my bare head (I didn't own such a thing as a sun hat, as I never needed one back home in the UK). So, looking down at one of the beaches from way up high, the blue stretch of the sea had never looked more inviting. I was desperate to get my feet into that cool water, so I found a path descending to that beach and started to clamber down. The path was quite steep and precarious, with loose pebbles and few footholds, so all my attention was focused on staying upright – so much so that I only looked up as I came round a boulder onto the beach.

As I did so, all the dangly, wobbly bits of the human anatomy came into view – those bits we normally keep under wraps. It seems comic now, but stumbling onto a nudist beach was a bit of a shock at the time. I tried hard not to look at all that bare flesh, but it was no good looking at faces either – those who noticed me stared as if I was an alien from a distant planet. Those nudies nearest to me said, "You are not welcome here unless you get all your kit off."

I must admit I did consider complying. The thought of cooling off in the sea was a great temptation. If all these people could happily strip down to the altogether, what was stopping me? Especially as I didn't know any of them, and would most likely never set eyes on them again, right? Wrong! Just as I'd stripped down to my own 'unmentionable undergarments' I spotted one of the conference organisers not 50 yards away from me – and she was looking in my direction! Help!! I started double quick to fling my clothes back on. I made the quickest getaway possible – back on the slippery path, clambering back to the top.

The next day was the last day of the conference and I couldn't avoid bumping into the nudie colleague – I mean she was of course smartly dressed now in a blue skirt and print jacket. "Did you enjoy your time off yesterday?" I blurted out.

"Oh yes," she said nonchalantly, "wasn't the weather brilliant? Did you manage to do some sightseeing?"

I noticed now that she was wearing thick glasses, and realized that she hadn't seen me on the beach after all! That spared our blushes on both sides. Who knows, however? She may have been proud of her nudist tendencies rather than embarrassed. Attitudes to nudity are typically more liberal in the Western world.

A cocksure man

26 April 1970

A Marwari left his native village in Rajasthan and migrated to Calcutta in quest of wealth. So engrossed was he in the acquisition of wealth in that great city that he hardly had the time to return to his young wife. Many years passed before he could take a holiday and go back to his village.

Finally, when he did return, he was overjoyed to see his wife standing on the threshold of his house, with two toddlers playing on the steps.

Pointing to one of them the Sethji asked, "*Eh kiko hai*?" (Whose is this one?)

The wife answered with a blush, "*Eh Ghanshyamdasji ko hai.*" (This is Ghanshyamdasji's)

Pointing to the other the Sethji queried, "*O kiko hai?*"

The flustered wife blushed again and said, "*O Ranchoddasji ko.*" (That one is Ranchoddasji's.)

The Sethji was mighty pleased and said, "*Mharo ghano soubhagya.*" (This is my great good fortune.)

Obviously the philosophy of the Sethji was: what did it matter whose children they were as long as they bore his name!

****

The above story is one extreme. The other comes through a recent press report when a VIP lamented that, notwithstanding his having had a vasectomy, he had become the father of a child. Because of the importance of this person, the medical profession was agog and started researching how this could have happened. Some even doubted the efficacy of the vasectomy.

What we feel is that this man is too cocksure of himself. Whereas maternity is a matter of certainty, paternity is pure speculation, isn't it?

A prudent man

Perhaps the philosophy of the Sethji was prudent. It is certainly admirable that he didn't pick a fight with his wife, and that he was willing to raise children not his own. After all, Sir William Golding, British novelist, playwright and poet, is quite right when he says:

"I think women are foolish to pretend they are equal to men. They are far superior and always have been. Whatever you give a woman, she will make greater. If you give her sperm, she'll give you a baby. If you give her a house, she'll give you a home. If you give her groceries, she'll give you a meal. If you give her a smile, she'll give you her heart. She multiplies and enlarges what is given to her. So, if you give her any crap, be prepared to receive a ton of shit!"

The green-eyed Monster

13 June 1965

The first cocktail party of the season last night was a gay affair. The women were all beauties, the men all dowdies, and it looked as though our host, a crusty old bachelor, had chosen the men for the only reason that they were married to beautiful women. With gallons of Scotch whisky flowing, there was great *bonhomie*, and a rare geniality prevailed.

After the usual pleasantries were exchanged – a handshake, how-do-you do? nice-to-meet-you! – we betook ourself to the Bar and, as we were surveying the scene, two of our girl friends approached us with great affection and, as we are very deaf, cooed into our ears, "Oh Dada, congratulations. We are so happy, you are now the Steward of the Bangalore Race Club. How very wonderful." But being unable to hear much, and yet being aware that something pleasant was being said, we switched on our beaming smile and nodded acceptance of their felicitations.

At this stage a good-looking woman escorted by her husband was seen coming into the hall, and the eyes of our two 'lovelies' fell on her. In a jiffy all the graciousness and charm vanished and the inherent feline instinct took possession of them. One said to the other, "Oh my! Look at that Mrs X with her low-cut blouse. She is 50 if she is a day, but she tries to look younger than her own daughter. And doesn't she succeed?

Look at that beautiful Conjeevaram sari we wanted to buy at Vijayalakshmi Hall; she has already gone and pinched it. These women married to businessmen in the private sector never seem to be short of money. But our husbands manage these big government industries and get only a fixed salary at the end of the month. This is an unequal world indeed!"

The other rejoined: "How I hate that woman! Haven't you heard of the lovely house she has built on Ashoka Road?"

This was too much for the first one and with great vehemence she put in, "I don't think much of that house. That balcony they have is all out of perspective, and the garish colours and the bizarre decorations are absurd. I hate that house just as much as I hate that woman. She is flaunting the fact that her son got a first class in the BA this year. So what! My son also got a first class last year."

Just then we happened to say, "Now, now, don't fight over nothing" – and that shocked them into awareness. "What, Dada! Have you been listening to our conversation? We thought you cannot hear." We said that we were not listening to their conversation but observing the green-eyed monster of jealousy.

****

This morning, as we scanned the morning paper through a severe hangover, we found

Brezhnev pulling up Kosygin:

"Kosygin, you are absolutely stupid. I have all along pressed for the 'hard line' – that heavy industry should have priority over consumer goods and, a revisionist that you are, you divert our resources towards the production of silly things like clothing, footwear and other *bourgeois* needs. Now these Americans are already on our heels, sending their astronauts for a space swim, and they may well overtake us in the race. Their Edward White has taken a space walk for 20 minutes, and remained in space for nearly four days. It appears they have also perfected a cosmic pistol which enables them to manoeuvre themselves in space."

Kosygin: "Don't be silly, Brezhnev. That Gemini is not a patch on our Voskhod, and our Alexei Leonov has performed a greater miracle than White. Gemini has no television link with the earth and they have to maintain 26 ships, 129 planes and 10,000 men to retrieve their astronauts from their sea-landing. But we – we have perfected a system of returning to earth on solid ground. But oh, how I hate those Americans! They don't allow us any respite and, notwithstanding their decadent capitalism, they are pursuing us fast on our heels. I do hate them."

****

We thought there was much in common between the beauties of last night and the beasts of this morning: the green-eyed monster of jealousy.

The green-eyed monster is alive and kicking

Apparently the phrase 'green-eyed monster' originates from Shakespeare. The world-famous playwright describes jealousy in his play *Othello* as a monster that consumes the person who harbours this powerful emotion: Oh, beware my lord, of jealousy! It is the green-eyed monster which doth mock the meat it feeds on. (Othello Act 3, scene 3).

In Othello the character Iago is referring to a lack of fidelity in love. This is perhaps the most common reason that evokes personal jealousy. However, it is in the workplace that many women experience the worst professional jealousy. When women achieve success they seem to be subjected to a degree of scrutiny and criticism which wouldn't happen to a man. And women are just as likely to judge the behaviours of their female peers in terms of double standards such as "He's assertive; she's bossy." "He's confident; she's arrogant." Perhaps subconsciously both men and women are socialized towards male values in leadership and business matters.

In various jobs I've otherwise enjoyed, the green-eyed monster and its various siblings – envy, anger, insecurity, competition – have reared their ugly heads from time to time. Could this be because I was naïve about the dynamics of relationships? Too focused on creating the best version of my best self and giving 100% to my work performance? Not realizing that the rewards and awards on which I was thriving had an impact on my team mates who were striving for recognition and not feeling acknowledged?

Strangely enough, all my negative experiences have involved female co-workers and managers. This makes me wonder if women are conditioned to be biased against their own sex – to be more prone to insecurity, and therefore more likely to be jealous of other women who they perceive to be more popular and achievement-orientated. After all it is a lack of confidence, competence and self-esteem which leads people to manipulate, bully and back-stab.

I could tell you about a specific example, but it would be a long horror story. I would also probably be sued for character assassination by the woman who turned out to be a serial bully. She would recognize herself no matter how hard I might try to disguise and fictionalize the sorry tale. Or would she? Maybe she'd be too deluded or arrogant, or too indifferent to read anything I write. So maybe this is another story I may tell after all – in the not too distant future!

IN CONCLUSION...

When in Bangalore I sometimes liked to stand with Dada at the garden gate and watch our local world go by. He would speculate on the lives of the people he saw: "See that schoolboy carrying his *tiffin dabba*" he would say. "His mother must have got up early this morning to cook lunch for him. It looks as if she ironed his shirt and trousers very well..." and so on.

Or "I wonder where Mrs Kodanda Rao is off to so early. D'you know, she came to India way back from Poland. Mr Rao has long since passed away – she must be lonely, living on her own in our country – so far and so different from her own. She's a brave old lady!" Indeed, I thought the world of dear Aunty Kodanda Rao. She always wore a *sari* neatly and had her silver hair in an immaculate up-style.

On the morning of 2nd February 1983, Dada watched a dry leaf blowing past in the wind and said, "There goes Mr Hosali!" He then went in to take a shower and get dressed to go to the races. As was his habit of many years, he locked the dressing room door and then the bathroom door. But when he didn't emerge for well over an hour, Bhabi kept knocking and went from concern to consternation. The bathroom was in a corner of the ground floor, with an external wooden door as well as the internal door which opened onto the dressing room. From that external door she could hear the shower water falling ... and falling... on the concrete floor. She got the cook to help break down that door. Dada had suffered a fatal heart attack.

When news quickly spread by word of mouth in the neighbourhood and beyond, on that fateful day, the compound of our Basvangudi house began to fill with people who knew and respected my father for his community service and involvement. He had helped many; tributes came thick and fast. Also messages of support and sympathy for Bhabi, who would now be on her own. Our extended family had grown and flown the nest by that time.

I was back at my home in the UK when I received the telephone call that brought news of Dada's passing. I wanted to chuck that phone into the deepest part of a deep and murky sea. Maybe stormy waves would crash and drown out the message that reverberated in my ears. I understood for the first time that saying about shooting the messenger, but actually I don't even remember who called to give me the message.

Later I spoke to Bhabi and Rani. Bhabi advised I shouldn't leave my young children and my job to fly immediately to Bangalore. She said she would need me later, in the summer holidays, by which time she knew all the early concern and support for her would have died down. Rani told me they had already gathered the ashes from the cremation and scattered them into the Cauvery River, along with a little float carrying a *diya* lamp and a single orchid from the garden – Dada's favourite flower.

My heartbreak came most of all from thinking about all that he still wanted to do, and so much he still had to live for. At the age of 73 he was young at heart, still saying "I'm top of the world!" He had been in the shower, looking forward to a meeting at the Turf Club. I take the liberty here of reproducing an excerpt from one tribute that came from a racing correspondent:

"Dada was a keen painter, sculptor and journalist, but – whatever his first love – it can safely be said in racing parlance that his love for 'the sport of kings' was a very short head second. Be it live racing or inter-venue off-course doings, he was inevitably there. So much so that his absence for the session on the Bombay Meeting on 2nd February evoked surprise and speculation. It was not till late in the afternoon that the Turf Club was informed of his sudden death."

My sorrow and concern was also for my mother – they had been married for 42 years and she suddenly had to learn to live without him. I knew she would be devastated, despite her courage and resilience. My sister Rani had a close bond with Dada too – and I keenly felt my distance from them when this sudden bereavement hit our family.

Dada had long known he had heart disease, but he accepted the risks of being mortal. He used to say that the human body was a fine-tuned set of organs and functions that had evolved over millennia, so we had every reason to trust our amazing ability to re-balance and recuperate from illness and injury. Despite these powers, he'd say our survival was still a miracle because of the many potential risks the body encounters every minute of every day.

On his last visit to my family in the UK, we noticed he had shooting pains down his left arm. He had to stop every so often when we were walking to the shops. On my last visit to see the family in Bangalore, my boys were little and Dada tried to make a sailboat for them out of a coconut shell – a gift from the coconut tree in our garden. But again I saw him pause several times in this crafting process due to the pain from angina. We tried to persuade him to see a doctor, but he just wanted to carry on living and eating as he'd always done, and to die with his shoes on rather than languish in a hospital bed.

It is customary to place a dash between a person's date of birth and the date of death. So Dada's lifespan was 4 November 1910 – 2 February 1983. For Bhabi it was to be 20 March 1920 – 28 April 2013; it would be 30 years before her soul joined her soulmate (who knows in what spiritual realm?). Both of them 'lived the dash' (that space between birth and death) with so much loving energy and courage, and left us with a legacy of positive values and inspiration. They role-modelled the concept that what matters most is how we 'live the dash'.

In the grand scheme of things, life may be ephemeral. It can be blown away like that leaf in the wind Dada commented on at his garden gate. But where has the leaf gone to rest? Where have memories gone? Not totally obliterated. For we are still here: Dada and Bhabi's children, grandchildren, great-grand-children…all our extended family whose lives he touched at different levels of significance; and all our relatives and readers too. We all have our own stories and I hope you will ramble down your own memory lanes. Long may you 'live the dash' with peace, love and happiness.

ABOUT THE AUTHOR

Arti Kumar (née Hosali) was born and raised in Bangalore, and has lived in the UK for nearly 50 years. In London and St Albans she has studied, worked and seen her family grow.

Arti retired in 2010 from her role as Associate Director of the Centre for Excellence in Teaching and Learning at the University of Bedfordshire. She continues to volunteer and work freelance as an education consultant, trainer and mentor.

She has won many awards, including a National Teaching Fellowship, a Lifetime Achievement Award from the Association of Graduate Careers Advisory Services and an MBE in the Queen's New Year Honours list in 2008, for services to higher education. She is a Fellow of the Higher Education Academy UK.

Arti's main area of expertise is in developing pedagogy and a process of holistic student development linked to employability skills and attributes. The resulting meta-model – *SOARing to Success* – has proven beneficial to many cohorts of students, from different backgrounds and programmes of study in the UK and abroad. These approaches are in her main book and in many further papers and chapters related to employability development and action research.

Main publication

Book / e-book: **Kumar, A. (2008)** *Personal, Academic and Career Development in Higher Education – SOARing to Success* London and New York: Routledge Taylor and Francis

Companion website:
http://www.routledge.com/professional/978041542360-1/

"This book addresses a key and continuing need: how we support the transition from student to graduate, and lay the foundations for sustainable employability and a fulfilling life in an increasingly competitive world. Arti's book delivers both understanding and practical tools for enabling the shift our students need to make."

Rob Ward, Director, The Centre for Recording Achievement

Kumar, A (2015) *Enabling all learners to SOAR for employability: an inclusive, integrative pedagogy* Innovative pedagogies series York, UK: Higher Education Academy

https://www.heacademy.ac.uk/sites/default/files/arti_kumar_final.pdf

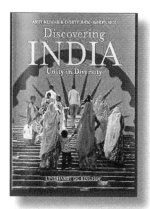

Kumar, A. & Baek-Sorensen, D. (2015) ***Discovering India – Unity in Diversity*** Copenhagen: Lindhardt og Ringhof

A textbook written for the Danish curriculum at Gymnasium (A-level) standard.

Companion website: http://www.lru.dk/discoveringindia

India is home to both Gandhi's non-violence policy and the giant Bollywood industry. How can anyone accurately know this large, evolving country in all its complexity and diversity?

We authors conducted field research in India and included 14 interviews which are available with transcripts on the companion website. In writing this textbook for young adults in Denmark, we encouraged teachers and students to explore with an open mind and gave them a variety of methods to build their own balanced concepts around knowledge-based content.

This type of discovery learning enables participants to bring creative appreciation and critical thinking to the topics, through their own research and reflection, proactive, interactive and collaborative learning. This is a rich resource in developing high level employability skills, and in creating self-awareness linked with inter-cultural understanding and communication – essential attributes in the multi-cultural and global context of work today.

Other related publications

Two modules created for an online programme: ***Skills and Attributes for Career Success: Developing an Enterprising Mindset*** (Epigeum, 2016). Kumar, A: **Module titles: Problem-solving and decision-making. Effective planning**.

Kumar, A. (2013) 'SOARing to success: employability development from the inside-out' in Bilham, T. (ed) *For the Love of Learning - Innovations from Outstanding University Teachers* (pp. 221-227) Basingstoke, UK, USA & Australia: Palgrave Macmillan Higher Education series

Threshold Concepts in Employability Curricula, Arti Kumar:
http://www.heacademy.ac.uk/assets/documents/employability/ArtiKumarEmployabilityArticle.pdf

Kumar, A. (2010) Chapter 18, p. 254 '**Supporting action research as a CPD process'**, in Atlay, M. and Coughlin, A. (eds.) ***Creating communities: developing, enhancing and sustaining learning communities across the University of Bedfordshire.*** Luton: University of Bedfordshire.

Printed in Poland
by Amazon Fulfillment
Poland Sp. z o.o., Wrocław